D1707942

Fumy/Sauerbrey   Enterprise Security

Enterprise
Security

IT Security Solutions:
Concepts, Practical Experiences, Technologies

Edited by
Walter Fumy and
Joerg Sauerbrey

Publicis Corporate Publishing

Bibliographic information published by Die Deutsche Bibliothek
Die Deutsche Bibliothek lists this publication in the Deutsche Nationalbibliografie;
detailed bibliographic data is available in the Internet at http://dnb.ddb.de.

www.publicis-erlangen.de/books

ISBN 3-89578-267-X

Editor: Siemens Aktiengesellschaft, Berlin und München
Publisher: Publicis Corporate Publishing, Erlangen
© 2006 by Publicis KommunikationsAgentur GmbH, GWA, Erlangen

Printed in Germany

Foreword

The global information society is increasingly dependent on electronic networking and exchanging "electronic goods" with high economic value, both in private life and in business. Whereas private individuals are used to managing their own risks, managers of organizations are made responsible for managing the risk in such a way that the organization will survive and will be able to continue its electronic business processes, even in the event of internal or external attacks or in the case of failure of networks, systems and components.

IT security is no longer an isolated issue for the IT manager, but requires attention at the top level of each organization. In this respect there is no difference between enterprises and public organizations, such as governments and healthcare. The view on IT security moves from product level up to solutions and process-driven business continuity. IT security changes from a cost factor to an investment factor. New auditing and consulting methods are centered around "Return on Security Investment" (ROSI).

Nearly every day newspapers publish stories about security breaches and damages being caused by systems failures. Just recently, we saw a major failure of a US airline computer leading to a complete shutdown and the grounding of all flights. A few months ago, an airline employee entered an incorrect code that led to a cascade of computer failures. The end result was a shut down, not only of the airline's entire flight operations but also of a second major airline. Why? Because both airlines outsourced their IT operations and the breakdown affected the entire network.

The danger is where one would least suspect it. Any high-tech company invests large sums in R&D. It's easy to see how a disgruntled employee could send valuable technical know-how to a competitor by means of a simple "mouse click" and earn more money in seconds then s/he can in years of salary. Patents can be passed on and revealed to competition. Imagine the risks pharmaceutical companies face. One could publish research and drug secrets prematurely, leading to a denial of a patent application, all because the technology was made available in the public domain.

Worldwide, the OECD Guidelines on the Security of Information Systems and Networks (Security Guidelines) propose the development of a "culture of security" to ensure the stable evolution of the digital economy and information society [OECD02]. The economic and social benefits have the potential to accrue on a global scale. In addition to the familiar concerns about the security of electronic commerce, hacking, privacy and cyber crime such as consumer fraud, there is the added vulnerability of society due to its dependence on information systems and the specter of cyber terrorism. The main policy impacts from the OECD are:

- Raising awareness of the importance of the security of information systems and networks for safeguarding critical infrastructures as well as business and consumer information.
- Highlighting and increasing knowledge of the Security Guidelines among all organizations who use information systems and networks.
- Providing guidance on the application of the Security Guidelines, using case studies of business, civil society and country experiences.
- Building awareness and, as appropriate, consensus on policy frameworks for the security of information systems.
- Exploring the use of technology and security standards in safeguarding information system infrastructures, as well as information stored in systems and networks.
- Encouraging the development and promotion of security architectures for organizations that effectively protect information systems, as well as consumer and business products that include "embedded" security features to enhance their use of information systems.

Enterprises operating globally may be subject to several legislations and local companies may be subject to legislation from entirely different regions of the globe. Laws are overlapping, jurisdictions are becoming irrelevant and corporate concern is growing. In the wake of prominent management failures, governments are under intense public pressure to pass more laws and regulations. The following issues must be addressed by any organization seeking regulatory compliance:

- Authentication: Who is the originator of the data? Who is the recipient of the data?
- Authorization: Are the sender and/or recipient authorized to send and receive?
- Transaction security: Are the data streams secure?
- Document security: Are the documents secured?
- Financial data security: Can the data be falsified? Is integrity assured?
- Monetary flow: Can funds be moved without proper authorization?
- Data storage security: Can documents be destroyed, ex-post changed or content be altered?
- Non-repudiation: Is the sent document legally effective and binding? Can the content and signature be relied upon?
- Last but not least, are the IT risks perpetually verified, evaluated and managed?

Management must identify the process-based relationships most critical to the company, pinpoint existing internal and outsourcing organization gaps in process and controls that may increase risk and enhance existing activities with a more encompassing framework for internal controls.

Furthermore, security has been included in the list of priority research topics in the EU Commission proposal for the 7th Framework Program for Research & Development (2007-2013). Security makes a timely entry into the list of research topics to be undertaken swiftly, in order to respond to highly societal demand in the face of new security challenges and to enhance the competitiveness of the security industry. Existing security-related research activities in Europe suffer from the fragmentation of efforts, the lack of critical mass of scale and scope and the lack of connections and interoperability. Europe needs to improve the coherence of its efforts by developing efficient institutional arrangements and by instigating the various national and international actors to cooperate and coordinate in order to avoid duplication and to explore synergies wherever possible.

In conclusion, my statement underlines that the importance of an integrated view on IT security incorporating concepts & trends, practical experiences, technologies & standards, as well as guidelines, legislation and research aspects cannot be overemphasized. This book will help us to cope with the actual and upcoming security issues in the right way and will give guidance for decision makers responsible for enterprise security and enterprise business continuity at all levels.

Prof. Dr.-Ing. Heinz Thielmann
Fraunhofer Institute
Secure Information Technology (SIT)

Contents

Introduction

Part I: Concepts and Trends

Part II: Practical Experiences

Part III: Technologies and Standards

Introduction

1 Challenges for Enterprise Security

Walter Fumy and Joerg Sauerbrey

Today's enterprises rely heavily on the use of information to conduct their business activities. Compromising the confidentiality, integrity, availability, non-repudiation, accountability, authenticity and reliability of an organization's assets is likely to have an unfavorable impact including the risk of financial losses. Consequently, there is a critical need to protect information and to manage the security of information and communication systems within an enterprise.

This requirement for enterprise security is particularly important because many organizations are internally and externally connected by communication networks not necessarily controlled by their organizations. In addition, legislation in many countries requires that enterprise management takes appropriate action to mitigate risks related to the business and the use of IT systems. Such legislation may cover not only horizontal aspects, such as privacy/data protection issues or accounting standards, but also specific sectors such as healthcare or financial services.

1.1 Threats

Over the past years, the number of vulnerabilities discovered within hardware, operating systems and applications has increased dramatically (see Figure 1.1). More than 3,500 new vulnerabilities are reported each year and registered with vulnerability

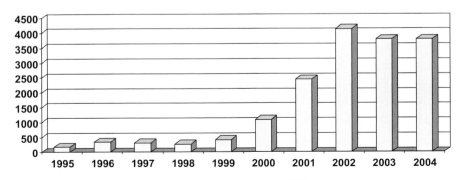

Figure 1.1 Vulnerabilities reported 1995 – 2004 (Source: CERT)

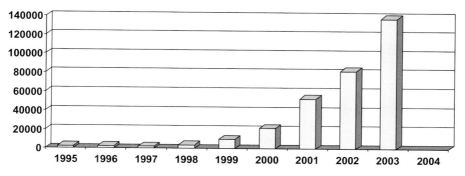

Figure 1.2 Incidents reported 1995 – 2004[1] (Source: CERT)

tracking organizations such as CERT[1]. The risk of attack against these security holes is greatest when security patches are omitted, awaiting deployment or not yet available.

Figure 1.2 shows the number of IT security incidents reported to CERT increasing more than thirty-fold between 1998 and 2003.

Attackers today have toolsets at hand that let them design exploits more quickly. Where it once took months to implement an attack, we now measure the duration from vulnerability to exploit in days, if not hours. Due to the widespread use of automated attack tools, the skill level required to commit IT crime is constantly decreasing and attacks against Internet-connected systems have become commonplace (see Figure 1.3).

As a consequence, enterprises struggle to keep up with the steady increase in vulnerabilities and attacks and to appropriately handle each individual malicious event. They are caught up in a contest of speed to keep the bad guys out.

Distributed Attacks

A major concern today is that the Internet is virtually everywhere. Thousands of unprotected computers connected to the Internet are at risk of being easily compromised by intruders and then used together for an attack. Such a scenario is known as a distributed attack.

From history we can see a trend toward threats affecting more and more sites and users at the same time. Advancements in security technology appear to move us closer to a cooperative analysis and response approach to identifying and improving attacks across the Internet.

This trend is likely to continue and begin to affect areas previously not tapped by cyber crime. It is expected that we will see threats evolve over the coming years to

---

[1] Carnegie Mellon University's Computer Emergency Response Team; see www.cert.org

[2] Note that, as of 2004, CERT no longer publishes the number of incidents reported. CERT feels that nowadays counts of the number of incidents reported only provide little information with regard to assessing the scope and impact of attacks.

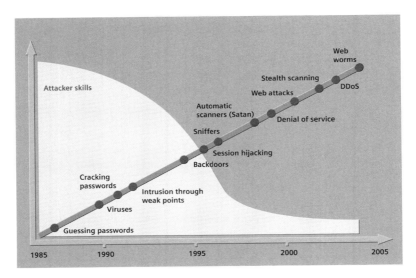

Figure 1.3 Development of attacks and skills

distributed attacks aimed at controlling assets and information rather than just denying services. Such attacks will attract intruders with far more resources at their disposal than today's hackers.

Insider Threats

Insider threats to information and communication systems are widely viewed as being of the greatest concern. In 2004, the Carnegie Mellon University's CERT Coordination Center (CERT/CC) and the U.S. Secret Service published the findings of an insider threat study focusing on people who have had access to and were responsible for harm using IT systems in the banking and financial sector.

For the purpose of this study, the definition of an insider includes current, former or contract employees of an enterprise. The cases analyzed involve incidents in which an insider intentionally exceeded or abused authorized access in a manner that affected the organization's data, daily business operations, system security or involved other harm.

Major findings include [USS04]:

- Most of the incidents were not technically sophisticated or complex. They typically involved the exploitation of non-technical vulnerabilities such as business rules or organization policies rather than IT vulnerabilities.

- In almost 90 percent of cases, the insiders employed simple, legitimate user commands to carry out the incidents and, in most cases, the insiders were authorized users.

- The majority of the incidents were devised and planned in advance. Furthermore, in most cases, others had knowledge of the insider's intentions, plans and/or activities.

- About 80 percent of the insiders were motivated by financial gain rather than the desire to harm the enterprise or the IT system.

- Insiders fit no common profile. Only 23 percent held a technical position, 13 percent had a demonstrated interest in "hacking" and 27 percent had come to the attention of a supervisor or co-worker prior to the incident.

- The impact of nearly all insider incidents in the banking and finance sector was financial loss for the victim organization: in 30 percent of cases, the financial loss exceeded $500,000.

- More than 80 percent of the incidents were executed physically from within the insider's organization and took place during normal business hours.

Most of these findings are likely to apply to other sectors as well.

Voice and Data Convergence

The requirement to reduce costs and keep enterprise technology performing optimally has led to combining data and voice networks into single converged networks. As a consequence, voice services become vulnerable to the same type of attacks as data networks – attacks that were unknown with previous circuit-switched networks. Therefore, this convergence leads to an increased need to improve the networks' overall reliability, availability and security.

There is no good reason to expect IT security threats to become stable. New protection techniques are followed by new vulnerabilities. Secured legacy technologies go along with new innovative and less secure technologies. For example, IP telephony meets business needs but also provides additional scope for malicious activities. The same can be said for other technologies including wireless, streaming multimedia and personal mobile devices. On one hand, technology advancements tend to provide faster, cheaper and more reliable ways to conduct business. On the other hand, however, they trigger new developments in the area of compromising attacks.

1.2 Enabling New Business Opportunities

While the original motivation for introducing IT security measures has often been security enhancements, appropriate security solutions also offer substantial potential for cost savings and for accomplishing new business opportunities. For example, advanced information technologies are increasingly being used to improve the effectiveness of business processes. Business transactions are processed over public networks without the need for being there 'in person'. This trend exists both in the business-to-business (B2B) and business-to-consumer (B2C) environments as well as in the context of enterprise-internal activities and communications.

Apart from the IT security threats discussed in the previous section, a number of key business objectives are driving IT security solutions for enterprises:

- *The move to e-business.* The use of the Internet to provide content and business processes to employees, subscribers, customers and trading partners became an essential tool for increasing productivity and streamlining collaboration. More and more enterprise IT applications and content are going online and secure access to these applications and content is required by an increasing and more diverse set of users.

- *Mobility.* Mobility has become a foundation of modern business. Users need to be able to work in environments ranging from the home to hotels, building sites or the back of a taxi. Business users are increasingly turning to small devices, such as Personal Data Assistants (PDAs) to use a subset of business data (e.g. calendar, address book entries, unread e-mail), wherever they are. Security issues have held back an early adoption of mobile data technologies, but growing use of security solutions such as Virtual Private Networks (VPNs, see Chapter 3) is beginning to drive business use of mobile data technology.

- *Fast and flexible change management.* IT systems and applications need to be flexible and responsive to dynamic changes in user populations and business processes brought about by mergers and acquisitions or the move to e-business. New users and users changing job functions must immediately get the access rights they need to be up and running quickly, while departing users must have their access rights revoked immediately to close security holes (for a detailed discussion, see Chapter 5).

- *Cost reductions.* Return On Security Investment (ROSI) recently became a topic of great interest, perhaps because security is traditionally such an enigmatic field. Today, several approaches exist, providing useful qualitative advice and rough quantitative methods. For specific examples, see Section 10.4.

1.3 Compliance

Enterprises are not just fighting the bad guys or enabling new business opportunities, they also need to show customers and competitors that they are properly protected. In addition, international and regionally mandated security and privacy requirements, directives and standards have shaped a higher level of security awareness and understanding.

Probably the most well-known regulation today is the Sarbanes-Oxley Act (SOA). Other compliancy mandates include:

- Health Insurance Portability and Accountability Act (HIPAA) – relevant for anyone in the U.S. with access to or holding patient information.
- Basel II – relevant for international financial service providers and for enterprises requiring a loan from such service providers.

- Gramm-Leach-Bliley Act (GLBA) – relevant for banks, financial institutions and insurance companies.

As security is such a strong component within compliance requirements, many organizations address this using international standards, including ISO/IEC 17799 [ISO17799] and ISO/IEC 27001 [ISO27001].

Sarbanes-Oxley Act

Following a number of major accounting and reporting scandals involving prominent companies in the United States, the *Sarbanes-Oxley Act* (SOA, also know as SOX) passed as U.S. law in 2002 to strengthen corporate governance and to restore public trust and investor confidence in accounting practices. SOA was sponsored by U.S. Senator Paul Sarbanes and U.S. Representative Michael Oxley and establishes new accountability standards and criminal penalties for Corporate Management.

The part of SOA that most directly concerns IT security is Section 404, which aims at strengthening internal control over financial reporting. Section 404 mandates that all public organizations demonstrate due diligence in the disclosure of financial information and implement a series of controls and procedures to communicate, store and protect that data. Public organizations are also required to protect these controls from internal and external threats and unauthorized access, including those that could occur through online systems and networks.

As most financial activity is performed on IT resources, Identity and Access Management (IAM) plays a significant role in helping to maintain the integrity of a company's reporting process. Of course, IAM is just one element of the overall SOA compliance process, but it can help make that process significantly easier to implement, maintain and audit. Detailed information on IAM concepts and technologies is provided in Chapters 5 and 14.

With SOA, safeguarding internal controls and procedures for financial reporting as well as ensuring the confidentiality, integrity and availability of information, changes from a best practice to a legal requirement for many enterprises.

Health Insurance Portability and Accountability Act (HIPAA)

The U.S. *Health Insurance Portability and Accountability Act* (HIPAA) is a comprehensive piece of legislation that governs privacy, security and electronic transactions concerning healthcare data. This legislation stipulates that patients have significant rights to understand and control how their health data is used. Furthermore, it obliges healthcare providers to provide an explanation of how they comply with privacy regulations.

HIPAA's standards and regulations can be reviewed in the HIPAA Security Matrix which describes the tasks to be performed. HIPAA requires that as healthcare organizations adopt wide-ranging security standards, key individuals are assigned the responsibility for executing and documenting formal security practices, for example accurate accounting of all activities passing through firewalls, routers and Intrusion

Detection Systems (IDS) (for details on network security concepts and technologies, please refer to Chapter 3).

Basel II

Basel II is a mandatory standard for financial service providers [Bas04]. Its core set of regulations requires banks to analyze their credit portfolios, not only through traditional rating methodology (cash flow, liquidity, profitability, market risks, equity to debt ratio, etc.), but also through the identification and quantification of operational risks.

To achieve regulatory compliance, financial service providers have to formalize and adopt a process-driven approach to risk and information security management. These risk evaluations must encompass internal processes, systems, people and external events. The process of identifying, assessing and controlling operational risks will potentially reveal the need to remediate gaps. IT operations may need to change or update processes and systems to demonstrate effective internal IT information risk management practices to the regulators (process-driven risk management is discussed in Chapters 2, 7 and 15).

The accumulated effect of these rating changes across a bank's entire lending portfolio may necessitate an adjustment of the bank's capital reserves. Therefore, Basel II will have a significant impact on the ability of banks to grant loans and the interest rates for loans.

The Gramm Leach Bliley Act (GLBA)

The Gramm Leach Bliley Act (GLBA) is a wide-ranging U.S. law requiring financial institutions to protect the security, integrity and confidentiality of consumer information. GLBA requires an advanced level of security understanding and awareness.

GLBA has an impact on enterprises, such as banking institutions, insurance companies or credit card companies.

ISO/IEC 17799

The International Standard ISO/IEC 17799 [ISO17799] is intended to serve as a reference for identifying the range of controls necessary for secure information and communication systems.

ISO/IEC 17799 applies to large, medium and small organizations and requires processes to ensure that the security controls for a system are fully matching its risks. This embraces the analysis of relevant threats, vulnerabilities, controls in place and potential impacts. Under ISO/IEC 17799, an enterprise must have a system for the following:

- Monitoring access to systems.
- Retaining the integrity of unaltered logs.
- Reporting material events to both upper management and the board of directors.
- Establishing sufficient audit trails to address threats and problems.

ISO/IEC 17799 stems from an original publication from the UK Department of Trade and Industry (DTI) in 1993. In 1995, this DTI publication became British Standard (BS) 7799 and in December 2000 ISO/IEC 17799. A 2nd revised edition of ISO/IEC 17799 was published in 2005. It is anticipated that ISO/IEC 17799 will be renamed to ISO/IEC 27002 at some point in the future, thus creating an ISO/IEC 27000 series of information security management standards.

ISO/IEC 27001

International Standard ISO/IEC 27001 [ISO27001] provides a model for establishing, implementing, operating, monitoring, reviewing, maintaining and improving an Information Security Management System (ISMS). ISO/IEC 27001 can be used in order to assess conformance by interested internal and external parties.

The adoption of an ISMS should be a strategic decision for an enterprise. The design and implementation of an organization's ISMS is influenced by their needs and objectives, security requirements, the processes employed and the size and structure of the organization. These and their supporting systems are expected to change over time. It is expected that an ISMS implementation will be scaled in accordance with the needs of the organization, for example. a simple situation requires a simple ISMS solution.

The process approach for information security management presented in ISO/IEC 27001 encourages its users to emphasize the importance of:

- Understanding an enterprise's information security requirements and the need to establish policy and objectives for information security;
- Implementing and operating controls to manage an enterprise's information security risks in the context of its overall business risks;
- Monitoring and reviewing the performance and effectiveness of the ISMS;
- Continuous improvement based on objective measurements.

ISO/IEC 27001 adopts the "Plan-Do-Check-Act" (PDCA) process model, which is applied to structure all ISMS processes. Detailed information on this approach is provided in Chapters 2 and 15.

1.4 Why this Book?

Almost all enterprises connect electronically to exchange information with other organizations such as business partners, customers, outsourcers or regulators. Unfortunately, business processes are still often designed for speed and convenience, not for security. With more than 600 million individuals now connected worldwide to the Internet, the risk of attacks taking advantage of unsophisticated users and enterprises and unsecured machines has become extremely large.

Enterprises and other organizations need to act if they want to guarantee the integrity, confidentiality and availability of their business information. This is particularly true if they use security-critical delivery channels, as in e-business, or if they process sensitive information subject to data protection requirements, as in the healthcare sector.

Most enterprises have focused their attention on security solutions that are designed to "keep the bad guys out" (for a discussion of defensive security technology, see Chapter 3). However, e-commerce and business-to-business activities as well as teleworking and other mobile applications demand security solutions designed to "let the good guys in".

The business value of information security can be calculated on the basis of risk reduction, as a decreasing cost of doing business and a return on investment via enhanced trust relationships and improved business opportunities. In general, the cost to mitigate the damage from a successful attack is much higher than the cost to prevent an attack.

On the other hand, IT security solutions play an essential role in assisting enterprises to achieve and sustain a compliance environment. Strong authentication based on smart cards (see Chapter 4) or biometrics (see Chapter 6) and digital signatures as well as identity and access management (see Chapters 5 and 14) help to verify that the controls are in place and working.

Our general recommendations include:

- Enterprises should review their information security requirements on a regular basis.
- Enterprises should assume that legal liability for poor security practices is on the horizon and act accordingly.
- Enterprises should establish a security-aware culture. The foundation for such a culture requires management commitment, implementation of a security policy and employee training (see also Chapters 2 and 15).
- Enterprises should take steps to secure themselves against insider attacks.

This book helps enterprises to address these issues and can be used as a first guide to identify requirements and opportunities.

1.5 How to Read this Book

This book provides broad knowledge of the major security issues affecting today's enterprises and presents state-of-the-art concepts and current trends. It is organized in three parts.

Part I "Concepts and Trends" covers key areas including information security management (Chapter 2), network and system security (Chapter 3), and identity and access management (IAM, Chapter 5). User authentication based on smart cards is discussed in Chapter 4, biometric authentication is addressed in Chapter 6.

Part II "Practical Experiences" complements Part I by providing in-depth information on practical experiences implementing enterprise security solutions in selected sectors, including risk management in the financial services industry (Chapter 7), public key infrastructure and digital signatures for e-government (Chapter 8), identity management for an insurance company (Chapter 9), and IT security management in a global enterprise (Chapter 10).

For those interested in specific details, Part III provides an in-depth discussion of relevant technologies and standards. Areas covered include cryptographic techniques (Chapter 11) and public key infrastructure (PKI, Chapter 12), smart card technologies (Chapter 13), identity and access management technologies (Chapter 14), and information security management systems (Chapter 15).

Acknowledgements

Apart from the individual authors, many people have helped make this book possible. In particular, the editors are grateful to Gerhard Seitfudem from Publicis for guidance and support given throughout the project. Our thanks are also due to Elmar Rothenwöhrer for his vision and encouragement.

Part I:
Concepts and Trends

2 Information Security Management

Sabine Kornprobst and Roberto Pillmaier

2.1 Goals of Information Security Management

Finally! The day on which you can pick up your new car has arrived. The salesperson takes you to the delivery lot to present your dream car to you. He explains all the fancy features, and you can barely wait to finally jump in and take it for its first spin. Once all the formalities have been taken care of, you take off on your first drive. You head for the nearest freeway, give a signal and move into the passing lane. The stereo pumps out high-fidelity sound, and the car's interior fully matches your expectations. Everything is new and beautiful.

Unfortunately, you are not the only person on the road, and the unexpected happens. Suddenly you have to hit the brakes hard and notice after a moment of shock that your car's safety features don't quite work as you expected ...

You had expected that the manufacturer would have taken care of this ...

The automobile industry tries to counteract all kinds of malfunctions, threats and hazards with sophisticated safety features like on-board computers, airbags, ABS and intelligent control components. Various checkups are supposed to make sure that all these features are present and operational. The risk of driving should be minimized without taking the fun out of it. To accomplish this, the industry executes sophisticated planning and develops expensive concepts. Based on precisely documented specifications, the entire production process is executed as safely and traceable as possible in line with various legal and regulatory requirements. Nevertheless, there will never be total safety, but only as much as can be accomplished with reasonable effort.

Quality control has developed into a competitive factor. Each company must be able to fully rely on its own data and the claims related to it, especially when it comes to the issue of functionality. This is one of the reasons why manufacturers have their processes certified according to international quality standards. This strict monitoring of processes on the one hand and consistent product quality controls on the other have led to the high standard of quality the industry has already achieved. No wonder that manufacturers often decide to issue recalls when there is a reasonable suspicion of a problem – they don't want this high standard to be threatened by potential risks or accidents.

Our little example from the automobile industry is an impressive example of the effort which manufacturers undertake to maximize the potential level of safety. On the other hand, the above scenario also demonstrated that, even with the greatest precautions, technical problems or human misconduct cannot be completely avoided.

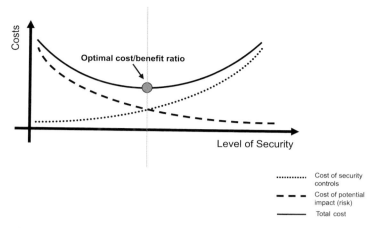

Figure 2.1 Optimum investment level

The right size of an investment relative to its benefits (= safety level) must be found again and again. There is no fixed value. Rather, each organization must re-evaluate this optimum investment level at regular intervals (see Figure 2.1).

Unfortunately, comprehensive information security in process can still not be taken for granted. Our example from the automobile industry is merely the tip of the iceberg. Again and again we encounter companies which – consciously or unconsciously – disregard security in a negligent manner and limit their entire security management to say installing a virus scanner.

However, the general awareness of information security is undergoing a significant change. While a focus on individual objects and access protection for the data of these objects was sufficient only a few years ago, today's conscientious security officer makes certain that his entire production chain is covered by comprehensive and consistent security. Whether the chain consists of complex assembly lines in the automobile production or an auction site on the internet is more or less irrelevant. Each has its special requirements on the basic pillars of security which we are all familiar with in terms of integrity, confidentiality, availability and liability.

Knowing your own processes in detail is indispensable for the general idea of information security. In many cases, the documentation is incomplete, process owners are not defined, interfaces insufficiently specified, data flows unknown and potential threat scenarios ignored – apart from the fact that potential security measures, escalations and workarounds are not described. Having solid process knowledge enables you to carry out clearly defined security analyses and audits which, when executed in regular intervals, provide you with information about the security status, potential security trends and a lot more.

The idea of a process-oriented information security analysis is also reflected in the various security standards which are increasingly being used and accepted, such as ISO/IEC 17799 at international level [ISO17799].

The logical consequence of this information security approach is to analyze security comprehensively, proactively, strategically and as a continuous process. Getting proper support from management is an essential prerequisite for a comprehensive implementation and acceptance among the employees. Besides, what good are the best processes and regulations if management does not set an example by actively practicing security itself?

Since 100-percent security cannot be achieved despite all the efforts in the field of information security, a cyclical controlling process must be introduced. Only with such a process can you take the constantly changing security requirements into account and respond with adequate measures – just like the virus scanner which requires almost daily updates in order to keep up with the constant stream of new threats. For more details concerning the continuous controlling process see Chapter 15.

2.2 Starting Point / Current Situation

The starting point for the introduction of an effective information security management system[1] can vary considerable from company to company. The organizational development can range from very active and competent (Experienced Company) to less developed (Greenfield Company), especially in areas where information security was neglected in the past. The approaches to implementing effective information security management differ significantly in the different company types. There is no single approach. For each scenario, the procedures and objectives for planning, design and implementation must be coordinated individually.

In addition to the wrong assessment of information security (many companies still mistake information security for individual security issues like virus protection or firewalls), there is still no basic awareness of information security in general terms. This starts with top management and flows like a red thread throughout the entire enterprise.

Greenfield Company. The "greenfield company" has significant shortcomings, particularly with respect to its organizational environment. In the field of security standards and regulations as well as security policies or guidelines, these companies are in dire need of putting some structure and content into their security organization, if one already exists. Developing the company from a low to an acceptable level of security takes time, which the company also needs to understand and start practicing the necessary processes and to build the required organization and infrastructure.

Developing information security in a company is a process that can take years (see Figure 2.2).

---

[1] An information security management system (ISMS) is a management system to establish policies and objectives for information security within the context of the organization's overall business risk and the means by which these objectives can be achieved.

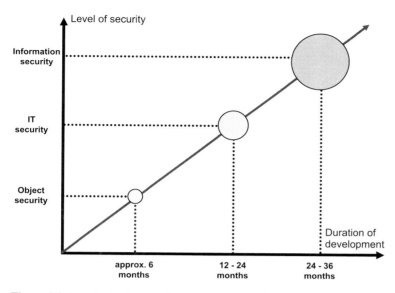

Figure 2.2 Developing information security within the company

Experienced Company. The "experienced company", on the other hand, already has some concrete ideas with respect to information security management. Security policy, security rules and regulations, risk management, security organization and business continuity management are terms the experienced company can deal with and may have already implemented more or less.

For this type of company, starting "from scratch" would not make sense. Companies like these want to make sure that the work they have already done in the area of security management will be considered. That's why the foundation for all future activities should be a thorough current status analysis, from which the strategy for maintaining and improving the current level of information security will be developed in line with the company's requirements (see Figure 2.3).

The experienced company generally has dedicated and explicit requirements. In most cases, the existing security officer has already collected some experience and expertise in aspects of security and will be only too happy to contribute his knowledge to any kind of security project. The trick is to channel this knowledge to provide the maximum benefit for a potential security project.

Ideally, the experienced company already has a security organization and can provide solid facts and input for various types of analyses. Often, the organization actively participates in security committees and therefore has excellent access to security studies. What's important in each case is the company's benchmark position relative to its market and its competitors. To improve its position relative to its competition, the experienced company demands to get support from a functioning, active security management system.

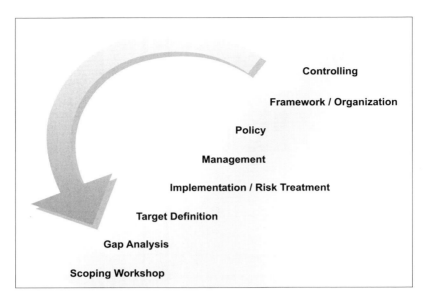

Controlling

Framework / Organization

Policy

Management

Implementation / Risk Treatment

Target Definition

Gap Analysis

Scoping Workshop

Figure 2.3 Typical steps for experienced companies

2.3 Drivers for Information Security Management

Legal Regulations. Independent of the company's development status w.r.t. security management, legal regulations are another major factor that plays an important role. Different countries have different laws and regulations governing information security which range far beyond data protection.

Security management must take these regulations into account. Working closely with corporate legal and auditing departments, should they exist, makes the security officer's job a lot easier. Complying with these regulations is becoming more and more a challenge particularly for internationally operating companies.

Specific Requirements (Compliance, Competition, Certification, Standards, etc.). Another driver for security management is the competition. Certifying that it handles its customer data securely can give a business a decided competitive advantage. Who would like to entrust his account information or patient file to a company that does not know how to handle it? And, to get back to our earlier example, who would not want to have the manufacturing processes in the automobile industry based on standards that certify compliance with all applicable safety standards, that the acceptance certificates reflect real results and that the vehicle will operate safely at all times?

Such compliance checks are performed by accredited companies in the form of certification audits. If the results are positive, the authorized auditor confirms on a certificate that the respective scope of certification complies with the selected security standards and is actually being practiced.

These certifications apply to many different kinds of standards. The company must evaluate and decide whether the certification should focus more on secure technology or on secure process management. In each case, certificates signal to the customer, partner or supplier that the company takes security seriously and can prove a certain security status.

In addition to complying with recognized international standards, each company can of course set its own internal standards, rules and regulations. Actually, a healthy mix of multiple standards and in-house regulations is quite common.

Figure 2.4 presents a simple classification of some popular standards for information security management. FIPS 140 and ITSEC / Common Criteria are technical oriented and concentrate on development aspects.

- FIPS (Federal Information Processing Standard) 140 specifies security requirements for cryptographic modules [FIPS140]. The standard covers 11 areas related to the design and implementation of a cryptographic module, and defines a security level rating (1-4, from lowest to highest), depending on what requirements are met.
- ITSEC (Information Technology Security Evaluation Criteria) is a European standard that assesses software and computer systems concerning their functionality and trustworthiness with data and computer security.
- The Common Criteria for IT Security Evaluations (CC), also known as ISO standard 15408 [ISO15408], provide for a broad range of assurance for many types of commercial and government use IT security products. The purpose of independent CC evaluations is to establish confidence and trust that a security product or system actually does what the vendor claims.

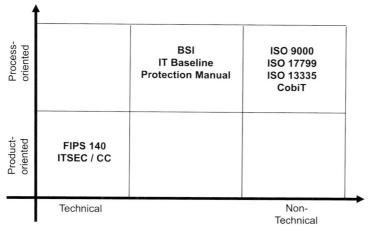

Source: Initi@tive D[21]

Figure 2.4 Overview of security and quality standards

A number of standards exist, which are less technical oriented and concentrate more on process aspects.

- The German IT Baseline Protection Manual aims to achieve a standard security level for IT systems based on infrastructural, organizational, human resources and technical standard security measures [BSI03].

- The ISO 9000 series of quality standards provide requirements and guidelines for quality management system elements and quality assurance and involve two basic actions: establishing proper quality management and documenting of controls.

- ISO/IEC 17799 intends to serve as a single reference point for identifying the range of security controls needed for information systems used in industry and commerce [ISO17799]. The standard can be used by large, medium and small enterprises.

- ISO/IEC 13335 is a five-part technical report giving guidance to define and describe the various concepts associated with the management of IT security [ISO13335].

- The Control Objectives for Information and related Technology (CobiT) contain control objectives that have been designed to help companies maintain effective control over IT.

Formal certification is not always needed. Despite the fact that achieving compliance is the main effort, many companies currently do without the official certificate, although the costs of preparing for the official certification are relatively minor compared to the cost of becoming compliant. The costs of a pure certification audit are estimated to make up only 2-3% of the overall cost.

Many companies advertise their compliance without having the official certification (a practice referred to as "self-declaration"). While this may provide some benefits, it is not considered equivalent to a "real" certification in the industry. Below is a list of the possible path towards certification:

- *Compliance*
  The company strives to operate its processes in accordance with selected security or other standards. It does not have an official certificate.

- *Self-declaration*
  A small step after compliance is self-declaration. The company officially claims that it operates its processes according to selected security standards. Again, there is no official certificate.

- *Manufacturer's Certificate*
  The company undergoes preparation programs in order to achieve compliance. In some cases, software or hardware manufacturers or information security consulting companies state that processes are documented to comply with standards.

- *Certificate*
  The highest level is an official certificate. Such a certificate can only be issued by accredited institutions. It provides the highest advertising benefits and the greatest competitive advantage.

These stages don't necessarily have to be traversed one after the other in order to conclude a certification. Since the terminology of the individual stages is not always consistent (only a few standards like, for example, the German BSI IT Baseline Protection Manual [BSI03] specify the names for the individual stages), companies still have a good amount of freedom with respect to their standard compliance claims.

2.4 What's the Best Way?

Since there is no single method or "best way", the greenfield company has to do a lot more in order to get the process going. After a basic orientation (scoping and roadmap), its first tasks include building a security organization and creating a top-level security policy, followed by additional analysis and management issues.

The experienced company, on the other hand, is a step ahead. In most cases, it already has at least a partial security organization and at least rudimentary security guidelines or policies in place. In the best possible case, the experienced company can make decisions where it wants to start out with the security process, which concrete analyses it wants to have and/or which areas need a more thorough examination based on objective and strategic aspects and not on the basis of the administrator's good instinct (see Figure 2.3).

However, the fact that there is no 100% security applies for both, despite all analyses and management efforts. All information security endeavors try to achieve a maximum amount of security with reasonable effort. Often the last 20% of security are so expensive that they are simply not worth the huge investment in security measures. And in addition to the cost factor that makes 100% security virtually impossible, there is still another factor that can never be completely controlled: people and their behavior.

2.5 Object-Oriented vs. Process-Oriented Approach

In the past, finding current risks was mostly the domain of IT managers or administrators. Because of their technical knowledge, functional or hierarchical level and, last but not least, the availability of methods and tools, their risk analysis tended to focus on objects, i.e. it was object-oriented. Objects can be workstations, clients, servers, host computers and even networks – at least as far as their components are concerned. Objects also include other infrastructure equipment, most of which falls into the area of building protection and access.

The object-oriented analyses therefore focused on singular objects. For each object, common analyses like vulnerability, threat and risk analyses were performed. Finally, dedicated security measures were recommended – again for each specific object. For larger analyses, the resulting document could become quite voluminous.

Ultimately, the specialist had to create a homogeneous security concept that pooled all the recommendations, eliminated redundancies and checked for interoperability problems. This was often done manually, opening the door for errors. The company was also unable to figure out what would happen if one of the analyzed objects failed.

Which brings us to a critical question: What does the failure of an object mean for my business, i.e. for my business processes?

More and more companies ask themselves this question, which is why the development of methodologies and tools is moving towards process orientation. In detail, this means: don't focus on the individual object, but analyze and asses the entire process. The benefit for the company is that it can play through or simulate various threat or failure scenarios. Based on these scenarios, it can then make adequate recommendations, point out potential damages and put a financial value on them.

Particularly the new security standards like ISO 27001 [ISO27001] (based on BS7799-2 [BS7799b]) are pushing security consulting in this direction and affect tools and methodologies accordingly. This starts with the fact that interviews and visits are no longer limited strictly to the operational level, but place tougher requirements on management as well. Management contributes actively, is involved from the very start, gets asked questions, is informed of the results and affected by the measures which are finally determined. This is the only way to achieve sustainable results and raise the acceptance for information security among the staff. Management's role model function is an important factor for the success or failure of the entire information security idea that should not be underestimated.

Of course, this process orientation also demands a transformation of the information security idea itself. While having detailed knowledge of an object or operating system (Windows, Unix, router software, network protocols, etc.) was sufficient in the past, today's security specialist needs to have wide ranging expertise of many information security aspects as well as broad business know-how, particularly with respect to processes. Being able to model a company's processes is essential for the object-oriented approach. The art is to model the processes as small as possible but as large as necessary if you want to come up with a logical result that ultimately produces practical security improvement recommendations for the company.

This transformation is also reflected in the information security tool environment. Until recently, mostly technically oriented tools were being offered that focused on the scanning and administration of IT systems. Today there are more and more suppliers to try to support not only the technical aspects with their tools, but also organizational and non-IT issues. There are lots of useful modeling tools for the process analysis as well.

2.6 Strategic Comprehensive Approach

Up to this point, we have discussed what drives information security management (legal aspects, standards, competition, etc.), that there is no single best method, and that the transformation from the object-oriented to the process-oriented approach continues unabated.

All these factors make information security management not exactly a no-brainer, which is why the call for a strategic, comprehensive approach is getting louder all the time. Companies need and want more security from soup to nuts and not just spot checks. That's why a security roadmap must be created and driven forward in small, manageable steps for each specific area of requirements.

A system of solution packages simplifies this approach. For example, workshops and smaller analyses can be conducted first in order to determine the project's scope in detail and find major shortcomings. Based on the results, more focused and detailed analyses and security management programs can then be set up.

We must always remember that information security management is about much more than technical concerns. Especially in the organizational field there are often major gaps and flaws. Only companies who are really well-developed (from a security standpoint) have a top-level policy or even an information security framework. In such cases, management needs to be convinced of the need to continuously meet or even exceed the minimum security requirements in order to gain a competitive advantage in addition to actually improving the level of security.

What's also important in any case is to treat information security management not as a one-time project. You should always view it as a control loop in which sensors (= analyses) continuously measure the current status and where appropriate measures are constantly taken (= management) to keep things from drifting off-course.

For the company, this means that security must be a regular project to be performed either in-house of by outside parties (outsourcing). In each case, you must make certain that a control loop has been established and is being practiced. In ideal cases, the company provides special capacity, even if only to check the security relevant work of outside parties. For more details concerning the continuous controlling process and outsourcing issues see Chapter 15.

2.7 Solutions

Practicing comprehensive information security management requires a harmonized portfolio of methodologies, i.e. a toolbox:

- that takes the needs of different and individual starting points into account,
- that takes object security as well as process security into account,
- that supports proprietary as well as standardized procedures.

As shown in Figure 2.5, the consulting solutions in information security management can be divided into five major activities.

Initiation and Scoping. *Initiation and scoping* provides the starting base for security management projects and defines the following points:

- What are the project limitations?
- What are the scope limitations?

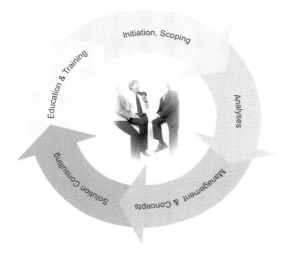

Figure 2.5
Consulting activities

- What is the schedule?
- Which project results must be created?
- Does a gap analysis have to be performed?

All of these questions are answered in a scoping workshop. In most cases it is not really known what the area of the investigation is until the scoping workshop has been completed.

With larger objects, an additional gap analysis is performed in order to back up the planning before the actual work components can be scheduled and started.

The scoping phase is useful for all types of security programs since it specifies key values and defines the procedure including expected results in detail. This cuts down on interpretations and the time-consuming discussions they inevitably lead to.

Analyses. In this section, various customized analyses can be performed for different requirements. The list shows these analyses in order of their level of complexity:

- High-level business process analysis
- Gap analysis
- Penetration test
- Audits as per individual specifications
- Object-oriented risk analysis
- Process-oriented risk analysis
- Examination and analysis of security-relevant documents (policy assessment).

A *high-level business process analysis* focuses on the most important processes. Having access to the managers of these processes (= process owner) for interviews is essential, because only they can provide the information needed to determine the precise scope of the analysis. The processes are then weighted and prioritized before a decision is made which processes will be subjected to a security analysis.

The *gap analysis* provides in only a few days a security-related overview of certain, previously identified business processes. It makes it possible to determine where concrete action is needed and to create a logical roadmap, i.e. a type of schedule for achieving the desired level of security.

Penetration tests or intrusion attempts into computer systems or networks are already being performed by many companies proactively and in-house, using commercial tools as well as freely available exploits from the internet. The results provide information about current vulnerabilities so that administrators can fix them immediately. Penetration tests differ in the way in which they are executed.

The *white-box test* simulates an internal attacker who already has access to the company's local network. The *black-box test*, on the other hand, simulates a hacker who attacks from the outside, for example over the Internet. This attacker usually knows not much more than the company's name. In addition, *social hacking* is becoming increasingly more important. With this version of the penetration, an attempt is made to gain information on an interpersonal level, for example by pretending to be a service technician who supposedly needs the administrator's password for his work, or by trying to gain access to the company through areas like the receiving dock, cafeteria, etc.

When such tests are performed as part of a preparation program for the certification according to a certain security standard like ISO/IEC 27001 or BS 7799-2, they must be preceded by so-called *gap analyses* in which the differences between the actual security status and the desired security standard are determined. This step makes a detailed estimation of additionally required work packages possible.

It is also possible to perform such analyses according to company-specific requirements. In *audits as per individual requirements* best-practice approaches are taken into account, but the focus is primarily on company-internal specifications. Here, too, the difference between the actual security status and the selected specification is determined. This step can also lead to a detailed determination of additionally required work packages.

The *object-oriented risk analysis*, as shown in Figure 2.6, focuses primarily on the security status of individual objects to find vulnerabilities and threats. From this information, the risk level is calculated on the basis of each object's importance and the likelihood of the threats to which the object is subjected.

The analytical methods range from simple inspections to interviews, questionnaires, self-assessments and complex, tool-supported network analyses. The results document the vulnerabilities, threats and risks which can then be responded to with appropriate security measures (see below).

The various risk ratings as well as any proposed security measures are often not related to each other. The results should instead be applied to the individual object being analyzed.

On the other side, we have the *process-oriented risk analysis*. The process-oriented risk analysis first models the business process to be examined on the basis of the assets involved (= rateable objects). These include computer systems as well as build-

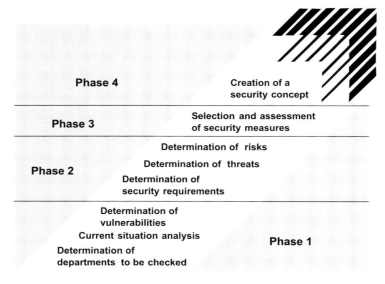

Figure 2.6 Risk analysis (object-oriented)

ings, data and applications, infrastructure and people. Once the business process models have been created, the involved assets can be subjected to business impact analyses in order to find out how important the individual assets are for the entire business process.

In subsequent interviews and surveys, any vulnerabilities and threats are identified. Based on this information, the risk value can be determined as shown in Figure 2.7.

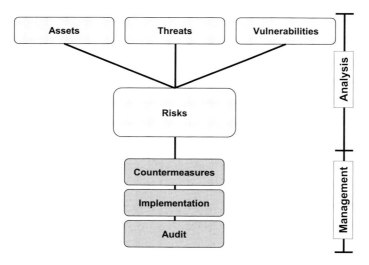

Figure 2.7 Risk analysis (process-oriented)

The *examination and analysis of security-relevant documents (policy assessment)* looks at the security documents and regulations within the company and provides the basis for the information security policy framework. It consists of information security rules and regulations which specify detailed, company-wide and mandatory security instructions, processes and guidelines based on a top-level security policy.

The goal of this set of regulations is the publication of mandatory policies which must be complied with by employees as well as outside suppliers. The document analysis confirms that this documentation is available and identifies what needs to be updated, improved, redeveloped or removed.

Management and Concepts. Management uses the results of the preceding analyses. These results can be used to document that risks exist and have been recognized. On the other hand, they can also be used to take appropriate action.

At this point it is important to check whether the results are still valid and applicable. Security analyses have a very short "shelf life". When in doubt, it is recommended to make spot checks and, if necessary, repeat parts of the analysis to make sure that the findings still apply.

If you want to base your security management on a solid foundation, you face the fundamental decision how you plan to respond to the individual risks. The following options apply:

- Accept the risks
- Transfer the risks
- Avoid the risks
- Reduce the risks.

Accepting the risks means to knowingly and objectively accept risks, providing they clearly satisfy the organization's policy and criteria for risk acceptance.

By *transferring the risks* you delegate them and their handling to third parties such as insurance companies, service providers or suppliers.

If you want to *avoid the risks*, you prohibit activities that would cause the risks to occur.

In most cases, you will prioritize the recognized risks and respond with appropriate security measures in order to *reduce the residual risk* to an acceptable level (see Figure 2.1). But keep in mind that the one-time implementation of a measure will not take care of the problem forever. It takes continuous controlling to make sure that the measure keeps working and is used appropriately.

The results of the controlling activities are transmitted via the defined reporting paths to the appropriate decision-makers. Ideally, they will lead to a renewed analysis with adjusted activity recommendations.

At this point, it is recommended to have a strategic plan for information security investments so that you don't just put out fires but maintain the level of information security over the long term with the help of a coordinated and visionary concept (long-term roadmap).

Another important criterion that determines whether the idea of information security throughout the company will live or die is the commitment of management. In addition to providing the necessary budget for information security measures, it is absolutely necessary that management openly stands behind the issues. If management does not accept them, it will be virtually impossible to convince the staff that the measures are necessary and need to be used.

Solution Consulting. Solution consulting plays a role at the end of larger security programs. After a product-independent analysis and management phase (s. below), product-specific consulting services can be provided on the basis of the insights which have been gained. In most cases, this phase consists of several issue-oriented workshops, similar to the scoping workshops at the beginning of the cycle. The goal of these workshops is to get as much developed output information as possible so that follow-up programs can be based on this information. Follow-up activities could include the detailed creation of requests for proposals for the next security implementation phase (for example, the introduction of a PKI).

Education and Training. Education and training is a major component of any security program. It can be particularly beneficial for employee awareness.

Continuous Process. Information security on paper is far from real information security. Its processes and behavioral patterns must be "lived". This is why it may be praiseworthy if a company has a lovely set of information security regulations, but they are of little use if they are not being practiced; the processes don't really work and the employees don't follow them.

The concept of information security is based on the seamless and smooth interaction of all the parties involved (processes, people and technology), where everyone knows his job, where the processes are seamlessly integrated into the company's mission and

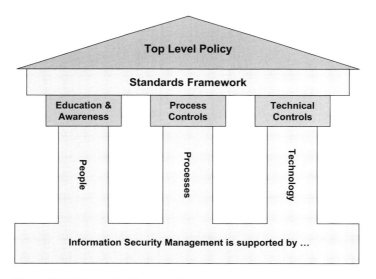

Figure 2.8 Information Security Management

42

where security is not viewed as an obstacle but as an enabler. Persistent threats in all areas of security (availability, integrity, confidentiality and reliability) manifest the permanent challenges facing a functioning information security management system (see also Figure 2.8).

The information security management must be supported by powerful and effective controlling. The trick is to limit yourself to a few methods and tools, but to use them consistently and permanently. The best central controlling tools have an indicator system for evaluating risks and benefits and a related reporting system. The job of controlling should never be intermingled with information security per se. The security manager is responsible for making the right security decisions, while the controller is responsible for supplying the manager with the information he needs to make these decisions. Both can be compared to the roles of a ship's captain (= management) and pilot (= controlling).

A good controlling system can significantly improve the information security management system's performance.

2.8 Conclusion

"Too many cooks in the kitchen" is a good description of the multitude of standards, methodologies and tools in the field of information security management. Many consulting offerings in the field of information security management only add to the confusion – and make it even more difficult for the user to make a decision.

Our experience has shown that *the ideal solution* does not exist. In many cases, a mix of various standards is used, enhanced by in-house regulations, guidelines, tools and methods. Each company must arrive at its own decision. What all standards have in common is that they view information security management as a comprehensive, strategic process that must be equipped with sufficient manpower and constantly monitors the latest developments and trends (new standards, tools and methods) and integrates them into the control loop. Information security management must be an ongoing process that can also meet the proprietary requirements at any time. What's important in any case is that the information security management processes are properly documented in order to meet various auditing requirements.

All companies which have recognized that security is an important factor for the success of their business must (re)act. There are many ways of making your business processes secure. If you feel that you don't have sufficient in-house expertise at your disposal, don't hesitate to get competent consulting help from the outside.

In the end of the day, it's the early bird that catches the worm and the smart company which has a certain level of information security installed before anything bad happens. Of course it's always easier to justify investments in security measures after incidents occurred, but it might be very much more expensive, too. Or even too late.

3 Network and System Security

Uwe Blöcher

3.1 Challenges and Requirements

Computer criminality is widespread. The U.S. Federal Trade Commission has calculated that the annual loss runs to $48 billion[1]. This damage is caused, for example, by computer viruses, worms, sabotage and misuse of confidential data. The threat is growing year by year.

For most companies, networks and the connected systems are some of their most important means of production. If they are down, considerable costs can be incurred very easily. Information and the know-how of the enterprise are no less valuable. Protecting them can ensure its economic survival. That's why there must be four objectives at the core of every security concept:

- Confidentiality: Business information is not intended for everyone's eyes. Confidentiality means that unauthorized persons cannot read the protected information.

- Integrity: Data can be easily manipulated in the network, but there are secure methods for ensuring the integrity of data and communications. Changes to data are detected reliably.

- Authenticity: Many situations demand verified proof of a communication partner's identity. The means of providing this range from a simple user ID and password to a complex public key infrastructure. Electronic signatures show reliably who is communicating with whom.

- Availability: If a network is protected against sabotage internally and externally, the reliability of the means of communication increases significantly.

Of course, not only the security requirements are important. Other requirements include:

- High Performance: The deployed security solutions must not degrade performance in an unacceptable way.

- User Friendliness: A security solution will only be accepted by the user if it is easy to use.

- Maintainability: A security solution will only be effective if it is kept up to date. This means that a security solution must be easy to maintain.

---

[1] "The Globe and Mail" October 24, 2003

- Cost Effectiveness: Not only the product price is important but the Total Cost of Ownership including implementation, administration and maintenance.

3.2 Solution Components

We will introduce the most important solution components below.

Firewalls – the key technology in network security – monitor communications at the interfaces between private corporate networks and the Internet.

Virtual private networks (VPNs) can be set up via public networks as an inexpensive and very secure means of ensuring that enterprise communication is protected. VPN-based solutions also give field personnel and small branch offices secure *remote LAN access* (RLA). Today, VPN functionality is typically integrated into firewalls.

To ensure the confidentiality and integrity of sensitive company data and IT systems within the corporate network, *intrusion detection and prevention systems (IDS/IDP)*, *content security* and *antivirus* technologies are used. Small enterprises can be secured by all-in-one communication platforms.

Figure 3.1 shows the typical components of a network & system security solution.

Professional services, lifecycle services and managed services offer efficient protection against new threats because counter-measures such as installation of up-to-date versions, patches and updates of configurations are performed in time.

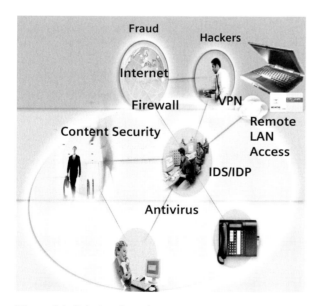

Figure 3.1 Solution Overview

3.2.1 Firewall

Purpose

A firewall is intended to block unsolicited traffic at the network boundary. Unsolicited traffic includes attempts by hackers to break into the private network, i.e. the corporate Intranet. The firewall therefore has the important task of keeping the private network free from intruders. This is usually not easy because the distinction between harmless and intended traffic on one hand and malicious traffic on the other hand is difficult and can often only be seen from the context.

Principle

A firewall decides which data packets are allowed to cross the boundary between the private Intranet and the Internet, offering two-way protection. The firewall uses a pre-defined set of rules, which are usually adapted by a specialist to the enterprise-specific security objectives.

Technology

Firewalls may be dedicated hardware devices, called appliances, or software programs running on standard HW. There are different types of firewalls.

A *packet filter* intercepts all traffic to and from the network and checks it against the rules provided. Typically, the packet filter uses the source IP address, source port, destination IP address and destination port. These are the filter criteria for allowing or disallowing traffic from certain IP addresses or on certain ports.

Another type of firewall is the *application proxy*. The internal client first establishes a connection with the application proxy. The application proxy determines if the connection should be allowed or not and then establishes a connection with the destination computer. All communications go through two connections – client to application proxy and application proxy to destination. The application proxy monitors all traffic against its rules before deciding whether or not to forward it. The application gateway is the only address seen by the outside world, so the internal network is protected. Application proxies are not designed to allow for new types of protocols. To pass a new protocol through a proxy server, you must develop a workaround. Because the application proxy terminates the connections passing through, the performance of application proxies can be bad, because this requires effort.

Stateful inspection is a new firewall technology that simplifies the configuration of new protocols. Stateful inspection enhances packet filtering by adding state information from past communications and other applications. Some of the new stateful inspection firewalls allow new protocol definitions to be added simply to the firewall. Much like a packet filter firewall, stateful inspection firewalls can be easily configured to allow new protocols to pass through the firewall via defined ports. In addition to this ease of configuration, the stateful inspection firewalls can provide added security to these new protocols by performing packet inspection for the packets moving through the firewall. Some stateful inspection firewalls, for example Checkpoint Firewall-1, have a scripting language that allows customers to write and add scripts for packet inspection. This gives an extra layer of security above packet filtering while maintaining ease of configuration. The stateful inspection firewalls are able to inspect all levels of the TCP/IP packets allowing inspection scripts to be as simple or complex as required. In addition, stateful inspection firewalls typically offer higher performance than application proxies.

Combination with other Solutions

Modern network firewalls typically also have VPN and remote LAN access gateway functionality included. Firewalls can often interact with content security and antivirus products to block malicious content at the network boundary.

Scenarios

Firewalls are usually set up in DMZ (Demilitarized Zone) configurations. A DMZ is a computer or small subnetwork that sits between a trusted internal network, such as a corporate private LAN, and a non-trusted external network, such as the public Internet.

Typically, the DMZ contains devices accessible to Internet traffic, such as Web (HTTP) servers, FTP servers, SMTP (e-mail) servers and DNS servers (see Figure 3.2).

Useful Hints

Packet filters do not represent state-of-the-art today. Sophisticated attacks cannot be detected and blocked by pure packet filters. Application proxies and stateful inspection firewalls can be equally secure. However, stateful inspection firewalls are today the most common because of the ease with which new protocols can be added and the higher performance offered. However, even the best firewall is only as good as how it is administrated and maintained. Updating the firewall software on a regular basis and

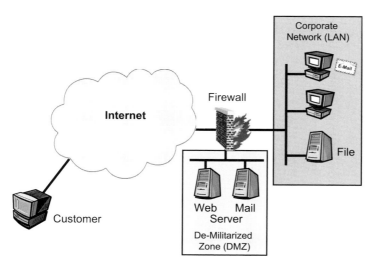

Figure 3.2 Typical DMZ scenario

adjusting and keeping the firewall rules up-to-date is essential for maintaining effective protection.

Because all traffic to and from the outside world passes through the firewall, its availability must be assured. High availability can be achieved by redundant configurations, like hot standby or load sharing.

3.2.2 Virtual Private Networks

Purpose

A virtual private network can be compared with a tunnel that links two communication partners through a public network. The VPN protects this connection, for example against eavesdropping, modification of data and unauthorized access.

Principle

Security protocols for ensuring confidentiality, integrity and authentication are used for implementing such VPNs. Today, either IPSec or SSL/TLS are the de-facto standards for the security protocol. A distinction can be made between site-to-site VPNs, linking two or more sites, and remote LAN access VPNs. Remote access VPNs are addressed in the next section.

Technology

Site-to-site VPNs are realized with VPN gateways, which can be hardware devices, software programs or a combination of the two.

The Secure Sockets Layer (SSL) or the similar Transport Layer Security protocol (TLS, standardized by the IETF) and the IP Security protocol IPSec are the two most important security protocols in the secure VPN area.

The SSL/TLS protocol is specified as a protocol that sits on top of a reliable transport system and offers the security service connection-oriented confidentiality, connection-oriented integrity and client and server authentication.

IPSec is defined as an extension of the IP protocol and can protect IPv4 as well as IPv6 traffic. It offers the security service connectionless confidentiality and integrity, optional replay protection and authentication of the IPSec peers.

Both protocols are specified as protocols that are independent of the specific application that uses their services. Consequently, they can provide secure tunnels through the Internet that can be used by a variety of applications.

SSL/TLS

SSL/TLS is designed as an application-independent security protocol operating on top of a reliable transport protocol (e.g. TCP). It offers the security services

- connection-oriented data confidentiality,
- connection-oriented data integrity,

- unilateral as well as mutual authentication of the SSL/TLS peers.

SSL/TLS defines not only an encapsulation protocol but also provides a protocol for key management. SSL/TLS is a session-oriented protocol, i.e. the SSL/TLS key management establishes security sessions that define the security parameters applied for protecting higher-level application data.

IPSec

IPSec comprises two protocols for data protection – IP Authentication Header (AH) and IP Encapsulating Security Payload (ESP) – and the key management protocol Internet Key Exchange (IKE).

The authentication header offers connectionless integrity, data origin authentication and protection against replay. The encapsulating security payload provides connectionless confidentiality and integrity, data origin authentication and protection against replay. According to the IPv6 design, both protocols define specific extension headers of an IPv6 packet that convey the security protocol specific information. These headers can also be integrated into an IPv4 datagram. The protocols support two modes of operation: transport mode and tunnel mode. In transport mode, the protocols provide protection primarily for upper layer protocols; in tunnel mode, the protocols are applied to a 'tunneled' IP packet that is encapsulated into another IP packet. Tunnel mode is used for site-to-site VPNs.

IKE is defined as a key management protocol for IPSec. IKE distinguishes between two different phases. In the first phase, two IKE peers set up a secure connection between themselves which is then used to establish security sessions for other security protocols like IPSec in the second phase.

Usage

SSL VPNs are better suited for enabling secure access by individual users to a private network (remote LAN access VPNs) than for connecting entire network segments (site-to-site VPNs).

Combination with other Solutions

VPN gateways are often parts of firewalls. A public key infrastructure (see Chapter 12) is useful for effective key management of larger installations. VPN gateways can be used for site-to-site and remote LAN access (cf. next section).

Figure 3.3 VPN site-to-site scenario

Scenarios

Figure 3.3 illustrates the site-to-site VPN tunnel through the public network (e.g. Internet).

Useful Hints

IPSec is the de facto standard for site-to-site VPNs. One differentiating factor for the solutions on the market is how easy they are to manage.

3.2.3 Remote LAN Access

Purpose

Field personnel or teleworkers are linked securely to the corporate network by means of encryption and authentication. Remote LAN access means that the remote computer is actually like a host on the LAN. The only difference between a remote host and workstations connected directly to the LAN is the slower data transfer speed. Figure 3.4 shows a typical scenario.

Principle

As explained in the previous section, IPSec or SSL/TLS based solutions can be used.

Technology

The main difference between IPSec and SSL/TLS based solutions is on the client side.

IPSec requires installation of an IPSec client. Because IPSec works on the IP layer, it can be used for all IP-based protocols. Its performance is good. However, it is dependent on the individual configuration of the client PC (e.g. operating system, application, network interface cards, access router). Larger installations may be difficult to maintain if there is no standardized hardware and software for the client.

SSL/TLS can only be used for protocols on a TCP basis. Because SSL/TLS is almost an application layer protocol, it is not dependent on the way the client is connected to the network. This makes SSL/TLS based solutions easier to maintain than IPSec based. SSL/TLS VPNs may use the built-in SSL/TLS functionality of browsers. No SW installation is then required on the client side. However, the drawback of this is that there is no control of the security of the client (Antivirus installed? Spyware?), especially if clients in public spaces (e.g. Internet cafes) are used. Therefore, it may be advantageous to use SSL/TLS products, which use dedicated client software.

Combination with other Solutions

Authentication is critical for remote LAN access. There are different authentication methods possible, ranging from limited security to high security. Popular are

- User name/password authentication
- One time token (e.g. SecurID)
- Smart cards.

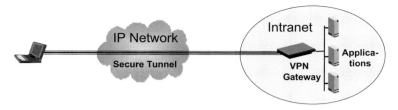

Figure 3.4 Remote LAN access scenario

For more information on the authentication mechanisms see Chapters 4 and 6.

Information on users – for example which users are allowed to have access, which access rights – must be administered. Directories come into play in this context (see Chapter 5).

Useful Hints

Both IPSec and SSL are used today for remote LAN access. Both have their advantages.

Characteristics of IPSec-based solutions:

+ Support all IP-based protocols
+ Better performance
+ Better control of client security
− Software installation required
− Standardized client hardware and software is recommended for avoiding problems with larger rollouts

Characteristic of SSL-based solutions:

+ May not need software installation
+ Lower rollout costs
− If no client is used, the security status of the client is uncertain

3.2.4 Intrusion Detection and Prevention Systems

Purpose

Intrusion detection and prevention systems monitor the network to identify or prevent misuse of communication channels.

Principle

An intrusion detection and prevention system (IDS/IDP) inspects all inbound and outbound network activity and identifies suspicious patterns that may indicate a network or system attack from someone attempting to break into or compromise a system.

IDS systems are characterized by the fact that they simply identify suspicious patterns whereas IDP systems also actively take counter-measures.

Technology

There are several ways to categorize an IDS/IDP (according to Webopedia[1]):

Misuse detection vs. anomaly detection: in misuse detection, the IDS analyzes the information it gathers and compares it to large databases of attack signatures. Essentially, the IDS looks for a specific attack that has already been documented. Like a virus detection system, misuse detection software is only as good as the database of attack signatures that it uses to compare packets against. In anomaly detection, the system administrator defines the baseline or normal state of the network's traffic load, breakdown, protocol and typical packet size. The anomaly detector monitors network segments to compare their state to the normal baseline and look for anomalies.

Network-based vs. host-based systems: in a network-based system, or NIDS, the individual packets flowing through a network are analyzed. The NIDS can detect malicious packets that are designed to be overlooked by a firewall's simplistic filtering rules. In a host-based system, the IDS examines the activity on each individual computer or host.

Passive system vs. reactive system: in a passive system, the IDS detects a potential security breach, logs the information and signals an alert. In a reactive system, the IDS responds to the suspicious activity by logging off a user or by reprogramming the firewall to block network traffic from the suspected malicious source. Reactive IDS is called intrusion prevention.

Combination with other Solutions

Though they both relate to network security, an IDS/IDP system differs from a firewall in that a firewall looks out for intrusions in order to stop them from happening. The firewall limits access between networks in order to prevent intrusion and does not signal an attack from inside the network. An IDS evaluates a suspected intrusion once

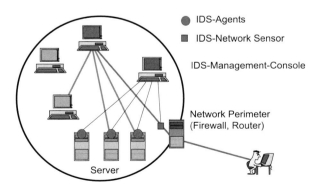

● IDS-Agents

■ IDS-Network Sensor

IDS-Management-Console

Network Perimeter
(Firewall, Router)

Server

Figure 3.5
Intrusion detection

---

[1] http://www.webopedia.com/TERM/I/intrusion_detection_system.html

it has taken place and signals an alarm. An IDS also watches for attacks that originate from within a system.

Scenarios

Figure 3.5 shows a typical intrusion detection scenario.

Useful Hints

As IDS/IDP systems may generate a high rate of alarms, it is crucial to define the rules precisely in order to keep the rate of false alarms low.

3.2.5 Filtering Content: Content Security and Gateway Antivirus

Purpose

Content security systems control the content that leaves and enters a corporate network. Important purposes include, for example, blocking viruses, spam, trojans, malicious code and blocking unsolicited e-mails, called spam.

Principle

Content security systems analyze the flow of data in the network in terms of its content. In this way, they can prevent certain sensitive data from leaving the corporate network without having been protected. At the same time, they keep unwanted content out of the network. Typically, the most critical applications are e-mail and web.

Technology

A distinction can be made between web and e-mail solutions:

Web:

Many solutions are based on extensive databases that categorize all web sites in the Internet, for example. Legally problematic content or content that is not related to employees' work is blocked reliably by so-called URL filters. In addition, the products analyze the web http traffic for key words and malicious content.

E-mail:

In just a few years, e-mail has grown from a novelty to a mission-critical means of business communication. Topics to address include:

- Anti-spam solution
- Anti-virus solution
- Anti-spyware solutions

but also

- Employee time-wasting
- Circulation of pornography

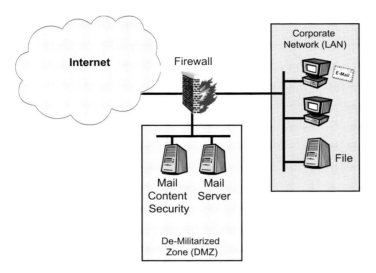

Figure 3.6 Content security configuration

- Breaches in confidentiality
- Legal liability and
- IT resource misuse.

Combination with other Solutions

Content security solutions may interface with firewalls.

Scenarios

Figure 3.6 shows a typical content security configuration.

Useful Hints

The implementation of content security solutions often requires legal advice because of potential monitoring and restriction on employees.

3.2.6 All-in-One Communication Platforms

Operating dedicated security systems does not always pay off for smaller companies. That is why all-in-one communication platforms are attractive. They can offer an end-to-end solution that enables secure e-mails and secure access to the Internet via a firewall-protected server. This can be attractive, particularly in combination with managed services. The enterprise does not need to train any personnel of its own in information security and keeps its operating expenses low – but its level of security high.

3.3 Integrated Solution for Data and Voice Communication

The protection of real-time applications, like voice-over-IP (VoIP), poses new challenges to network and system security.

Figure 3.7 shows an example of a secure voice-over IP infrastructure and illustrates the integration of different technologies into an end-to-end security solution.

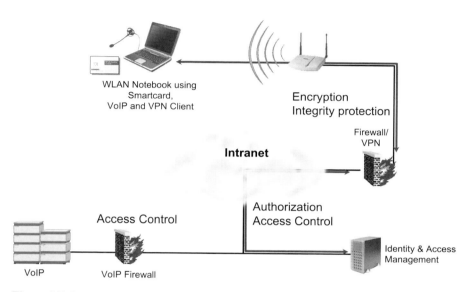

Figure 3.7 Integrated security solution

In the solution presented here, mobile employees can use their notebook to phone into a virtual private network via WLAN, the Internet and an Intranet. To enable this, a VoIP client and a VPN client are installed on the notebook. The former enables telephony, while the latter handles the encryption of the data as it traverses its protected tunnel through the public network.

Users authenticate themselves to the VPN with their employee ID card (smart card). Their user profile and individual access rights are checked by the firewall. The profiles are maintained in a central identity and access management system and made available to the systems that check them. The VoIP system itself is protected by its own VoIP firewall, which controls VoIP data traffic to and from the Intranet.

3.4 Conclusion

Computers are used for everything from doing e-commerce to accessing human resource data and communicating with others through e-mail. Although enterprises may not consider their communications "top secret," they certainly do not want strangers reading their e-mail, using their computers to attack other systems, sending forged e-mail from computers, or examining personal information stored on servers (such as financial statements).

Establishing a secure network infrastructure is essential to enable trusted communications and to ensure secure access to applications and resources.

4 Smart Card Solutions

Axel Pfau

4.1 Introduction

Any security solution must be child's play to operate and administer if it is to be used willingly and reliably on a regular basis. That is why a smart card solution is the ideal basis for enterprise security. It protects information, speeds up work processes and demonstrably helps to cut costs. The latest-generation multifunctional smart cards are very easy to handle and can be used in a wide variety of ways – for instance as secure storage for secret keys, passwords, certificates and access codes. The example of an intelligent employee ID card shows how a smart card-based security solution can make a wide range of processes at a company simpler, more secure and thus cheaper, day in and day out. A typical scenario could go like this:

An employee, let's call him Bob Smith, arrives early one morning at the barrier in the company's parking lot. As soon as his smart card comes close enough to the reader, the barrier opens automatically, since the card has the necessary permission stored on it. The building door is opened with the smart card in the same way – and the current time recorded simultaneously. Bob also uses the card to log on to his PC. Together with his PIN (personal identification number) or his fingerprint, the card can also release his PC and individual applications for Bob's use.

These applications may include Intranet portals or the company's central CRM (customer relationship management) solution, for example. Bob creates an invoice to which he attaches a legally binding digital signature and then simply e-mails it to the customer. The integrated electronic purse function dispenses with the need to fiddle around with change in the cafeteria – because he also pays for lunch electronically. In the afternoon, while visiting a customer, Bob sets up a connection secured by the smart card from his laptop to the company portal in order to download the latest information (see Remote LAN Access, Chapter 3). After returning to the office, he completes his travel expense form and digitally signs it using the smart card.

Before Bob can use his smart card, several decisions are necessary. The right type of smart card must be chosen. A smart card infrastructure must be built up and a set of applications must be designed.

4.2 Types of Smart Cards

A smart card is a plastic card with an embedded chip. The size of the card and the position of the contacts are standardized according to ISO/IEC 7816 [ISO7816]. Smart cards can be distinguished by the means of communication with the chip and by the type of chip used.

4.2.1 Communication with the Chip

In principle there are two different types: The chip with contacts and the contact-less chip.

Contact-less Chip

A contact-less chip has a transmitter and receiver onboard. It uses radio waves to communicate with a reader, an electromagnetic interface through which it obtains its power supply and sends and receives data. There are chips for different ranges and applications.

Close coupling chips according to ISO/IEC 10536 [ISO10536] are for distances of about 2 mm. Today those chips have a very small market share.

Proximity chips according to ISO/IEC 14443 [ISO14443] operate on a 13.56 MHz frequency, are suitable for distances of about 10 cm and are typically used for access control, e-purse or e-ticketing. Mifare or Legic are examples of proximity chips. Recent ICAO (International Civil Aviation Organization) standards for machine-readable travel documents specify a cryptographically signed file format and authentication protocol for storing biometric features (photos of face, fingerprint, see Chapter 6) in ISO 14443 chips.

Vicinity chips according to ISO/IEC 15693 [ISO15693] also operate on a 13.56 MHz frequency and offer a maximum read distance of 1.5 meters. Today these chips are mainly used for event management or product tags. Typical examples are my-d chips.

The term *RFID* (Radio Frequency Identification) chips is often used today for these chips.

Contact-less chips are very convenient for users and very robust because no direct contact with the reader is required. Today's chips are comparatively simple and therefore cheap. They are predominantly used for secure physical access solutions.

Chips with Contacts

In this case, the communication and power supply use lines with direct physical contact. The layout of the contacts for the interface is standardized in ISO/IEC 7816 [ISO7816], so any ISO-compliant card reader can talk to any ISO card. Chips with contacts are used for example in PCs and notebooks.

Contact-less chips and chips with contacts have pros and cons. For example for mass applications like physical access to a stadium, a contact-less chip is much better suited because inserting every single chip card into a reader takes too much time. On the other hand, the radio interface between the contact-less chip and the reader can be eavesdropped. Therefore, appropriate cryptographic protection is necessary when exchanging data for security-critical applications. For more information on cryptography see Chapter 11.

Combinations of Contact-based and Contact-less Cards

Hybrid cards are cards with two different chips, one for contact-based and one for contact-less applications. Typically, these cards are used in scenarios with existing contact-less applications like physical access where contact-based applications like PC logon are introduced.

Dual interface cards are cards with one chip and both interfaces. They can be used for applications where both interfaces are needed and where the applications need to access the same data.

4.2.2 Type of Chip

Different types of chip suit different applications and different security requirements.

There are memory chips and processor chips, both of which are described below.

Memory Chips

Memory chips can be used to read and write information from/to the chip. In general, access control to the chip is based on PIN checks or cryptography. All the functionality of a memory chip, including security functions and even cryptographic algorithms, is hardwired into the chip. Typical applications where memory chips are used today are phone cards and other prepaid cards.

Processor Chips

Processor chips differ from memory cards in that they have a freely programmable microcontroller. The chips have a working storage RAM (Random Access Memory), a permanent program storage ROM (Read Only Memory) for storing the operating system and a rewriteable data storage EEPROM (Electrically Erasable Programmable

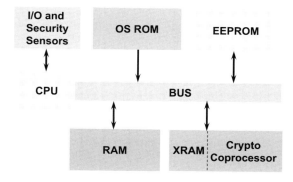

Figure 4.1
Processor chip

Table 4.1 Examples of smart card chips

	ROM (kByte)	EEPROM (kByte)	RAM (Byte)	Crypto Co-Processor
Hitachi H8/3114	32	16	2048	yes
Infineon SLE 66CX322P	136	32	4098 + 256 Byte 700 cryptoRAM	yes
Philips Smart XA	32	32	2048	yes
Samsung S3C49C9	96	32	4096	yes
SGS Thomson ST19SF32	32	32	1088	yes

ROM). Some processor chips optionally have an arithmetic crypto co-processor for asymmetric encryption algorithms like RSA (Rivest Shamir Adleman) [RSA78], which supports modular exponentiation (see Chapter 11). Figure 4.1 provides an overview of a typical processor chip.

Today's processor chips have a standard operating system (OS) designed for a wide range of applications. The OS offers transport protocols, cryptographic algorithms and a set of application-independent commands. There are a number of card operating systems on the market for chips with contacts. Usually chip cards with a processor chip are called smart cards. We use the term smart cards exclusively below. Table 4.1 provides an overview of typical smart card chips.

There are two different approaches for smart card operating systems, the ISO/IEC 7816 [ISO7816] file-based OS and the JAVA-based OS.

File-based OS consist of several different files according to ISO/IEC 7816-4 [ISO7816].

The MF (Master File) is a root directory in the smart card file tree. The MF contains the data, PIN and keys relevant to all card functions.

The DF (Dedicated File) is a file directory which generally corresponds to an application.

The EF (Elementary File) is a smart card file system that stores the useful data. EFs may also contain keys and PIN. Access to EF is controlled by access conditions.

File-based OS communicate through a command-response dialog. The smart card never initiates any activity. Once contact has been made, the reader resets the card, which then switches to its power-on state, stands by and waits for an external command. When an APDU (Application Protocol Data Unit) arrives, the card checks its authority, processes the command if appropriate and outputs the result to the caller as a response APDU. Once it has processed (or rejected) a command, the card returns to its power-on state to await further instructions. Typical APDUs are read, update, write data in files or perform cryptographic operations like generate a signature or authenticate the card.

JAVA cards have a different concept. Java cards contain a JAVA interpreter. They allow application-specific JAVA Applets (Cardlets) to be downloaded to the card. The Cardlets perform application-specific functions. JAVA Card technology provides an environment for applications that run on smart cards and other devices with very limited memory and processing capabilities. Multiple applications can be deployed on a single card and new ones can be added to it even after it has been issued to the end user. Applications written in the JAVA programming language can be executed on cards from different vendors.

The positioning of file-based OS against JAVA cards is as follows. Cardlets need more EEPROM space than pure data. Cardlets are interpreted, which means they are slower than pure OS code. Security features of Cardlets need to be implemented, which is more complicated than setting access conditions. When using Cardlets, the hardware should support memory management for secure separation of application data. New card applications can be easily realized by Cardlets and they provide a certain level of independence from the supplier. But not each Cardlet runs on each card.

To use it, the chip has to be embedded in the plastic card. The embedding is usually performed by specialist companies. The quality of embedding is important for trouble-free use. Before the card can be used for the dedicated applications, a smart card infrastructure has to be created.

4.3 Smart Card Infrastructure

The smart card infrastructure typically consists of a Card Management System (CMS), a Public Key Infrastructure (PKI) and smart card readers.

4.3.1 Card Management System (CMS)

The CMS is an administrative infrastructure for personalizing and administering the smart cards during the entire smart card life cycle. It recognizes every single smart card and is always aware of the current status of each smart card. It controls card issuing, sets the card status to 'active' or 'blocked', withdraws the card from circulation and declares it 'terminated'.

The CMS starts the card personalization process. In the first step, all card data is written to all components of the smart card. Optical data like card layout, personal inscription data, possible picture data and further optical details like holograms are written on the plastic card. Electronic data like chip file system, definition of access rights, general keys, general data, personal keys and personal data is written on the smart card chip.

The CMS typically has several interfaces. The cardholder's name, staff number and other details are imported via the interfaces to the existing human resources databases

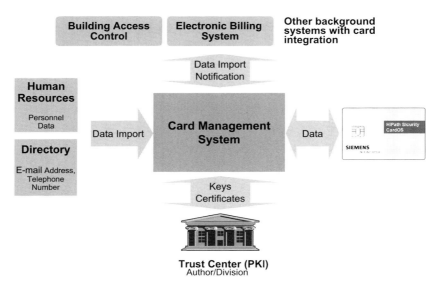

Figure 4.2 Card management system

and directories. Application-specific data including requests for card blocking is imported from the corresponding application databases. All information regarding the cards produced and issued is exported from the CMS to the applications that need it. The number of blocked cards is forwarded from the CMS to the applications in order to prevent a malicious user entering restricted premises. Public keys created on the card can be exported via the interface to a Trust Center and certificates from the Trust Center can be imported. Figure 4.2 provides an overview of a CMS with its typical interfaces.

The ultimate security of a smart card enabled application depends on the card management process. The CMS concept should therefore deservingly be regarded as a key component of the overall security structure because:

- Personalization data must be consistent when gathered from several sources
- It must not be possible to bring two cards for the same user into circulation
- Access to card data is only allowed via the card administration system, and no direct access via a database interface must be possible
- Not everyone may import data
- Protection against multiple distribution of cards must be guaranteed.

Today all organizations that want to introduce a smart card solution need an adequate CMS for managing the smart cards. In general there are CMS for low/medium scenarios with up to 100,000 smart cards and high-end CMS, which are used for mass administration of several million smart cards.

4.3.2 Public Key Infrastructure (PKI)

A PKI is necessary when security applications based on asymmetric cryptographic algorithms like RSA are used (see Chapter 11). The user gets at least one private/public key pair for the relevant applications as well as the corresponding certificate which guarantees the authenticity of the public key. A Certification Authority (CA) is a trusted third party whose signature on the certificate vouches for the authenticity of the public key bound to the subject identity. A CA as part of the PKI can generate and distribute asymmetric key pairs. It is also possible to get the certificate from the CA for key material not generated by the CA. This is dependent on corresponding procedures required, for example, by digital signature laws.

There are several different standards for the certificates, for example X.509 [X509] and OpenPGP. X.509 certificates are in general provided by LDAP (Lightweight Directory Access Protocol) directories of CA or Internet providers. OpenPGP certificates are provided by PGP key servers of CA or Internet providers.

Many application requirements can be fulfilled based on a public key system with corresponding key pairs (public and private key) and certificates.

The following list provides some typical requirements for applications, like setting up a protected connection to the corporate network from outside or signing of documents:

- A company's internal and (if possible) external communication should be protected against eavesdropping or corruption.
- Access to system resources should be made more secure.
- The login process for the internal network and for remote connections from outside the company should be made more secure.
- The login procedures for different applications (single sign-on) should be standardized.
- Workflow processes should be digitized, but with the same traceability and binding character as traditional paper-based processing.

The secure association of a key pair with a user, or the smart card of this user, is necessary for all these requirements. The user must be authenticated when issuing a certification request or transferring key material. The private key must be kept secure in the user's environment.

The smart card as a portable security token is ideal for meeting these requirements of PKI-based applications. The smart card can handle a range of functions:

- It can generate private/public key pairs.
- The cardholder's private key can be securely stored in the smart card.
- A smart card with a cryptographic co-processor can handle the asymmetric algorithm and use the key within the chip.
- Moreover, the smart card is able to support the certification process with the CA, as it is integrated in the CMS process. If the key pair is generated in the smart card, the corresponding public key is sent to the CA, certified by the CA and the

certificate stored in the smart card. If the key pair is generated outside the smart card, for example at the CA, a secure end-to-end protocol (e.g. secure messaging) between the CA and the smart card guarantees that the private key never appears as plain text outside the CA or the smart card.

Some major business applications today use digital certificates and cryptographic operations, for example Check Point VPN Client or Microsoft Windows Smart Card Domain Logon. There are two interface modules for integrating smart cards into these existing PKI-based applications.

PKCS (Public Key Cryptography Standards) are a series of industry standards from RSA Security, which deal with public key cryptography. PKCS#10 is a cryptographic token interface standard and describes the format for a certification request [PKCS10]. PKCS#11 specifies an API (Application Programming Interface) to devices that hold cryptographic information and perform cryptographic functions, for example smart cards with a cryptographic co-processor [PKCS11]. PKCS#15 is a cryptographic token information format standard and describes a file structure for smart cards in a PKI [PKCS15].

CSP (Cryptographic Service Provider) is a software module that carries out cryptographic operations. The CSP interface is the standard Windows interface for smart cards with a cryptographic co-processor.

4.3.3 Smart Card Readers

A wide variety of smart card readers are offered today for supporting contact-less, contact-based, hybrid and dual interface chips. Typical contact-based readers are provided in manifold ways:

- Integrated into the PC (provided by PC manufacturer)
- Integrated into the keyboard (provided by keyboard manufacturer)
- PCMCIA plug-in card for notebooks
- Stand-alone reader (serial or USB)
- Readers with integrated PIN pad for secure PIN input
  (for high security requirements).

The reader is an interface device for the smart card. It establishes contact with the card, supplies it with the necessary electrical energy and acts as a clock for the card processor. It also processes the transport protocol as a service to the card application, which usually runs outside the reader. The application passes its commands to the reader for transport to the card and vice versa.

Card reader specifications vary considerably from manufacturer to manufacturer. Therefore, technology independent solutions are highly valuable. One option is the PC/SC architecture (www.pcscworkgroup.com), an application-side solution that defines an industry standard for integrating smart cards and smart card readers into the PC world. The PC/SC architecture is OS-independent in principle, but has in practice established itself primarily in the Microsoft Windows world. Access to different card readers is controlled by the Resource Manager, which is provided by the manufacturer of the PC operating system. The main advantage of PC/SC is that applications do not have to be aware of the details regarding the smart card reader in order to communicate with the smart card. Moreover, the application can function with any reader complying with the PC/SC standard.

4.4 Smart Card-Enabled Applications

Smart card-enabled applications for information security are compelling, primarily for two reasons.

Firstly, they are very easy to use. A company's employees are convinced right away when they discover that all they need for recurring daily activities, such as access to rooms, authentication at their PCs or buying their lunch in the company cafeteria, is a card with a PIN number.

Secondly, they demonstrably help to cut costs in enterprises. And the cost savings grow with the size of the company. Experience shows that smart cards reduce costs mainly due to three factors:

- Simplification of authentication processes (single sign-on, process optimization).
- Increase in the level of security (physical and logical protection) and
- Bundling of various security functions (multi-functionality).

Since the pressure to cut costs on organizations is enormous, the merits of smart card-enabled applications in this area are particularly easy to convey.

The cost savings that can be expected are so persuasive that not only Germany is thinking aloud about introducing a health card. The region of Lombardy in Italy, for example, is opting for a smart card-enabled solution for its health service. The new information system improves patient care and cuts costs. Nine million multifunctional health cards are in use by the end of 2005.

For the same reasons, universities or hospitals also profit from introduction of the card. They can even leverage a far larger range of functions than currently envisaged for government agencies.

Each of these organizations – government agencies, hospitals and universities – makes certain demands of its security infrastructure.

Information must be easy to access, but not by everyone, and tailored to traditional workflows based on differentiated authorization levels. The security concept should reliably repel threats arising from the use of modern means of telecommunication and IT. Finally, the aim is to simplify and speed up work processes where possible and thus make them cheaper.

These are essentially the same objectives that a company's management has its eye on when the issue of information security is raised.

4.4.1 One Card, Many Functions

The following examples show how a smart card-enabled security solution makes the wide range of very different processes in enterprises simpler, more secure and thus cheaper day in, day out.

Physical Security – Access Control

The typical working day of an employee – let's again call him Bob Smith – starts at the gate in front of the company parking lot. Bob Smith passes his corporate card by the contact-less reader and is authorized to enter the grounds. After parking, he gains access to the building in the same way. The smart card-enabled solution logs all access to buildings and rooms, as well as any errors and alarms. All events are easy to reconstruct. Of course, the system only grants Bob Smith the defined access rights he needs for his work. For more information on Identiy & Access Management see Chapter 5.

Time Data Collection

When Bob Smith enters the building, he can also record his time and forward it to the central administration department if that is desired.

Secure Access to PCs and Applications

At his workplace, Bob Smith inserts the smart card in the reader next to his PC. He logs on to the local system and authenticates himself to gain access to specific network resources. Apart from logging on to the computer by means of a smart card and PIN number, a biometric method optionally ensures that the employee is authenticated by means of his fingerprint.

File and Hard Disk Encryption

In addition, Bob Smith can encrypt files on the local hard disk, on portable data media or on shared volumes so that they are protected permanently against being viewed by unauthorized persons.

Electronic Signature

The smart card provides the possibility to improve business processes significantly by replacing the handwritten signature with an electronic equivalent. Thus, costly and time-consuming paper-based processes can be avoided, for instance:

Bob Smith prepares a proposal for a customer, signs it electronically using his smart card, sends it to the customer by e-mail and archives it electronically.

Due to the electronic signature, the customer can be sure that this is an official offer and Bob Smith can be sure that nobody can modify the offer without being detected.

At the end of the day, Bob Smith calculates his travel expenses using a web-based application in his company's Internet portal. As proof of act, he signs the data using his smart card. His boss gets notification, checks the data and also signs it using his smart card.

Secure E-Mail

Bob Smith looks in his mailbox and finds a new e-mail. As it contains important contract information, the mail was encrypted. He can decrypt it using his smart card and read the e-mail. But can he be sure that the e-mail is actually from the specified sender? Once again, a smart card-based technology helps. The sender is identified beyond doubt by means of an electronic signature.

Secure and Remote LAN Access

Later, Bob Smith has an appointment with a customer. He calls on the customer and discovers during their talks that it would be a good idea to show a recent presentation that he has not stored locally on his laptop. He quickly sets up a secure remote link to the company network over the Internet and downloads the data to his mobile system (see Chapter 3).

Secure Payment Transactions

Bob Smith even uses his corporate card in breaks from work. In the cafeteria, at the kiosk or at various machines, he can make intra-company payments quickly and easily. He can use the smart card reader at his PC to inspect the latest transactions on his account. He can reload the card at a loading station. The amount drawn can be debited directly from his salary account.

Biometrics – Secure Authentication by Smart Card

A state-of-the-art method for physical and logical security is biometrics (see Chapter 6). An unmistakable digital template that is stored securely on a smart card is created for example from Bob Smith's fingerprint. If Bob Smith attempts to gain access to a PC, for example, his fingerprint is scanned again by a sensor and compared with the reference on the card. The card now decides automatically whether Bob Smith has authenticated his identity or not.

The advantage of biometrical methods is that users of a security infrastructure do not have to remember anything. They do not need a PIN or password to prove their identity to applications, at doors or on PCs. At the same time, their ID card remains forgery-proof and unique.

4.4.2 The Argument for Single Sign-On

Smart card-enabled solutions also permit improved forms of access management. The term 'single sign-on' subsumes various ways of simplifying secure access to networks and applications. They range from a simple login with a user name and password to smart cards with certificates. A common feature of all of them is that after logging on once to the network, users have access to all the resources for which they have authorization. They only have to remember a single PIN, but can perform various authentication activities, such as in the company portal or to use a protected application. The most important advantages:

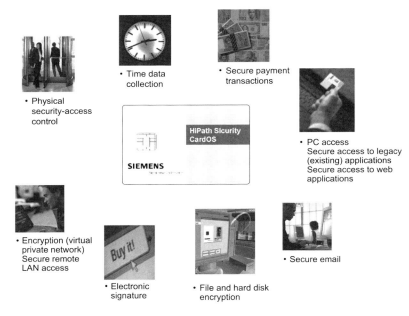

Figure 4.3 Smart card-enabled applications

- Added security, because a complex password is used instead of several simple, easily guessed passwords. Login data and passwords can be stored securely and especially conveniently on a smart card.
- Time savings thanks to faster login
- Fewer inquiries to help desks from people who have forgotten their passwords
- Simpler and more reliable administration, particularly in conjunction with an identity and access management solution (see Chapter 5).

4.4.3 Return on Investment for Smart Card-Enabled Solutions

In a detailed study [Dat04] addressed the question of the return on investment from using smart card-enabled solutions in enterprises.

Enterprises with a workforce of 50 or more can expect significant annual savings if they use smart cards to ensure physical and logical security. The cards protect access to buildings and rooms, as well as PCs and networks. Finally, they enable secure e-mail in a simple way. The precise return on investment that can be expected must be calculated on an individual basis. Costs are cut primarily in the following areas:

- Password inquiries to IT staff
- The time needed for signing on
- The time required for access control
- The personnel costs of access control
- The issue of temporary access permissions.

There is additional savings potential in the area of security:

- Fewer violations of IT security policies
- Less system downtime due to sabotage.

4.5 Conclusion

Smart cards are becoming established in more and more areas of enterprise IT as part of a security policy. This comes as no surprise when you think how many functions such a smart card can perform and yet just how simple it is to use. A smart card solution is therefore the ideal basis for security in enterprises. It protects information, speeds up work processes and demonstrably cuts costs.

5 Identity and Access Management (IAM)

Rudolf Wildgruber

5.1 Challenges

Today's business environment is a challenging one for identity and access management in the enterprise. Business relationships are growing more complex, blurring the line between internal and external business processes. They are also more dynamic, requiring greater flexibility and responsiveness in the enterprise's business practices, policies and processes. Companies are under pressure to open up their IT infrastructure to an ever-increasing number of users, both inside and outside the company and to ensure the highest productivity and privacy for these users, all while controlling IT administrative costs and leveraging existing investments wherever possible. Now more than ever, granting the right people the right access to the right resources at the right time is an essential element of enterprise security as companies strive to protect their corporate data and systems and remain innovative, productive, responsive, compliant and cost-effective business entities.

In the conventional IT infrastructure used in most big companies today, there is a one-to-one correspondence between a function or resource available to users and the IT application/system that provides that function. Consequently, user management, access management, password management and auditing are carried out on a per-IT system basis. IT staff must administer users and their access rights on each IT system in the network, usually by manual administration. Users get one account and one password for each IT system they need to use. Each IT system has its own audit or monitoring function to track changes to users and their access rights on that system.

This structure has negative consequences for identity and access management:

- Decentralized user management and provisioning means that identity and access data is duplicated across IT systems and usually becomes inconsistent over time, making it difficult to find correct and up-to-date information and to de-provision users.

- One password per IT application means that users must remember a lot of different passwords, one for each system they need to use. Password proliferation leads to more help desk and hotline calls, lost productivity as users wait for password resets and increased IT administration costs.

- Manual administration is expensive and leads to delays in provisioning and de-provisioning users, which decreases productivity, jeopardizes security and leads to data inconsistencies.

- Decentralized auditing and monitoring makes it difficult to track changes to users and their access rights. There is no way to tell what a single user's total access rights are across the enterprise, making it difficult to audit for regulatory purposes.

Overcoming the present limitations requires an enterprise-wide, cross-platform, centralized and automated user management, provisioning and access management system, which controls access to IT resources based on business roles, policies and processes. The system must provide ways to align itself with business processes and off-load routine administrative functions and decisions from IT staff to users and their managers so that decisions about what users really need are made by the people who know best. Identity and access management (IAM) technology has evolved to a well-defined market category and has reached the depth and breadth to offer an effective way to satisfy these requirements.

5.2 Use Cases

Identity and access management (IAM) is an integrated solution that makes user and access management transparent across the different systems that make up the enterprise's IT infrastructure. The Burton Group defines IAM as "the services, technologies, products and standards that enable the use of digital identities". *Identity management* addresses the need to administer users and security policies across the IT infrastructure, while *access management* addresses the real-time enforcement of the security policies in force for each user of the enterprise IT infrastructure. A *directory server* is most commonly used as the data repository for identity and access management solutions.

Here are some real-life scenarios that illustrate how IAM works.

5.2.1 Making a New Employee Productive Quickly

Figure 5.1 illustrates how the IAM system works when a new employee is hired:

- The personnel department enters the master data for the new employee into the human resources (HR) system and the master data is automatically synchronized with the IAM system's identity store.
- The IAM system automatically assigns the appropriate privileges to the employee based on the rule-based security policies (called provisioning rules) established and saved in the identity store.
- An identity administrator optionally assigns individual privileges to the employee.
- According to the employee's privileges, the IAM system automatically determines the IT systems that the employee needs to have access to and the access rights for these systems.
- The IAM provisioning system automatically generates accounts in the IT systems and sets the access rights. For example, the IAM system generates an account for Intranet and Extranet access, a mailbox as well as accounts for other enterprise IT systems.

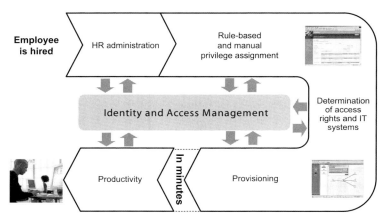

Figure 5.1 Making a new employee productive quickly

- The IAM provisioning system also sets the employee's access rights in the central web access management system for the portals s/he will use.

The new employee has now access to the relevant IT systems with the access rights defined in the privileges assigned to him/her.

5.2.2 Changing an Employee's Job Function

In this use case, an employee is switching from the Sales department to the Marketing department effective February 1st. S/he is currently authorized to perform sales activities in the sales portal, but will need to use the marketing portal as of February 1st. The IAM system handles the required access rights changes as follows (see Figure 5.2).

- The personnel department enters the change in department into the HR system and the change is synchronized with the IAM system via a "department" user attribute.

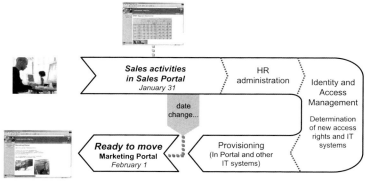

- ■ MARKETING PORTAL released
- ■ SALES PORTAL is no longer accessible

Figure 5.2 Changing an employee's job function

- The IAM system records the departmental change in the entry for the employee in the identity store (in the "department" user attribute) and automatically determines the employee's access rights based on the new value.
- The IAM system revokes the access rights associated with the privilege "Sales".
- The IAM provisions the access rights associated with the "Marketing" privilege.
- The Marketing portal is made available to the employee and the Sales portal is no longer accessible to the employee.

5.2.3 Changing a User Password

Figure 5.3 illustrates what happens in the IAM system when a password that can be used for several applications is changed:

- A user changes his/her password on first logging in to a Windows system.
- The IAM system discovers the password change and saves it in the entry for the employee in the identity store.
- The IAM system synchronizes the changed password on the employee portal.
- The changed password is available to authenticate against the employee portal.

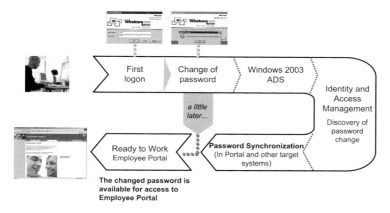

Figure 5.3 Changing a user password

5.2.4 Authorizing an Order

In this use case, a sales employee needs access to an analyst report and this access must be authorized. The IAM system handles this case using a request workflow (see Figure 5.4).

- The sales employee orders the report.
- The IAM system runs a request workflow that handles the authorization process and automatically forwards the request to Sales management.
- Once Sales management has authorized the request, the IAM system provisions the changes in access rights in the Sales portal.

- Sales employee is informed by e-mail via the request workflow
- The needed report is then obtained via the Sales Portal

Figure 5.4 Authorizing an order

- The IAM system informs the Sales employee via e-mail that access to the analyst report has been granted.
- The employee then obtains the analyst report from the Sales portal.

5.2.5 Web Single Sign-On

In this use case, sales employee Mr. Maier wants to generate his monthly order income report, enter a new customer contact and report recent travel expenses. The IAM systems support these tasks with web single sign-on (see Figure 5.5).

- The sales employee Mr. Maier accesses the employee portal.
- The employee portal requests Mr. Maier to authenticate with user name and password. The web access management system creates a session for Mr. Maier.
- Mr. Maier opens the order income application. The web access management system grants access and supplies the session information to the order income application in the background. Mr. Maier fills in the report parameters and generates the report.

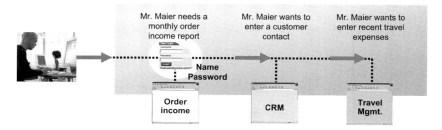

Figure 5.5 One-step authentication for accessing multiple applications

- Mr. Maier now opens the CRM application. The web access management system grants access and supplies the session information to the application in the background. Mr. Maier creates a new customer record.
- Mr. Maier now opens the travel management application. The web access management system grants access and supplies the session information to the application in the background. Mr. Maier enters travel details and costs.

Mr. Maier had to authenticate only once to have access to multiple applications. The web access management system made authorization decisions when Mr. Maier tried to open the applications and granted access according to central security policies.

5.3 Components

5.3.1 Directory Services

Directory services are critical components of today's highly interconnected business environment. Directory services provide the foundation for identity and access management across the ever-widening boundaries of the enterprise:

- In the Intranet environment, the directory service provides a global repository for shared information about employees, organizations and resources such as applications, network devices and other distributed services, accommodating hundreds of thousands of users.
- In the Extranet environment, the directory service maintains profile information about customers, trading partners and suppliers, accommodating millions of users.

For both these environments, the directory service must be able to manage user identities and control access to the information and services offered to its users, and it must provide fast, constantly available, authenticated access to the information and services, potentially to a vast number of users. The ideal directory service for today's enterprise:

- Integrates the disparate service- and platform-specific databases, profiles, policies and provisioning processes within the enterprise's infrastructure into a centralized service- and platform-independent model that is always up to date
- Supports advanced, complex identity management services to guarantee data security
- Provides the performance and scalability required to manage user identities and control access to information and services by potentially tens of millions of users.

Directory services are often complemented by virtual directories or LDAP proxies.

A virtual directory is a middleware solution, acting between directory-enabled clients on one side and database systems or multiple directory servers on the other side. The virtual directory appears as a single directory server to the client. Internally the data is collected from distributed sources and technologies but presented as having originated from one source. To retrieve data from database systems, the virtual directory translates directory queries and commands into SQL statements for read/write operations. Like an LDAP proxy, a virtual directory is not a repository and does not have a persistent store. Virtual directories are used in environments where

- Identity data that is stored in multiple repositories needs to be merged on-the-fly
- The application data format needs to be reconciled with the infrastructure format.

An *LDAP proxy* is a directory server front-end that simply redirects directory requests to other directory servers. An LDAP proxy is often used for load balancing or to provide a single point of access to multiple directory servers. In contrast to a virtual directory, an LDAP proxy redirects a single directory request to only one directory server and does not merge data from multiple sources.

5.3.2 Identity Management

The **process** of identity management includes identity creation and clearing, privilege assignment, provisioning and auditing.

Identity Creation and Clearing. The first step in the identity management process is to create a unique digital identity for every user of the enterprise IT systems. Information about users is usually managed in authoritative systems like HR systems (employees), CRM systems (customers and partners) and SCM systems (suppliers). The IAM system imports the user information from the authoritative sources into a central repository where all the privileges of the users are maintained during the lifecycle of the user. Importing of user information goes along with consolidation of user data, like normalizing or correcting misspelled certain user attributes. The creation of a unique user ID and the synchronization of that ID with the source systems help to keep the user information consistent in all connected systems. For example, if a user changes his/her surname as a result of marriage, the unique user ID allows the related user information to be found in the central IAM repository and the name change to be adopted from the source system.

Privilege Assignment. In an IAM system access rights to IT systems are established based on privileges. Therefore, the next step in the identity management process is to assign one or more privileges to users. Provisioning rules can be used for automated privilege assignment. The rule-based provisioning model works well when access rights depend on the values of user attributes – like a departmental or managerial function. Thus, a change in a user attribute value triggers an immediate de-provisioning and reprovisioning. Manual assignments of privileges are necessary when access rights are more static – when they depend on the person's job, for example, educational services trainer or quality manager. In this case, privileges don't need to change when organizational attributes change. In reality, rule-based assignment is often combined with manual assignment.

Provisioning. Provisioning is the dynamic process of establishing the target system-specific access rights to which a user-to-privilege assignment ultimately resolves. Provisioning is a two-step process:

1. Calculating the accounts, the groups, the target systems to which the groups belong and the account group memberships that result from the privilege assignments to users and creating the account, group and group membership data in the identity store – this process is called privilege resolution and can involve the matching of user attributes to provisioning policies, permission parameters or role parameters to determine the appropriate groups and target systems.

2. Synchronizing the access rights data in the identity store with the target systems – this process physically transfers the access rights data from the identity store to the target systems.

Auditing. The identity audit collects information on all user and privilege management actions; for example a change in a user's data that affects a privilege assignment. Auditing functions include writing audit records for access requests and decisions, evaluating these audit records and generating reports. The audit ensures that the activities associated with identity management are logged for day-to-day monitoring to prove regulatory compliance and for corporate knowledge purposes.

The main **services** of identity management include user self-service and delegated administration, password management, user management, privilege and policy management, request workflow, provisioning and metadirectory.

User Self-Service and Delegated Administration. *User self-service* allows users to perform simple user-oriented identity management tasks that must typically be carried out by technical IT administrators in the traditional enterprise IT infrastructure. With self-service, users can manage their own data, including their own passwords and request privileges – user access rights to resources in the IT systems in the enterprise network – for themselves.

Delegated administration allows users to delegate their identity management tasks (or a subset of these tasks) to other users. Delegation allows an enterprise to distribute identity management tasks according to business functions and to create a hierarchy for identity management that reflects its business structure.

Together, self-service and delegated administration permit the enterprise to balance the user management and access rights administration load across the enterprise and to off-load identity management tasks from IT, hotline and help desk staff to the people who really need to be able to perform them.

Password Management. Password management allows users to maintain a single password that will automatically be synchronized with all relevant IT systems in the enterprise. Password management functions allow users to change and reset their passwords in one or more systems – for example in an LDAP directory or in Windows, notify users when they need to change their passwords to comply with password policies established for the enterprise (for example expiry of a password's lifetime) and synchronize these password changes in real time to all the relevant IT systems. Forgotten passwords can be reset by the user through a challenge-response procedure, or by an administrator.

User Management. User management includes all activities related to the creation, maintenance and use of user accounts, user attributes, privileges, etc., encompassing the different directories, user databases and application-specific repositories that make up the fragmented, heterogeneous enterprise IT environment. User management consists of two main tasks: maintaining an accurate and up-to-date directory of users to be provisioned and assigning users to privileges. The task of maintaining a consistent user directory is handled by request processes from the users themselves and/or their managers (user self-service and delegated administration) and by data synchronization workflows (e.g. with the enterprise HR system) provided by the metadirectory.

Privilege and Policy Management. A *privilege* is a set of access rights based on either business semantics or on IT system specific semantics that permits users to access enterprise IT resources. The enterprise can structure its privileges in a hierarchical model according to its business roles and functions or based on other considerations. Privilege management establishes a logical layer for the modeling and management of authorization (access control) information that is generic enough to cover many of the relevant IT system's authorization/access control methods:

- Group-based IT systems control access rights via account membership in groups. Making an account a member of a group gives the account the access rights that have been granted to the group. User groups, profiles, and application-specific roles are examples of group-based methods of access control.
- Attribute-based IT systems control access rights via attributes in the accounts. For example, in Active Directory, a set of account attributes defines a user's mailbox; there is no concept of group membership.
- Some systems, like Microsoft Active Directory, provide both types of access control.

Privilege-based access management allows managing access control on each IT system in a uniform way. Privilege management also simplifies and structures access rights administration. High-level managers can assign privileges to their staff without needing to know the lower-level details, and IT personnel can administer the access rights in the IT systems without needing to know the higher-level details.

Policy Management comprises the management of security and administrative policies. Policies are composed of one or more rules and each rule defines the objects subjected to the rule (e. g. a set of users), the action to be performed and a priority to handle conflicts with other rules properly. Administrators define rules for consolidation of user data, privilege assignment, reconciliation and audit to determine how the identities and their access rights will be managed.

Request Workflow. Request workflows allow users to request privileges, which in turn must be authorized by various approvers according to the security policies in force in the enterprise. Administrators set up an approval path based on business policies; the workflow then notifies each person in the path – for example, by e-mail – that s/he has an approval request to handle. The approver uses a web browser to access a web interface to grant or deny the request.

Provisioning. Provisioning is the fully automated process of calculating user access rights and distributing them to IT systems based on the privileges assigned to the user. The provisioning process automatically grants, changes and revokes access rights in IT systems in response to privilege assignment, re-assignment and revocation.

Provisioning automates the time-consuming process of managing access rights across many different IT systems over the user life-cycle and permits fast activation and de-activation of access rights across these systems for multiple user identities.

Provisioning provides a single point of administration for the enterprise's total identity and access control information and implements the services that keep the identity and access control data in the IT systems consistent and up-to-date, allowing the enterprise to ensure the security of its data, reduce administration overhead, accelerate its business processes and improve its customer service as well as protect its investments in existing IT systems.

The validation of IT systems is a periodic comparison between the account and group data in the IT system and the central IAM repository. Validation is necessary to check for and detect local changes to the IT system data that have occurred independently of changes initiated by the IAM system. Deviations are reconciled either manually or automated through rules.

Metadirectory. Metadirectory is the set of services that integrates the disparate directories, user databases and application-specific information repositories in the enterprise IT network into a centralized data store and provides the connectivity, management and interoperability functions that unify the user data ("join") and ensure the bidirectional attribute flow (synchronization) in this fragmented environment.

In an IAM system, the metadirectory provides an infrastructure for automated enterprise-wide user management that addresses the problem of decentralized multiple user identities and user administration functions. Metadirectory services:

- Integrate user data from multiple authoritative sources – human resources directories, enterprise resource planning (ERP) systems, customer relation management (CRM) and supply chain management (SCM) databases – into a single, unique digital *identity* that represents the user to be provisioned in the IT systems
- Maintain an accurate and up-to-date *identity store* of these identities and synchronize identity data from the identity store back into the authoritative sources.

5.3.3 Access Management

The **process** of access management includes authentication, authorization and audit.

Authentication. Authentication is the step of identifying users and verifying their identity. Various authentication methods can be used, including basic or form-based authentication using username/password, secure tokens, digital certificates and smart cards. Authentication ensures that authorization is performed for the identified user who accesses enterprise resources.

Authorization. Authorization is the real-time enforcement of user access requests to the enterprise IT systems and resources. When a user tries to access a resource, a decision is made if the access is granted or denied. Access decisions are usually based on security policies. Authorization ensures that users can only access enterprise resources according to the policies in force.

Audit. Audit in access management collects information from all enforcement points in the access management process and evaluates and reports this information. Auditing functions include writing audit records for access requests and decisions, evaluating these audit records and generating reports. Audit ensures that the activities associated with access management are logged for day-to-day monitoring, to prove regulatory compliance and for corporate knowledge purposes.

Information can be provided about:

- Which tasks have been performed by an administrator
- Which operation has been performed by an identity
- Which events have occurred
- Which specific operations have been performed successfully or unsuccessfully.

The main **services** of access management include authentication, authorization, audit as described above and policy management, web single sign-on, enterprise single sign-on, federation, web services security, auditing and reporting.

Policy Management. Policy Management is the administration of the security policies. Policies are composed of one or more rules and each rule implements part of the policy. Administrators define authentication, authorization and audit rules to determine how the applications and resources will be protected and managed.

Web Single Sign-On. Web Single Sign-on (Web SSO) gives every user a one-step authentication for access to multiple web resources or applications. Having authenticated a user, Web SSO creates a single sign-on session using an encrypted cookie to store user authentication and session information. The user is freed from the need to authenticate multiple times.

Enterprise Single Sign-on. Enterprise single sign-on is the enlargement of single sign-on to non-web resources. This typically comprises host and terminal as well as database and application-specific authentication. To achieve this functionality, the client needs SSO-specific software, which takes care of the login procedures for these enterprise applications.

Federation. Identity federation permits an enterprise to share trusted identities with autonomous organizations outside of the enterprise, like trading partners or suppliers. The goal of federation is to integrate identity information across enterprise boundaries to allow the enterprise to build business communities.

Web Services Security. To allow business integration with partners, customers and suppliers, applications expose service-oriented interfaces, commonly known as web services. Web services security deals with securing the web services based integration of applications across enterprise boundaries. Specifically, web services security allows access to the services to be controlled, the service level and quality of service agreements to be enforced and monitored and the source of failures to be diagnosed.

Reporting. Reporting in contrast to audit and logging is used to retrieve static information about data in the repository. It can be viewed as an extended view of certain objects or attributes.

5.4 IAM for Heterogeneous Environments

An IAM solution provides uniform and business-oriented management of identities and enforcement of access control, especially in situations where a heterogeneous IT and application infrastructure exists. The focus here is on supporting a large variety of systems and applications, for example

- Platforms like Windows, Linux and Unix
- Applications like SAP R/3, mySAP ERP, SAP NetWeaver, Siebel, Peoplesoft
- Databases like Oracle, MS SQL, IBM DB2 and
- Others like communication systems and content management systems.

Figure 5.6 shows a typical scenario in a heterogeneous environment.

- Portals are already in widespread use as cross-domain, process-oriented interfaces. Whether as employee portals for access to internal applications, partner or supplier portals for collaboration along the supply chain, or customer portals to improve customer relationships – portals are always the interface to a series of applications.
- Internal and external users have access to the applications through the portal. Access management authenticates all access via the portal centrally and enables single sign-on. Access management then controls which user is allowed to access

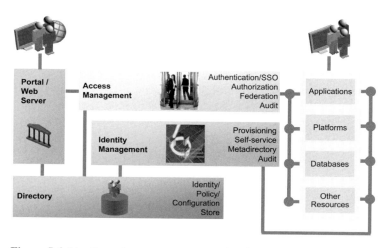

Figure 5.6 Identity and access management in a heterogeneous environment

81

which application and how by means of guidelines, policies and rules. A directory service stores identity, policy and configuration data.

- Identity management centrally manages all internal and external users and their privileges. The portal and all applications are provisioned with user accounts and access permissions. By assigning cross-platform privileges the identities are granted access rights in the portal and all applications in one step. In addition to using a portal, internal users can access applications directly from their desktops.

5.5 IAM and Regulatory Compliance

An often underestimated problem in connection with identity and access management is compliance, i.e. the clear and demonstrable observation of legal regulations. The debate here is currently centering on US standards such as HIPAA in the health sector or the Sarbanes-Oxley Act (SOX) for accounting (see Chapter 1). These are also of importance for many European enterprises.

However, one point that is overlooked is that European and German regulations, such as KonTraG (Corporate Control and Transparency Act), BDSG (German Data Protection Act), the European Data Protection Directive, as well as regulations on risk management in the German Law on Limited Liability Companies and Stock Corporation Law and the strict guidelines on risk management under Basel II, form a closely meshed network of compliance requirements.

An IAM solution can ensure that an enterprise does not become entangled in this web. This is because a consistent view of "who" is necessary to ensure that the question "Who is allowed to do what where and who did what where?" can be answered. If an employee has different digital identities in a number of systems, it is difficult to obtain a complete overview of the authorizations assigned to the employee and his or her compliance-related actions. The IAM solution can ensure that defined and stringent processes for managing identities and access permissions are implemented. Users must not be created and given access authorizations in an ad hoc fashion. Every change to user information and every assignment of rights must be structured and documented. Internal IT processes are optimized and standardized by means of self-service functions, delegated administration and request workflows. The creation of users in different systems and their assignment to roles and groups is controlled centrally and always carried out in the same way. Access decisions can be controlled and monitored centrally. Together with the auditing and reporting services in an IAM solution, this creates the foundation for compliance.

5.6 Conclusion

Enterprises and other organizations need to be able to identify everyone involved in their business processes – unambiguously. They have to control which persons with which rights can access which resources and when.

Information about users is typically stored in numerous distributed directories, while the applications and services to be protected are based on heterogeneous platforms. In such a situation, ensuring compliance with legal requirements is a very complex task. If communication security policies and compliance requirements are to be enforced permanently and throughout an enterprise, all directories must first be kept up-to-date and consistent – on the fly. Secondly, it must be possible to update the user authorization profiles for all systems from a central point of administration and across all platforms. These two requirements can only be met by comprehensive identity and access management that provides user data centrally, grants permissions dynamically – and controls access securely.

Identity and access management also opens up new possibilities for strategic partnerships. Joint and trusted use can be made of identities with partners outside the enterprise network (federated identities). Users can easily switch between the partner's domains and applications without having to sign on again.

6 Biometric Authentication

Gerd Hribernig and Peter Weinzierl

"Biometrics is the science and technology of measuring and statistically analyzing biological data. In information technology, biometrics usually refers to technologies for measuring and analyzing human body characteristics, such as fingerprints, eye retinas and irises, voice patterns, facial patterns and hand measurements, especially for authentication purposes."[1]

Generally speaking, biometrics describe different ways of measuring biological data, for example blood pressure sensing. In terms of security, biometrics is usually used synonymously with biometric authentication. The task is to find out someone's identity by analyzing characteristic parts of his/her body, biometric features, like the shape of the face, the structure of the fingerprint pattern etc.

These characteristic biometric features in an ideal biometric system have the following properties:

- Singular within all humankind (past, present, future)
- Stable from birth to death
- Independent of personal and environmental conditions.

Good biometric features arise from genetic heredity in combination with chance in early embryonic phases. Chance is a very important issue, otherwise there would be no difference between identical twins and similarities between blood relatives would be very high. Real biometric systems fulfill these requirements on different levels.

6.1 Biometric Systems

6.1.1 Types of Biometric Systems

Biometric systems use different sets of characteristic features of the human body. There are various systems on market that use a large variety of features. Important for usage in authentication systems are[2]:

---

[1] www.securitysearch.com

[2] International Biometric Group: Market and Industry Report 2004-2008

84

- Fingerprint (45%)
- Face (14%)
- Hand Geometry (10%)
- Iris Recognition (9%).

The following section will discuss these different types of biometric systems.

Fingerprint. Fingerprints have been systematically used for identification since the end of the nineteenth century. The basic structure of a fingerprint is described by the flow of ridges (i.e. elevations) and valleys (i.e. depressions). The ridges form a personal pattern, individual for every finger and every person. They end and unify in characteristic spots. These spots are called minutiae (see Figure 6.1).

A collection of these spots is called a minutiae list or feature vector. You can usually find 20 to 50 minutiae on a fingerprint, while the feature vectors comprise 100 to 200 bytes of data. Due to distortions, moisture, sweat and elastic deformation of the skin, a single minutia is not stable over a set of fingerprint images. Therefore the comparison between two feature lists is a tricky task.

More advanced systems use additional information, like the flow of the ridges or parts of the grey level image. These additional features lead to lower error rates and better performance. On the other hand, the template size grows up to more than 20 kBytes.

Fingerprints have a high discrimination rate, therefore they can be used for large scale identification tasks (thousands to even millions). Sensor devices are comparably cheap and small, the image capture process is easy to use as the user only has to press his/her finger on the sensor. New sensor types allow outdoor application and there are even devices on the market that do not need contact between finger and device. For all of these reasons, fingerprint recognition systems are the most popular biometric systems.

In some regions, like South America or the Arab countries, fingerprints are part of everyday business life, for example banks use them for identification of bank accounts. In other regions, like Europe, acceptance is not yet that high as fingerprinting is still associated with criminal investigations. As fingerprint systems spread, acceptance will also increase rapidly.

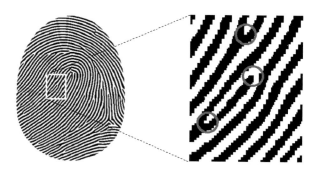

Figure 6.1
Minutiae – elementary
features of a fingerprint

Figure 6.2
Face with primary features

Fingerprint systems have a wide range of applications. These applications range from PC/network access, physical access or time and attendance systems to all kinds of machinery protection or convenience applications.

Face. Face recognition is the most natural way of identifying humans as images of faces are part of all identity cards. In biometric face recognitions systems, the images are usually captured by a video camera or a still image camera. Significant features of a face and the interrelation between these features are detected from this two-dimensional image, such as for example the position of eyes, mouth and ears as well as the shape of the eyes and the face (see Figure 6.2). The data of these features is stored in a feature vector of typically 100 bytes.

The discrimination of face recognition systems is quite fair, as there might be a strong similarity between blood relatives. It is obvious that identical twins cannot be distinguished. In addition, face characteristics vary in time (compare a child to an adult) and in conditions. Variations in hair cut or eye glasses influence the recognition rate.

For that reason, systems for three-dimensional data acquisition are being developed. Patterns, like spots or stripes, are projected on the face and a camera takes a two-dimensional image (see Figure 6.3). A three-dimensional data set can be derived from the distribution of the projected patterns on the face. These systems promise a high level of accuracy, as many more features of the face, like the position of the tip of the nose or the base of the ears, can be used for the identification task.

As the cost of face recognition systems is rather high, they are used in applications where many people use a single system, like in physical access systems. The most important applications are biometric identity cards. The next generation of passports

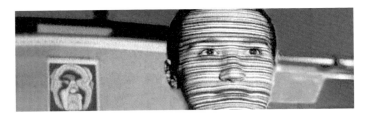

Figure 6.3 3D Face image acquisition

will be biometric extended. The International Civil Aviation Organization (ICAO[1]) has set up a standard for biometric travel documents. Face is the prime biometric feature, fingerprint is second.

Hand Geometry. Hand geometry systems scan the back of the hand and use height, width and structure of the hand and the fingers. The advantage of these systems is resistance to dirt and other environmental influences, but the accuracy and therefore security is not that high. Hand geometry is quite popular in the USA for physical access control, while in Europe hand geometry systems are very rare. Due to the limited security level, the importance of these systems is decreasing.

Iris Recognition. Iris scan systems detect and compare the features of the iris like ridges, furrows and striations. The capture devices range from small inexpensive cameras for PC/network access to high quality, specialist apparatus with active light.

Like fingerprint systems, iris recognition systems can be used for reliable 1:1 and 1:N searches. The accuracy of iris systems is very high, although large databases for evaluation are not available.

The usability of the available low-cost systems is rather poor, as users usually have to move into an inconvenient position to get access. As the high-end devices use active light, which is not that pleasant for the user, the acceptance is not very good.

Overall, iris scan systems are appropriate for all kinds of access systems. As devices become cheaper and easier to handle, iris recognition systems will play an important role on the market.

Other Biometric Systems. In addition to the systems described above, there are a lot more biometric systems, like:

- Voice Verification
- Signature Verification
- Keystroke Verification
- DNA Analysis.

They all have some niche applications, but the maturity of the technology is not sufficient, especially for security applications. In the case of DNA analysis, the accuracy is very high, but the process of data acquisition is rather uncomfortable and therefore not applicable to IT security systems.

Fingerprint systems will be looked at in the next sections, as they are most common for biometric applications in enterprise security environments. In some cases, additional information is given for face and iris recognition.

6.1.2 General Working Scheme of a Biometric System

All biometric systems have a similar working scheme. The general scheme of a biometric system is shown in Figure 6.4. The biometric data is captured by a sensor

---

[1] www.icao.org

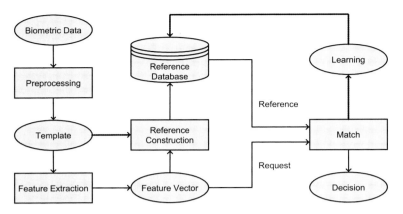

Figure 6.4 General working scheme of a biometric system

device. The pre-processing unit produces a raw *template*, which is an enhanced image containing the essential information. The feature extraction component generates the feature vector including minutiae and global structure information. Pre-processing and feature extraction are called the *encoder* unit.

The *feature vector* is stored in the reference database. Some systems store an additional raw image for compatibility reasons. This procedure is called enrolment.

For verification, the feature vector of the biometric feature just captured is matched with the corresponding reference in the database. The system has to make a decision if there is correspondence between the queried feature and the reference. Some systems use the outcome of the so-called *matcher* to improve the reference in the database.

6.1.3 Components of a Biometric System

The components of a biometric system have to be carefully adjusted in order to ensure satisfactory performance. In most cases it is advisable if all components come from one supplier. As standardization steps progress (see Section 6.5 Software), free choice of components from different suppliers is becoming more accessible. The following list provides an overview of properties of the components required.

Biometric Devices

- *Usability*: The device should come with a practical user interface including feedback.

- *Integration:* Some devices are delivered as standalone devices, some need integration into a case. Properties: Data interface, electric supply, volume, software drivers.

- *Cost:* Devices range from about 50 USD (low-cost fingerprint device) to more than 2000 USD (high-end face recognition kiosk).

- *Throughput:* Some devices are designed for high throughput (e.g. fingerprint, 2 seconds per user), some need more than 30 seconds (e.g. iris scan).
- *Trigger:* External trigger signal needed or automated trigger
- *Acquisition time:* Images per second
- *Data transfer rate:* Images transferred per second
- *Ergonomic design*

Encoder

- *Device connectivity:* Which devices are supported? Is the output data independent of the input device?
- *Data output format:* Proprietary or standardized
- *Data output size:* Depending on the biometric feature and the required performance, the feature vector size may range from 100 bytes to more than 20 kBytes.
- *Runtime:* Encodes per second

Matcher

- *Device connectivity:* Which devices are supported? Is the output data independent of the input device?
- *Data output format:* Proprietary or standardized
- *Runtime:* Matches per second
- *Biometric error rates:* See Section 6.2.3

Template

- *Size:* Bytes, compressed or plain data
- *Format:* Standardized or proprietary
- *Data storage:* Centralized or decentralized

6.2 Deployment of Biometric Systems

Successful deployment of a biometric system requires intensive attention to all components, starting at the user's expectations and ending with the system integration. Before starting the deployment, the requirements must first be clarified.

6.2.1 Requirements

When developing a biometric (fingerprint) application the following issues have to be considered:

- Is the application more of a convenience type or does it need high level security?
- Application of a verification or identification scenario? (See Section 6.2.2)
- Application of one or two factor authentication? (See Section 6.3.2)

- Small group of users using the system quite often or large group using the system quite rarely?
- Supervised enrolment or user self-enrolment?
- Centralized or decentralized storage of templates?
- Feedback opportunities
- Computational performance requirements
- Biometric performance requirements (see Section 6.2.3).

There is not one single biometric system that meets all these requirements. The more users are left alone with the system and the more rarely they use the system the more good usability is essential. Relevant feedback (optical or acoustic) is a must for applications where users access the system on their own.

6.2.2 Verification versus Identification Scenario

Verification is a 1:1 identity check. The user enters a unique identifier (personal number, user name) or provides a smart card with that identifier. The system checks if the biometric feature matches the stored template of the user.

Identification is a 1:N identity search and approval. The user just supplies his/her biometric feature, the system searches all users of the database and comes up with the best matching biometric data set. For positive authentication, the similarity must exceed a defined limit.

In general, verification scenarios are more reliable, because the number of possible false acceptance errors increases with the size of the reference database. Identification scenarios are feasible for small groups (e.g. small office or family), while groups of a thousand or even more users result in response time of some seconds.

Identification scenarios are more convenient. Convenience of verification can be increased if you combine verification with a token or a smart card holding a unique identifier (see Section 6.3.3). Another way of applying identification is to form smaller groups, for example departments in an office.

6.2.3 Performance of Biometric Systems

The level of security and convenience of a biometric system are directly linked to biometric performance. It is therefore essential to strictly define the required error rates and test them in real-world applications.

Error Rates. Different error rates are used for evaluating and improving biometric systems. These error rates apply in general in a similar way for all kinds of biometric systems.

The output of a biometric system is usually a measure produced by the matcher unit, the so-called quantity match score. The match score describes the similarity between the matched templates (i.e. feature vectors); 100% corresponds to absolute identity.

In commercial applications, the system output is always true or false, as you need a clear decision for granting access to a system. The decision is controlled by a threshold; match scores higher than the threshold lead to a positive answer, match scores lower than the threshold result in a negative message.

There are two types of errors in access control systems (positive recognition system).

- Two different fingers have a match score higher than the threshold, i.e. false match.
- Two measurements of the same finger have a match score lower than the threshold, i.e. false non match.

In general, error rates can be measured on two levels:

- *Biometric engine level rates*, taking just the inputs and outputs of the engine (i.e. software).
- *System level rates*, considering all the errors between user and non-biometric application.

Biometric Engine Level Error Rates. A well-known database that uses fingerprint images or templates as input is usually used for testing biometric engine level error rates. Output is the match score. The following error rates are used for evaluation of biometric engines:

- *False Acceptance Rate (FAR)*: Count of false match in relation to all matches of non-identical fingers.
- *False Rejection Rate (FRR):* Count of false non-match in relation to all feasible matches of identical fingers.

If you draw these rates for each threshold value on a chart you get the typical FAR/FRR curves (for an example see Figure 6.5).

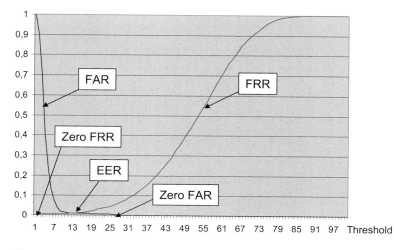

Figure 6.5 Curve of false acceptance rate (FAR) / false rejection rate (FRR)

There is no threshold in real systems where FAR and FRR curves are both zero, therefore other interesting points on these curves are taken to characterize the performance.

- *Equal Error Rate (EER):* Point of intersection of FAR and FRR curve in percent. EER is quite a fair measure if you need to describe the performance of a biometric system using only one figure.
- *Zero FAR:* Lowest FRR where no false match occurs.
- *Zero FRR:* Lowest FAR where no non-false match occurs.

Zero FAR and Zero FRR are never equal, as there is no threshold value where FAR and FRR are zero in common.

These FAR/FRR values are sufficient if you want to set up a biometric system. Depending on the application, you set the threshold to a higher value (e.g. more secure) or a lower value (e.g. more convenient). In the first case, you would rather accept having to check your fingerprint sometimes twice than accept a false match and vice versa.

System Level Error Rates. The whole workflow must be taken into account when evaluating a biometric system:

- User interaction,
- Ergonomic design of the sensor device,
- Sensor,
- Biometric engine,
- Application integration,
- Enrolment scenario and
- Verification/identification scenario.

At system level therefore, more characteristic measures (i.e. error rates) must be considered in addition to the FAR/FRR curve of the engine. These errors are additional to the errors of the biometric engine and overall they determine the performance of the biometric system.

- *Failure To Capture Rate* (FTC): Depending on the sensor and the triggering mechanism of the biometric device, image capture can sometimes fail. The better the ergonomic design of the device, the lower the FTC rate.
- *Failure To Enroll Rate* (FTE): This is the percentage of attempts that do not lead to a valid template and a successful user enrolment.

Some more interpretations of the results of the FAR/FRR evaluations are necessary for developing a biometric application.

- *Stability:* Slight variations in image capture conditions should not lead to severe alternation in results. Quite a good measure for stability is the shape of the FAR and FRR curve near the EER point. The lower the gradient, the more solid your system.
- *Error distribution:* During evaluation every test has the same implications. It makes quite a difference for applications if the biometric system has constant error

distribution over all fingers or if there are some "general keys" that often match with other fingers. These "general keys" usually occur if fingerprint images with bad image quality are accepted at enrolment. Therefore, advanced systems check the image quality carefully before accepting the fingerprint template in the database.

- *Enrolment quality:* Because the enrolment process determines the performance of the system, you have to consider the FTE rate by comparing different systems. The higher the FTE rate, the easier it is to get good FAR/FRR, because critical fingerprint images are already excluded during enrolment. In real applications however, users do not accept not being enrolled.

6.3 Biometrics Security – User Authentication

6.3.1 General

Biometrics introduces a new option for identifying users as they interact with computer systems and networks. Biometrics also provides a new quality of accomplishing the identification task by directly recognizing people requesting access to a protected resource. So the machine adapts to the requirements of the person and the person does not use authentication methods like passwords and certificates, which can easily be understood by computers but are complicated for people to apply.

The computing power offered today by standard PCs and also embedded systems offers the possibility to capture unique biometric features, calculating the characteristic features and matching against known reference patterns, thus deciding who is trying to interact with a system.

Biometrics only takes care of authenticating a person, authorizing access or authorizing the use of a resource does not change compared to standard authorization technology.

Although identifying a person by a biometric feature exclusively will be useful for many applications, some may call for two or even multi-factor authentication depending on the level of security required and on the nature of the biometric feature used.

Single factor biometric authentication is limited today to a number of "strong" biometrics like fingerprint, iris, retina and DNA. But if identification (1 to many search) is to be used for authentication, even these "strong" biometrics have limits, for example in terms of potential false acceptance or also response time to return with the identification result.

6.3.2 Two- and Multi-Factor Authentication

Although two and multi-factor authentication may be designed by using either different biometrics together like face recognition plus fingerprint etc. or using biometrics together with a PIN or password, those latter combinations still suffer from the drawbacks of either discomfort or a potential security risk.

The combination of possession and biometrics, however, provides a number of advantages:

- Binding the physical authentication medium (smart card, token, badge, ...) reliably to the owner. For example a smart card is typically bound to the owner by a secret PIN, yet both authentication means can be transferred deliberately to another person.
- Changing a biometric identification task to a biometric verification task. By using a smart card as either an identifier or even a storage media, the biometric authentication can be reduced to a 1:1 comparison of a presented biometric to a single reference biometric pointed to or even stored on the smart card.
- The physical authentication means can provide other useful functionality for providing digital signatures or encryption tasks. This applies especially to smart cards or tokens that carry a crypto controller for carrying out advanced cryptographic tasks in a secure environment.

6.3.3 Combining Possession and Biometrics

Physical authentication means are well established in our everyday life. Everybody uses keys to open doors of buildings, flats, cars, safes etc. These simple keys are typically not personalized, so normally it cannot be decided if a key is used by the authorized owner or by an impostor.

People are identified by their passports, driving licenses, identity cards, employee badges and thus gain access to countries, areas, places and buildings. Typically the holder of the identity document can be authenticated by comparing the photo on the document with the person presenting the identity document – this is done using a biometric feature to bind an identity document to a person.

The most important property of such proof of identity is that it is unique and authentic, i.e. issued based on correct data by the appropriate authority.

Most of the existing identity documents rely on a person to check the photograph on an identity document. By enhancing the document to be machine-readable and also adding "machine processable" biometrics, new scenarios of automated identity checks can be accomplished.

Identity proofs can be combined with biometrics in different ways depending on the type of identity card and the application it is used for:

- Identifier on card (IoC)
  This is the easiest way of combining smart card and biometrics, especially for improving security of existing smart card systems, as existing smart cards do not have to be replaced. The card carries a unique identifier (e.g. employee number); this identifier is sent to an external biometric system, where verification is calculated between the request biometric and the stored template.

  Even simple non-transferable paper tickets can be protected against fraud by this combination with an external biometric authentication system, for example a server-based system, which keeps the biometric reference templates in a central database.

- Template on card (ToC) / Biometric image on card/chip
  The biometric template is stored on the card itself for decentralized use. The biometric template size typically requires between 100 bytes to some kilo bytes for a single feature. Also, as this biometric template data would be readable for any application, the template data is therefore usually encrypted for privacy reasons. Templates on card systems require a smart card file structure, which can accommodate the template data.

  The upcoming biometric passports are different to the template on the card structure referred to, because international standards require that the biometric feature is stored as compressed image data on the chip embedded into the e-passport. Storing the image data ensures the interoperability of biometric passports all over the world. The international standards therefore also cover access protection and optional encryption to protect the stored "plain text" biometric image data.

- Matching on card (MoC) / System on card (SoC)
  Matchers on card systems use the processor of the smart card for the matching process. The image capture and the encoder functionality are executed by an external device like an embedded system or a PC. During the enrolment, the template is stored in the secure memory of the smart card. The requested fingerprint is encoded for verification purposes in the external system and the template is forwarded to the card. The card matches the requested template with the stored template and releases the data protected by the "biometric access condition" or it directly triggers functionality like applying a digital signature.

  The advantage of this matching on card principle is that the reference template on the card is highly secure as it never leaves the card.

  However implementation of a matching on card system requires that existing smart card operating systems be enhanced to cover the biometric matching function. Secondly, the memory capacity and processing power required only allows for modern, powerful and as yet quite expensive smart cards.

Table 6.1 Comparison of the combination of tokens and biometrics

	Biometrics	Security Level	Sensor	Template	Encoder	Matcher	Smart Card (min. Requirements)	Advantage
Identifier on Card	Centralized	Medium	Device based	Server based	Device / PC based	Device / PC based	Storage Card (typ. 8 Byte)	Compatible to all existing Card systems
Template on Card	Centralized/ decentralized	High	Device based	Card based	Device / PC based	Device / PC based	Storage Card (typ. 1 kByte)	Compatible to recent Cards
Matcher on Card	Decentralized	High	Device based	Card based	Device / PC based	Card based	Processor Card	Privacy protections
System on Card	Decentralized	Very high	Card based	Card based	Card based	Card based	Biometric Processor Card	High privacy protection

The "system on card (Soc)" concept implies that all components of the biometric system (i.e. sensor, encoder and matcher) are located on the smart card – an ideal combination of biometrics and smart card. Because of the technical difficulties concerning power supply, processor power and sensor device integration there is no technical implementation available as yet.

Table 6.1 gives an overview of the properties of the different combinations.

6.3.4 Fraud and Mitigation

Several reports have been published as to how biometric security systems have been overcome by applying fake biometric features to biometric sensors and subsequently gaining access to protected resources. Those reports have been published for a number of biometric types including the most successful ones like fingerprint, face and iris recognition.

However most of these reports have only shown that a copy of a biometric feature could be produced in presence and with the support of the owner of the biometric feature. This copy was successful to some degree for overcoming a biometric sensor and the recognition engine.

These experiments were typically carried out in a lab environment, where there was no limit in terms of available time, the number of trials and of course abundant knowledge about the biometric system properties.

Naturally real-world attack scenarios would differ from these laboratory conditions and would hardly be that successful. The reasons for this are:

- Collecting biometric information suitable for producing fakes is often difficult. Although the situation differs regarding the type of biometric feature (some are more public than others), it is even hard for biometric types like fingerprints that leave traces (e.g. latent fingerprints).
- The impostor needs to find the correct trace, which will eventually be suited to gain access in terms of the correct feature (e.g. which finger ?) and in terms of the quality of the trace.
- Secondly, the impostor needs to have knowledge about the biometric system technology being used, s/he needs to know how the sensor works and what processing is being applied to the data collected.
- Producing a good fake is also complicated, many types of fakes do not have enough mechanical stability or stability over time, so that fakes may only work in a very limited way.
- Most importantly, the impostor must have the option to test and tune the produced fake, which means s/he needs to have
  - Unobserved access to the biometric recognition system
  - Enough time to test and tune a fake.

The prerequisites, which would make a potential attack successful, also show useful ways of mitigation.

The best way to prevent fake attacks is to design the scenarios for biometric identification in a way that both situations, the enrolment and the subsequent identification / verification, are only carried out under observation of other people. This especially applies to the enrolment phase, in which the identity of a person has to be established by conventional methods (identity card, passport, etc.) and the reference biometric feature is recorded at a very high quality level.

Another building block for biometric security is to limit access to the biometric identification system to the moment of identification, limit the number of retries and to restrict feedback information about the quality of the identification achieved. Although this may harm the usability of a biometric system, it may be considered to strengthen the security.

Also, by implementing different biometric technologies (e.g. different sensor types) within the same application, this may also raise the bar for a potential attack. One step further in this direction is to combine additional security mechanisms with a single biometric. This could be another biometric or a token, which again makes it harder to bypass the access security.

Live detection for preventing attacks with fakes may be overestimated. Live detection typically involves the measurement of additional biometric parameters (like pulse, temperature, conductivity, etc. for fingerprint biometrics), which should help to differentiate a "real" biometric feature from a fake. However, given some knowledge about the "live" detection mechanisms involved, it is often possible to modify the application of a fake biometric to fulfill those additional conditions as well. On the other hand, these "live" detection measurements may adversely influence the standard operation and usability of the biometric system, so that the number of false rejections increases.

The basic question to answer is if the overall risk and potential damage will decrease by implementing a biometric identification system, and for most applications both will be reduced.

6.4 Systems

A number of typical systems may be constructed by architecting the basic functions of biometric identification systems in different ways.

These systems are characterized by the specific location of the biometric functions:

- Capture
- Encoding
- Matching
- Reference Storage

Different combinations of these functions provide different system properties in terms of on-/offline capability, availability, ease of use, privacy and security. Some may only support biometric verification whereas others may also provide biometric identification options.

This section does not cover biometric systems used in criminal identification (AFIS) or also in the homeland security sector.

Smart Card Oriented Biometric Systems

Smart card oriented biometric systems today typically use the smart card for reference template storage. Physical access control solutions employ contact-less cards or tokens together with fingerprint, face or iris biometrics.

The template storage normally needed is some hundred bytes so that transferring the reference templates from the card for comparison is quick.

Powerful card processors also allow for implementation of the matching algorithm additionally to the template on the card processor.

Pre-processing, encoding and interfacing to the biometric sensor are handled by an external device. In many applications this external device will be a standard PC, while in high security-critical environments the external device may be a dedicated specially-enhanced smart card reader, which provides for a greatly reduced attack surface.

The future of the matching-on-card technology may be the system on card approach, which seeks implementation of biometric sensors (typically fingerprint), encoding and matching functions and reference template storage on a standard ISO7816 card [ISO7816].

Embedded Biometric Systems

Embedded biometric systems allow for a self-contained complete biometric identification system. Powerful microcontrollers and digital signal processors together with flash memory may compose a complete biometric identification system at a size of 1 inch in square (see Figure 6.6). Those embedded biometric systems may include all functions of preprocessing, encoding, matching and reference storage together with application functions on a small printed board, thus making it very easy to integrate into everyday applications like door locks, safes etc.

Figure 6.6
Embedded biometric system

Most of the available embedded biometric systems offer biometric verification and also biometric identification, with reasonable performance for several hundred persons. Embedded biometric recognition systems are often found in access control solutions and use fingerprint biometrics, but also face and iris recognition.

PC-based Biometric Systems

Most of the simple IT-security related biometric systems make use of desktop PCs in the enterprise. Biometric sensors today come with standard PC interfaces, almost exclusively using the USB ports. The CPU and memory capabilities of a standard PC today allow for running sophisticated image processing, encoding and matching algorithms and can provide excellent performance. Reference template data is typically stored on the PC's hard disk, with biometric verification and some limited biometric identification functions being provided. In general, biometric recognition is used to perform user authentication within the operating system and to applications, thus replacing usernames and passwords with convenient fingerprint recognition. Some implementations of face recognition and iris scanners are also available for PC users, although fingerprint is the prevalent biometric technology on the desktop.

Network-based Biometric Systems for Enterprises

Although PC-desktop based implementations provide useful functions by replacing usernames and passwords for applications, they suffer from several limitations, like

- Biometric reference data is local to the PC. Although authorized, not every user can use any PC in the enterprise.
- Enrolment, credential management, security policy enforcement are local management tasks that are carried out by the user.
- Local desktop security and availability is limited due to the almost public accessibility of desktop PCs.

Enterprises will therefore use centrally manageable network-based authentication systems that interface with the enterprise-wide identity management infrastructure. Server-based biometric authentication systems provide control over enrolment, security policies, secure reference template and credential management. Biometric enrolment may be integrated into the standard user provisioning functions. Biometric verification and identification can be made available to a number of network-based applications like the Intranet, ERP systems and others for all employees at all locations, thus not only enhancing security by establishing true identity but also reducing password operating costs. According to a number of studies by renowned consulting groups[1], password reset costs add up to between 51 and 147 USD, illustrating that biometric authentication systems really pay off.

---

[1] E.g. Gartner Group Technology Report, T-15-6454

Convergence between Physical Access Systems and IT Security Systems through Biometrics

Biometric recognition systems are equally useful for implementing physical access systems as they are for implementing user authentication in IT applications. By integrating the biometric recognition system into a comprehensive identity management system (see Chapter 5), biometric identification may be used for door access and also as a replacement for the password-based application login on the desktop (see Figure 6.7).

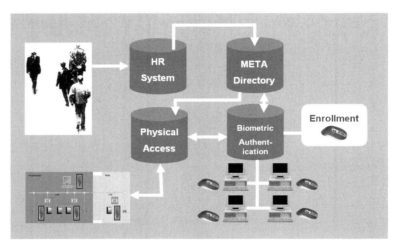

Figure 6.7
Example for the architecture of a converged solution for physical access and IT access

Due to privacy and security concerns also, it is desirable to have a single point of biometric data storage and enrolment. Feasible approaches are either networked systems with central template storage or decentrally organized access systems using tokens with embedded biometric templates. Token-based approaches are normally more expensive as tokens have to be handed out and their live cycle has to be managed (e.g. loss, destruction, etc.). Depending on the strength of the biometric feature chosen (e.g. face recognition) only biometric verification may be feasible so that a token might be necessary anyway. Fingerprint biometrics is equally well suited for physical access as it is on the desktop for IT security applications.

6.5 Software

Biometric recognition technology is composed of hardware and software components. Some vendors provide both, so that their biometric software algorithms are also dependent on using specific or licensed hardware, such as sensors.

Especially representative of this approach are all today's available iris recognition systems, which have to license Iridian's[1] patents to implement iris recognition cameras, which in turn are based on Iridian's software components.

Most other biometric types, like fingerprint or face recognition software, allow sensor technology from a vendor other than the algorithm manufacturer to be used. Mature and powerful biometric algorithms even allow use of a variety of sensors from different manufacturers performing almost equally well sometimes even in mixed operation within the same system.

Vendors therefore typically specialize either in providing sensors or software algorithms. For example, in the fingerprint biometrics market, there are around a hundred different vendors of sensors and algorithm producers competing with one another. Independent vendor tests[2] periodically provide some information about the abilities of specific vendors.

These tests are carried out at an academic level, however, and may characterize the biometric performance of a single engine with a number of predefined biometric databases. These tests will not provide information about the important issues of application integration options, user feedback and interface flexibility, which really decide if the engine performance can be transformed into real-world performance.

Biometric performance data in terms of error rates for FAR, FRR, FTE etc. of a specific engine may therefore only contribute on a subordinate level to the application performance of a real-world biometric recognition system.

Most biometric software vendors provide some kind of biometric SDK (Software Development Kit), which includes the basic biometric functions of biometric enrolment, verification and identification. Most available SW packages also include some kind of template or data store management. Some SDKs are simple libraries while some resemble complete frameworks including graphical user interface components and database capabilities.

SW Standardization

Several attempts at standardization of biometric software functionality have been made over the last decade, the best known of which are:

- BioAPI™ (Biometric Application Programming Interface)[3]
- HA-API (Human Authentication Application Programming Interface)[4]

The BioAPI standard has gained reasonable support from vendors and is now available in Version 2.0 (to become ISO/IEC 19794-1). BioAPI Version 1.1 was accepted as ANSI INCITS 358-2002 with several vendor implementations, especially regarding the biometric service provider level (BSPs), having being made available.

---

[1] www.iridiantech.com

[2] e.g. the International Fingerprint Verification Competition, see bias.csr.unibo.it/fvc2004/

[3] www.bioapi.org

[4] www.biometrics.org

Standardization covers a software framework implementing the interfacing to one or more biometric service providers. As regards BioAPI 1.1, only a single application is considered using biometric functionality through each instance of the BioAPI framework. BioAPI 2.0 overcomes some limitations of the previous definition by adding an abstraction layer of biometric function providers (BFP).

Standardization does not cover the representation of biometric template data in depth or algorithm internals so that biometric template data may be exchanged between different vendors' algorithms and databases. Special biometric data interchange formats have been defined to serve this purpose, such as CBEFF (Common Biometric Exchange File Format)[1].

Caveats for Implementing Biometric Applications

The all-dominant facts for providing a useful biometric application include:

- The correct design of the biometric application scenario
- Appropriate user guidance and feedback
- An observed and careful enrolment of biometric reference data
- Training and information for users of the biometric system

Poor biometric application implementations typically suffer from disregarding these facts and therefore have resulted in poor user acceptance. Another typical problem may arise if a single application implements biometric recognition in an isolated way. So even if the application design was appropriate, the user's request for adding biometric authentication to a number of additional applications within an enterprise will probably fail, thus again reducing user acceptance.

Biometric authentication systems for enterprises should therefore be planned and considered as an enterprise-wide service integrated into the overall identity management architecture.

6.6 Conclusion

Increasing numbers of human machine interfaces, global cooperation and cyber crime attacks need to be addressed by appropriate measures in rising security and convenience at the same time. Users expect security processes that are efficient in time, easy to use and take privacy concerns into consideration.

Biometrics is a good additional means of improving security without unpleasant complexity for users. The technology has proven maturity, in the near future we will all use biometrics as an everyday application in our private and official life, when traveling cross borders, when drawing money out of a cash dispenser or accessing the Internet.

---

[1] see Common Biometric Exchange File Format (CBEFF) at www.itl.nist.gov

Part II:
Practical Experiences

7 Risk Management in the Financial Services Industry

Roland Müller

This chapter describes how an international financial services provider manages information security in order to reduce potential risks and comply with legislation at a global, regional and local level. It shows how DaimlerChrysler Financial Services (DCFS) initiated a global project on information security to ensure that its local and regional entities are sufficiently equipped to face the threats of doing business via the Internet.

We first describe the problems that were identified after the merger of the financial organizations of the former Daimler-Benz and Chrysler corporations. These problems include legal requirements at a state, federal, national, regional and international level. We then develop the cornerstones required to overcome identified problems. Finally, we discuss the approach taken by executive management, which enables them to be sufficiently equipped for upcoming challenges.

7.1 The Merger of Two Automotive Corporations

In 1998, two of the most important corporations in the automotive sector merged and this merger of equals was considered one of the most risky but also most promising steps to revitalize American and European automotive manufacturing. There was Daimler-Benz AG who dominated the segment of luxury cars with its Mercedes-Benz brand but was also the largest commercial vehicles manufacturer in the world. Then there was Chrysler Corporation who had come to be the third largest car manufacturer in the United States after almost being bankrupt at the beginning of 1980. Daimler-Benz was manufacturing vehicles on all continents but its main focus was on Germany and Europe. Chrysler was strong in the United States, but almost non-existent in Europe or Asia. The situation regarding their car portfolio was similar: Mercedes targeted the luxury car sector with best of breed technology while Chrysler provided bread-and-butter cars with an appealing look but poor technology. Both corporations had divisions providing financing for vehicle customers.

These financial divisions are the target of interest for several reasons: each of these divisions is supporting the sale of vehicles by offering various financial services, such as car leasing, car financing or fleet management (e.g. for commercial vehicles). But due to the regional concentration and car portfolio, the customer base also differs: in the U.S. most customers finance their vehicles while this financial service is predominantly used by commercial customers. Therefore, car finance is important in the U.S., while commercial lease is more often used in Europe and other parts of the world.

After a successful merger of the manufacturing and development divisions where appropriate, the financial divisions were combined in the DaimlerChrysler Financial Services group which is managed out of Berlin, Germany. One of the first tasks to harmonize their business processes was the installation of a Corporate Information Technology Management solution, as the financial services rely heavily on information technology. This information technology management is now directing all IT initiatives throughout the group.

7.2 Legal Requirements for Financial Services Providers

DaimlerChrysler Financial Services provides financial services in 41 countries on five continents. The portfolio includes financing, leasing, fleet management, insurance brokerage services and structured financial services. These services have to comply with applicable law in all of these countries. These legal requirements can be structured as follows:

- Risk control legislation
- Data protection legislation
- Legislation fighting organized crime and terrorism

The following paragraphs will explain what implication each of these legal directives may have for a corporation, especially in the area of information security.

7.2.1 Risk Control Legislation

This legislation was always important for financial institutions as its primary goal was the protection of customers' money. It gained momentum in the last decade because of criminal activities initiated in major corporations. Bankruptcies like the Enron cause and WorldCom led to more rigid legislation to avoid similar incidents. The U.S. Sarbanes-Oxley Act is an example of these new laws.

Risk control legislation requires companies to sufficiently evaluate any risk they may face and to develop adequate strategies to control identified risks sufficiently, may they be financial or non-financial. With respect to information security, business continuity is an important issue in that area.

7.2.2 Data Protection Legislation

Data protection plays an important role in Europe but is also becoming more important in the U.S. and Asia Pacific. Examples of this type of legislation are the European directive on Data Protection 96/46/EC, the various national European privacy acts and the U.S. Gramm-Leach-Bliley Act.

The intention of this legislation is to protect personal information automatically processed by business. With respect to financial services, this focuses on protecting customer information and avoiding any misuse or disclosure without the customers' official consent.

With respect to information security, this legislation requires companies to protect customer data sufficiently and to provide methods and processes that prohibit misuse and disclosure.

7.2.3 Legislation Fighting Organized Crime and Terrorism

This legislation, also known as money laundering legislation, is a contradiction to the data protection legislation as it requires companies to disclose those customers who are assumed to misuse financial transactions for laundering money gained by criminal acts. In light of terrorism, this legislation was amended to include money transfers with terrorist organizations.

In terms of information security, it requires processes to supervise money flow and customer clearance and rating procedures.

7.3 The Decision to Use an International Standard

Due to the fact that the various entities of DaimlerChrysler Financial Services had no common understanding of information security nor had they followed any central initiative in the past, the IT Management of DaimlerChrysler Financial Services decided to make use of an internationally accepted approach. Various standards were taken into account:

- NIST Special Publication Series 800
- German Information Security Agency's Baseline Security Handbook (Grundschutzhandbuch) [BSI03]
- ISO/IEC 13335 Guidelines for the management of IT security [ISO13335] and
- ISO/IEC 17799 Code of practice for information security management [ISO17799].

The National Institute of Standards and Technology (NIST), an institute governed by the U.S. Department of Commerce, provides a lot of guidance material on how to establish information security. However, their primary target is the federal administration of the United States and this restricts the usability of their publications. On the other hand, the material provided is quite up-to date and offers valuable input for various areas of information security. The documents on business continuity, on the installation of an awareness program for employees and on technical material on how to protect an infrastructure are a substantial help for any organization dealing with information security.

The German Baseline Security Handbook follows a similar approach in primarily targeting the German federal administration. Their stronghold is technical guidance but they lack management guidance. In addition, due to their concentration on technical issues, they bear the risk of becoming outdated quickly as the German Information Security Agency cannot guarantee to keep their Handbook always up-to-date.

The guidelines for managing IT security published by ISO/IEC during the second half of the last decade focus strongly on managerial tasks with respect to information security [ISO13335]. Topics like the implementation of an information security organization, responsibilities and awareness are sufficiently well specified to enable an organization to fulfill its tasks. In addition, risk management is described in such a way as to establish it without strictly following just one methodology. Finally, guidance is provided on how technical issues as offered in the NIST series and by the German Information Security Agency, can be used to complement the series of standards.

The final candidate, ISO/IEC 17799, was derived from the British Standard BS 7799 and tries to cover the technical and the managerial aspects of information security within one document. Although it is not the perfect fit, it offers the best solution for international corporations as its areas of control range from policies as the fundament of information security to compliance with internal regulations and applicable law. Its weaknesses come from excluding risk management from the standard but it tries to overcome these weaknesses by stipulating risk management as a prerequisite. Its specific advantage is that it allows classification of the status of information security at a high level, which executive management prefers.

Table 7.1 shows the pros and cons of these information security guidance approaches. DaimlerChrysler Financial Services decided to focus on ISO/IEC 17799 knowing that the version from 2000 was to be revised within a few years.

Table 7.1 The DCFS policy development process incorporated into the DCAG information security process

	NIST Special Publications 800-x	**BSI Baseline Security Handbook**	**ISO 13335 Security Guidelines**	**ISO 17799 Code of Practice**
Audience	Technical and management	Primarily technical	Management	Management and technical
Content	Technical and management oriented	Primarily technical oriented	Management oriented	Primarily management oriented
Completeness	High	Technically high	Management aspects high	Management aspects high
Software Support	Only a few	Quite good	Not	Good
Pros/Cons	Very good quality of information	Good quality, not always up to date	Too extensive and sometimes poor quality	Good quality but requires additional guidance at technical level

7.4 Information Security Status Evaluation

In order to achieve an adequate status of information security throughout the whole DaimlerChrysler Financial Services group, the Corporate Information Security Officer intended to evaluate the status of information security for all entities of DC Financial Services. Therefore, an assessment process was set up based on the International Standard 17799 "Code of Practice for Information Security Management". This assessment process consisted of four components:

• Self-assessment questionnaire
• On-site assessment
• Remote penetration testing and
• On-site technical evaluations.

The self-assessment questionnaire was provided to all entities of the group and consisted of more than 200 questions derived from the ISO Standard. All ten security control clauses of the standard are covered to achieve a comprehensive status in all areas of a corporation. Due to the fact that the portfolio for the various entities of the group differed, each entity could select one of four different answers to each question (Yes-Partial-No-Not Applicable). The filled-out questionnaires were the basis for identifying appropriate actions at a corporate level as well as locally.

The on-site assessments were intended to verify the results achieved with the self-assessment questionnaire. An on-site assessment was set up in such a way that all areas of the questionnaire – the ten security control clauses of ISO 17799 – were evaluated. This way, not only did information security focus on those areas where IT is mostly involved but also on areas where the legal department or the human resource department was in the lead.

In preparing these on-site assessments, an agenda was proposed inviting all departments of an organization, where information security may play a role, for interviews. At the on-site assessment, the respective departments were interviewed and each answer had to be confirmed by evidence. For example, clauses in outsourcing contracts dealing with information security had to be provided for review. This way, all answers of the self-assessment questionnaire were verified. Each on-site assessment was finalized by an on-site assessment report detailing all findings. The outcome showed that in general the self-assessments were conducted quite diligently; deviations were caused by misinterpretations of specific questions.

In summary, six entities on three continents were visited and had to undergo an on-site assessment.

The remote penetration testing served as evidence to show with restricted efforts, how secure an entity was doing its business via the Internet. Due to the fact that it only concentrated on technical issues, the results were used to either confirm the proper setup of Internet connection or request immediate actions in order to protect an entity. However, it provided a well-accepted method to quickly verify information security weaknesses. The remote penetration testing was conducted at four locations on three continents.

The final component, the on-site technical evaluation, was intended to identify existing vulnerabilities within an infrastructure, regardless of whether accessible via the Internet or internally. This evaluation could help in closing security gaps at the border gateway, in server configurations and in workstation setups. The on-site technical evaluation was performed at four locations on two continents.

In summary, all four steps helped to achieve an accurate information security status but also allowed eminent gaps to be closed at the same time. The entities selected covered all five continents where DaimlerChrysler Financial Services was conducting business. The on-site steps were implemented so that interviews and technical evaluations were conducted by a service provider to achieve an unbiased result. Also, remote penetration testing was performed by that provider.

These results were compared with a best-practice benchmark in the financial sector (a Swiss financial services corporation acting globally). It clearly showed that DCFS had to increase its efforts in that area.

7.5 Derivation of Activities

All results were evaluated and offered a comprehensive picture of the information security status within DaimlerChrysler Financial Services. In order to present this information to the board of management, a graphical representation was selected that allowed easy understanding of the results achieved. Figure 7.1 shows this graphical representation covering all control clauses of the ISO standard.

In general, almost all entities were actively supporting information security but the outcome was not sufficient for an enterprise that considers itself to be a benchmark in its area of expertise. Those control clauses where technology plays a major role were usually executed quite well while other areas were lacking.

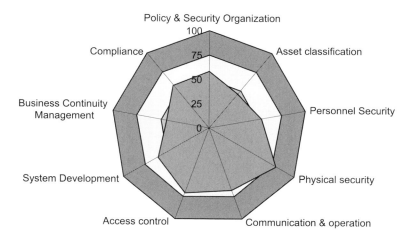

Figure 7.1 The information security status graph aligned to ISO 17799

In comparing all control clauses, Corporate Information Security organized the results into two domains: weaknesses requiring a local initiative and those demanding a corporate-wide approach.

7.5.1 Corporate-wide Activities

The results clearly pointed out that some areas that are the basis for practicing information security had not been provided to the entities in all countries. The following activities were identified for corporate-wide activities, which led to the definition of a set of work streams:

Risk Management: Neither a common methodology nor processes and guidelines existed to conduct risk management with a focus on information security. Due to the fact that risk management was identified as a prerequisite for establishing an Information Security Management System (ISMS) within an enterprise, this work stream had to provide a method and tools for conducting risk management at DaimlerChrysler Financial Services with a focus on practicability.

Information Security Policy Development and Adoption: Policies build the basis for information security as they define the goals of information security and propose appropriate measures to achieve those goals. As a start, a Corporate Information Security Policy was developed and signed by the board of management; it outlined the goals and principles of how information security should be established within DaimlerChrysler Financial Services. In addition, processes were required to guarantee that business and administration functions were involved in the policy development process. Finally, policies had to be developed in order to increase information security for all entities.

Education and Awareness: This work stream was directed at addressing various audiences represented in the group. These are management, IT administration (user help desk, network, system and application administration), developers and normal users. Other audiences may be added later, such as mobile users. The goal is to make them aware of what threats the financial services are facing and how all users may counter them. This work stream will make use of PowerPoint presentations, web-based training and other initiatives.

Asset Classification: An important prerequisite for directing information security initiatives is the classification of all assets. This work stream delivers a methodology and processes that help business to classify its information assets properly in order to derive appropriate measures for protecting them.

Tool Provision: In order to equip all entities with the adequate tools, Corporate Information Security initiated this work package, which concentrates on identifying information security tools for detecting vulnerabilities and improving the security status of the infrastructure. The identified tools have to be evaluated and properly configured to ease their use. In addition, training may be offered.

Business Continuity: This work stream is intended to provide a framework for developing a business continuity plan, which will be supported by various templates to advise management on taking the required steps to prepare for emergencies. In addition, a process must be developed.

Incident Management: In order to deal with an incident – this may be a virus, a hacking attack or even computer theft – a process is required that allows classification of the incident and initiation of appropriate measures.

Monitoring and Reporting: Because DCFS consists of many entities distributed across five continents, an important task is to record the progress and identify areas for support. This task has to be supported by a monitoring and reporting process applicable to all entities but also without putting too much burden on the respective management.

BS 7799 Certification: The final proof for entities within DaimlerChrysler Financial Services for achieving compliance with the ISO standard is certification according to the British Standard BS 7799 whose part 1 is identical with ISO 17799. Certification is intended for those entities providing IT services to other DaimlerChrysler Financial Services companies and for whom certification is a criteria for demonstrating its professional services.

All of these work streams were set up globally and were directed by the project team. In addition, it was agreed that a core team had to be established to support the project and provide guidance whenever required. This core team should meet at least twice a year but should also communicate on a regular basis to supervise the activities set up centrally.

7.5.2 Local Activities

In addition, the assessment identified a lot of activities to be left for the local companies. These activities were local for various reasons: they had to be aligned to the local infrastructure; they had to comply with regional and local law; they were aligned with local processes or they required specific cultural refinement.

For these activities, each entity received a draft action plan containing the identified local deficiencies. Each IT manager was requested to provide information on how and when s/he intended to work on this weakness and who would be responsible for the identified task. This way it was assured that local management was heavily involved in information security.

With respect to budget, every entity was requested to plan for mitigating identified risks in fulfilling compliance with the ISO 17799 standard. In addition, the target agreements of IT managers for the upcoming year were modified to include information security. This way, the fulfillment of information security had a monetary aspect for IT management.

7.6 Interim results

By the end of the first year, an additional assessment was conducted with an identical setup, i.e. the four components as introduced in Section 7.4 were performed. This time, other entities were evaluated to complement the picture of the 1st assessment.

In general, all entities had achieved progress, some only on a minor level, and some with remarkable results. Progress ranged from two percent to more than 140 percent. A few entities achieved worse results, which required explicit evaluation.

After diligent evaluation, the project team decided to modify its approach: in order to increase general progress and annual information security goals were defined for each entity. In addition, a support process was initiated to help the various countries in achieving their annual goals. Finally, more tools and guidance support was provided.

7.6.1 Support Process

Each country that was identified as being behind expected results was visited by the Corporate Information Security Officer who conducted an additional gap analysis. This gap analysis concentrated on those topics that were reported to be not in compliance.

For each topic, an action was defined to achieve compliance; the responsibility for fulfillment was clearly stated and could also be transferred to Corporate Information Security, and the due date for compliance was indicated. All due dates were within a time span of less than a year.

The support process identified that more guidance material was required for the local IT manager. This ranged from clauses for employment contracts covering confidentiality and data protection to job descriptions for administrative security functions. It also included regulations on how to harden systems, how to operate firewalls and intrusion detection systems and how to evaluate logs and correlate them.

7.6.2 Work Stream Results

In the meantime the work streams as defined had delivered some interim results. These results were first presented to the core team and then officially put into operation.

Policy Development and Adoption

With respect to policy development and adoption, a gap analysis was conducted, which identified that only minor activities were required to cover the specific requirements for a financial services provider. Primarily, the security officers of Daimler-Chrysler Financial Services had to ensure that the policies of DaimlerChrysler under development also covered the specific requirements of the DaimlerChrysler Financial Services group.

In order to achieve this, a policy process was established, which made sure that various groups were involved in developing and reviewing policies. The groups involved

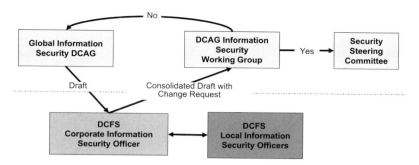

Figure 7.2 The DCFS policy development process incorporated into the DaimlerChrysler AG (DCAG) information security process

were business, legal, IT operations, audit and human resources. This way, policies were under development and received input and a broad consensus. Figure 7.2 describes the process and shows how it is incorporated into the policy development process of the parent company. For large organizations, such as the DaimlerChrysler Bank, a local process was also defined to involve the various groups of interests.

Education and Awareness

The most important task was to educate and train the employees of DCFS in the area of information security. Here, it was intended to provide support during the various phases of employment. Figure 7.3 demonstrates this approach. An employee should receive initial training after being hired. Induction training should inform the new employee in this case of the reasons for securing the enterprise, of the people to contact when requiring help and of general ways for complying with existing information security policies. Being aware that induction training has to be aligned to national law and has to be provided in the respective local language, a template was developed where general security issues were introduced. Those parts addressing local law had to be filled out by the Local Information Security Officers thus making them aware of existing legislation in their area of responsibility. They were also given the task of translating the training into their local languages. The induction training then had to be provided to local HR in order to include it in the whole introduction process.

In addition, web-based training was developed covering topics like virus protection, password security and a general introduction to information security. This should be reworked and updated on a regular basis to increase general awareness.

Management was first addressed by a presentation that showed examples of how the lack of information security had led to the bankruptcy of enterprises. This was supported by movie clips addressing the topic. In summary, it gave a stunning impression and convinced executive management that the topic was extremely important.

Regular reports on the progress of awareness helped executive management in dealing with information security.

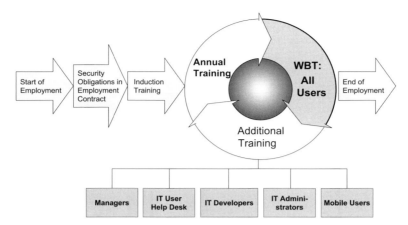

Figure 7.3 The incorporation of education and awareness into the employment lifecycle

Tool Provisioning

For achieving compliance with policies and for constantly evaluating the security status of an organization, a set of tools was required. In order to keep costs low, tools from the public domain area were evaluated and combined in such a way that their use was easily manageable for the Local Information Security Officers. The whole setup was certified for a specific laptop platform and distributed to the Local Information Security Officers. Their response showed that additional platforms are required as no single make of laptop is available worldwide. It also showed that training sessions are required in order to properly use the toolbox.

Monitoring and Reporting

From the very beginning, reporting played an important role. However, this did put quite a burden on the Local Information Security Officers. Therefore, the project team decided to develop an application to overcome this problem and also provide a medium for management for easily monitoring the success of the initiative. In addition, this application was intended to monitor according to the new ISO standard that was published in June of 2005 [ISO17799]. This application will be rolled out in the near future.

7.7 The Ongoing Information Security Process

DaimlerChrysler Financial Services has now implemented information security in various areas. One of the most important areas is the application development process. Quality gates were defined for this process, which require the respective Information Security Officer to verify that information security issues are properly taken into account.

In order to get the required information security issues covered, any new IT project proposal has to be reviewed by Information Security. The Information Security Officer has to validate which areas of information security may play a role in the new project. The result is presented to the proposed project manager who may ask for further guidance.

This way, information security is incorporated into the early process stages of the software development life cycle and will help to develop more secure applications.

In addition, the Corporate Information Security Officer is jointly heading the Infrastructure and Security Council where any infrastructure initiative is discussed and has to be approved.

Various initiatives are addressing information security issues. For example, the appearance of new worms and the existing countermeasures are publicly explained in order to increase better understanding of security problems. Also, the company magazine includes short articles on information security.

7.8 Conclusion

DaimlerChrysler Financial Services has established a process and initiated an information security project with the goal of making information security an integral part of business processes. In the meantime, good results have been achieved but there is no time to rest.

The ISO/IEC 17799 standard has helped considerably to include executive management into the process. This is based on the understanding that an international standard provides guidance accepted in many countries of the world and a certification scheme at an international level provides a way to compare the results.

In this respect, DaimlerChrysler Financial Services is waiting for substantial progress in the area of standardization covering the certification issues as well as metrics for various business areas.

As a final experience it was noticed that requirements derived from legislation, such as the Sarbanes-Oxley Act, could be fulfilled quite easily as the measures put in place helped to mitigate risks as addressed by this law. It is expected that upcoming requirements postulated in Basel II will be fulfilled more easily.

8 Digital Signatures for eGovernment Applications

Joacquin Galeano

8.1 Introduction

The Autonomous Community of Valencia is in the eastern part of Spain. It has a population of 4 million and an area of 23,255 km^2. The Generalitat Valenciana is its autonomous government and holds devolved powers in key sectors such as education, health, etc. There are a total of 95,000 public employees working for the Generalitat Valenciana.

Since 1995, the Generalitat Valenciana has been taking an interest in the use of information technologies that allow services to be provided for citizens in a quick, convenient way. Studies were begun on technologies allowing traditional procedures on paper to be converted to other processes that do not require the physical presence of the parties concerned.

Around the year 2000, the Generalitat Valenciana began to implement what is known as the 2nd Modernization Plan to cover basic security requirements to enable it to take on the development of real tele-government services.

The major goal of all project activities described in this chapter is: the introduction of digital signatures and development methodologies that allow the secure use of these technologies in the Generalitat Valenciana.

8.2 ACCV – The Certification Authority (CA)

The *Autoridad de Certificación de la Comunidad Valenciana (ACCV)* is the certification authority (see Chapter 12) of the Generalitat Valenciana.

The aim of the Generalitat Valenciana in creating the ACCV is to provide all those who will use services on the Internet with digital certificates for identifying themselves and for ensuring that interaction takes place in a trustworthy, secure way. The autonomous government provides this certification service as a free public service.

The certification authority of the Autonomous Community of Valencia is able to provide recognized, quality certification services and advanced digital signatures equivalent to a hand-written signature since it has:

- Legal support based on DECREE 87/2002, of 30 May, of the Valencian Regional Government, and Law 59/2003, of 19 December, on digital signatures
- A public key infrastructure (PKI)
- A declaration of certification practices and policies.

The public key infrastructure (PKI) is a group of hardware and software systems whose purpose is to issue and manage digital certificates and their associated keys (see Chapter 12). This is the nucleus of a certification authority and its components allow those services to be provided.

The staff of ACCV is responsible for the management and maintenance of the PKI to ensure that its activities comply with current legislation and to carry out the progressive introduction of new services. Other pillars of the ACCV are the declaration of certification practices and the certification policies.

The declaration of certification practices establishes the technical procedures and measures used to generate keys and issue digital certificates, guaranteeing the fulfillment of requirements relating to security, availability and functionality. The general rules of the declaration of certification practices are listed in a certification policy for each type of certificate.

The purpose of the ACCV is as follows:

- To provide citizens and public administrations with the necessary tools to guarantee the security and legal validity of telematic transactions
- To promote and contribute to the development of applications and services using digital signatures
- To provide training for citizens, public employees and application developers on aspects of digital signatures and provide the necessary support in their use
- To promote mutual recognition between the ACCV and other certification authorities with a view to achieving universal use of certificates.

8.2.1 What Can Be Done With the Certificates?

The ACCV's digital certificates can be used in the applications of the Generalitat Valenciana and of local and central government.

Some of the more significant applications are as follows:

- Telematic registration
- Payment gateway module that allows payments to various financial institutions to be made on the Internet
- Telematic notices module.

Furthermore, services aimed at Generalitat Valenciana internal procedures have been started up; for example:

- Public employees have an application available on the civil service portal for consulting their pay slips and personal income tax bills.
- Corporate electronic mail is based on secure messaging.

Other examples include:

- A health information system (Abucasis-II) that allows management of prescriptions, analysis reports and electronic case records for doctors.
- Remittance of documents to the Official Gazette of the Generalitat Valenciana.

8.2.2 Implementation Steps

The project was formally inaugurated in November 2000 and the first stages implemented were as follows:

- General training in the selected PKI product
- Training in development tools
- Planning of basic training for users
- Final design of the initial PKI architecture to be created
- Introduction of test and development environments.

This initial stage was simultaneous with a review of the pilots launched to assess the advisability of starting them up and work to publicize the project to allow new applications to be proposed by the various regional government ministries.

The following goals were established in the project up to mid-2002:

- Training of a nucleus of internal consultants in PKI solutions and the way in which they are used. This group was made up of specialists in PKI and legal specialists.
- Training of personnel engaged in planning and management of projects and also of personnel engaged in application development.
- Creation of a recognized certification authority, which allows certificates to be issued for advanced signature creation, as contemplated in the law. This certification authority is supported by a public key infrastructure that will initially be designed for the current pilots and will, in any case, have all the features of the selected technological solution.
- Start-up of current pilots and launch of applications that are currently at various stages, ranging from analysis to development.

Once the initial aims had been achieved, other new basic aims were established for 2003 and 2004, which are described as follows:

- Improvement in services from the PKI nucleus: The objective is to provide higher fault tolerance levels for certain critical services (basically certificate validation by OCSP), improving revocation and user information systems (on renewal, suspension, revocation, etc.)
- Development of new training plans: Despite the fact that it is some years since asymmetrical cryptography and digital signature technologies began to become more widely used, there is still a lack of basic knowledge on the part of final users of services (both citizens and public administration personnel). Specific training plans have therefore been designed with face-to-face and distance training courses.

- Review of procedures and regulatory support for the PKI: In view of the change-able nature of the technologies used and the fact that the legal and regulatory framework affecting the supply of certification services has not been fully established, it is necessary to review the methods for operating the PKI and the way in which services are provided and also to publish new rules or amendments of existing rules.

- To facilitate the launch of User Registration Points (local registration authorities, LRA) throughout the Autonomous Community of Valencia (see Figure 8.1): One of the main difficulties when launching electronic government services based on digital certificates is the convenient, secure distribution of the certificates themselves to users. For this purpose, cooperation has already begun with the provincial councils and municipal authorities and this will now be increased to ensure that these public administrations take part in launch processes through the creation of User Registration Points in each municipal authority and in the three provincial councils. The aim is to have between 80 and 100 additional public offices acting as registration authorities.

- To improve systems for processing and management of proprietary digital certificates: The systems existing on the market for introducing the necessary system of User Registration Points did not meet the requirements established for that purpose and therefore the decision was made to develop a group of proprietary tools.

- To establish systems and procedures to accept certificates issued by other certification authorities: The objective is to establish the requirements for official approval for other certification authorities so that applications accept certificates issued by them. It is also a question of providing access to the validation systems offered by these certification authorities.

- Support and assistance in developing applications and services using digital certificates: The objective is to increase the resources aimed at facilitating the development of applications using digital certificates both in the form of direct support for development teams and by supplying new high-level development tools and libraries.

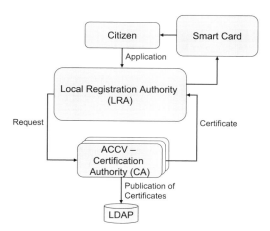

Figure 8.1
Process at a local registration authority (LRA)

8.3 Applications

One of the most important achievements of the PKI that was established is the number and quality of the applications using that infrastructure. It allows complete administrative procedures to be carried out online more quickly, while maintaining high security levels and strict respect for individuals' privacy and rights. Apart from services with high visibility due to the fact that they are aimed at citizens or companies, PKI infrastructures are also being used to develop and operate internal applications for the Generalitat Valenciana and other public administrations of the Autonomous Community of Valencia.

This section includes a review of some of the more significant applications that use digital certificates and the services of the PKI established in the ACCV[1]. A brief description is given of each application in terms of profiles and number of users and operational level of the service or application, along with a general view of the scenario in which the service is provided and the benefits that the application provides. The directions in which work is to take place in the future are described in some cases.

Applications for Small and Medium-Sized Enterprises

The first application is a package of solutions aimed at improving and speeding up communication between the Valencian Institute of Small and Medium-Sized Industries and small and medium-sized enterprises in the Autonomous Community of Valencia.

Distribution of Medical Information

This is an application of the Autonomous Ministry of Health for sending medical information generated at large hospitals, which is currently sent on paper, to small health centers.

Secure Exchange of Files with Payment Offices and the Land Registry

This application consists of a transport system based on S/MIME secure messaging for the transfer of sensitive information between Land Registry offices and the tax department of the Generalitat Valenciana (relating to property transfers and acts liable for stamp duty). Before this system was launched, the information to be transferred was recorded on tapes or CDs and was transported by specialist messenger companies. The benefits of this application range from a significant reduction in costs to faster transfer of information. Those benefits also give rise to significant improvements in data security.

Secure Corporate Messaging System

This is an extension of the use of S/MIME secure mail generally within the corporate messaging services of the Generalitat Valenciana and the bodies linked to it. As a secondary objective, it is a question of structuring the necessary user registration points

---

[1] www.tramita.gva.es shows an actual catalogue of services

throughout the Generalitat Valenciana and distributing certificates to officials for other subsequent uses, depending on each regional government ministry or department.

This service is fully operational. The group of users is made up of staff attached to the Generalitat Valenciana and other administrations for which messaging support is provided.

Work is being carried out to develop the service by integrating legacy X.400 messaging services.

Management of the Youth Card of the Valencian Institute for Young People

This is an application with transport based on S/MIME secure mail for exchanging information files on "Carnet Jove" (Youth card) holders between the banking institutions taking part and the Valencian Institute for Young People.

This application is fully operational.

Exchange of Data between Agents of the Waste Management Chain

The purpose of this application is to replace the current system based on paper – from which it is difficult to extract information – and establish a system for monitoring the dangerous wastes to be managed. This application makes the information much easier to use and, as a result, it allows a reliable system to be established for monitoring dangerous waste materials. Digital certification is used by the four types of users of the application (producers, managers, transporters and the administration) to allow web forms to be signed digitally with the type and quantity of waste produced. This also applies to transporters and, finally, to managers who receive the waste for storage or recycling.

This application is at the initial launch stage with a small number of companies involved.

Remittance of Documents to Be Published in the Official Gazette of the Generalitat Valenciana

The objective in this case is to establish an electronic system for secure transfer of documents between the bodies authorized to publish in the Official Gazette of the Generalitat Valenciana and the publications department. The basic security requirements consist of the ability to guarantee users' identities, the integrity of the documents sent and stored and, finally, the provision of a system for keeping all the information transmitted confidential prior to publication.

This application is being launched initially within the internal sphere of the Generalitat Valenciana and will then be continued in the other Valencian administrations.

Information System of the Valencian Employment and Training Service

This project aims to distribute digital certificates to the citizens registered as seeking employment or waiting for improved employment who wish to receive them for direct access to information systems on supply/demand for jobs and for sending CVs.

DIRECTORIO Project

The aim of this project is to create a database for citizens containing useful information for tele-government services and the creation of an official citizens' messaging system, in other words, to supply official e-mail accounts along with web-mail systems with S/MIME capacities and systems for secure electronic notices to citizens, among other things.

The digital certificates issued by the ACCV will contain the name of the official e-mail account in order to guarantee the usability of secure mail and avoid problems resulting from the variability of mail accounts and providers used by citizens. It is therefore a question of providing citizens with an electronic address in the same way as they already possess a postal address that is known by the administration.

The Tax Agency

Using a digital signature certificate, all types of tax procedures can be carried out through the Tax Agency, including submission of tax returns, payment of taxes, consultation of outstanding debts, receipt of tax certificates, telematic receipt of notices, participation in auctions and requests for deferred payment.

The digital certificates issued by the certification authority of the Autonomous Community of Valencia are valid for the implementation of these procedures since they comply with the conditions provided in the Order of the Ministry of the Public Treasury of 12 May 2003, which established the specific rules on the use of digital signatures for contact with the Tax Agency on taxation matters by electronic, computerized and telematic means, along with the relevant technical specifications.

Central Treasury for Social Security

The Central Treasury for Social Security offers 19 services at its Virtual Office on the Internet. The services allow users to consult and amend data, submit requests, check the processing status of requests, manage retirement pensions, etc. The following services are available: Reports: on work history, bases for contributions, work situation, correction of this data, medical treatment during temporary visits to other European countries, a range of services for pensioners and a range of requests for information and data on withholdings and payments on account of personal income tax.

Directorate General for the Land Registry

The Virtual Office is the telematic window of the Directorate General for the Land Registry for attending to users. Through this Virtual Office, citizens, public administration bodies, the judicial authorities and other institutions taking part, such as notaries public and land registrars, can submit enquiries, obtain certificates and carry out some of the procedures formerly carried on at Land Registry offices.

Users may submit enquiries on cartography and protected registration data and obtain telematic registration certificates for real estate properties owned by them.

SUMA Project

The SUMA Virtual Office is a service that this autonomous body of the Alicante Provincial Council provides for taxpayers to give them a fast, convenient method, available 24 hours a day, to carry out many of the procedures to fulfill their tax obligations with their municipal authority.

Using a certificate from the ACCV, they can carry out the following procedures online: submission of documents, requests and notices, domiciling of tax payments, amendment of personal data, enquiries on payment of debts and payment of debts in real time.

Official Association of Surveyors and Technical and Industrial Engineers

The main purpose of this project is the telematic acceptance of submissions of files relating to industrial installations.

It includes the telematic submission of the project (application, reports and plans, all signed digitally), the reply to the Official Association with confirmation of reception and the necessary data for payment of duty, receipt of messages from banking institutions stating that bills have been paid, stamping reports and making digitally signed bills and reports available to members of the association.

Valencia Municipal Authority

The User Services of the Valencia Municipal Authority are intended to provide citizens with secure online personal information and procedures relating to that information. The personal information supplied relates to the municipal register, bills, applications, etc. and the available administrative procedures consist of management of certificates and domiciling those services.

The purpose of the application is to provide citizens with a range of services that do not require them to visit the municipal offices. They can therefore initiate procedures and make administrative enquiries from home or work, 24 hours a day; 365 days a year.

Abucasis-II Project

This is an ambitious project by the Autonomous Ministry of Health whose aims include the creation of a centralized information system for electronic clinical files and records. Any medical treatment will result in a document signed electronically by the doctor being included in the medical records of the patient in question. There are higher-level security and confidentiality requirements for this information and therefore various parts of the project will require certificates, without which no member of the medical team will be able to carry out their duties.

The project Abucasis II ensures a connection of the ambulant treatment centers and of their information systems in the scope of the network dedicated to the basic and specialized medical care. Not only does it support administrative functions (such as the coordination of appointments, etc.), but it furnishes a complete management system for the end-to-end treatment process. All clinical and administrative patient data is centralized and is thus available from any point of the public medical care network (doctor's offices, health centers, policlinics and hospitals). Before taking this system into operation, part of the required infrastructure was implemented. For instance, the data processing center was redesigned and every workplace of all ambulant treatment centers was networked.

8.4 Some Relevant Data

Since it started in July 2001, the certification authority of the Autonomous Community of Valencia has issued over 47,000 certificates and has set up more than 165 User Registration Points distributed throughout the three provinces of the Autonomous Community, with one more in Madrid.

The Public Key Infrastructure of the Generalitat Valenciana is the first to be established in a Spanish regional government and one of the first in Europe.

The ACCV has signed recognition agreements with two certification authorities. Its certificates are also accepted by the Spanish Tax Agency (AEAT), the Directorate General for the Land Registry and the Ministry of Justice. Negotiations are being carried on with a further six central government bodies for acceptance of the certificates by those bodies.

The project has won several prizes and awards:

- November 2001: Prize for good practice in e-Government at the European Ministerial Conference – "From Policy to Practice".
- November 2002: Prize in the "Institutions" category at the 8th Conference on Information Technology (ETI) of the Autonomous Community of Valencia for work to apply and develop Information Technology, organized by the weekly publication "Computing" and PricewaterhouseCoopers in cooperation with SUN Microsystems.
- April 2004: Prize in the "Public Bodies" category at the first Edition of the SIC Prizes awarded by the prestigious Spanish magazine "SIC – Seguridad en Informatica y Comunicaciones" [Computer and Communications Security].
- June 2004: Prize at the First Conference on the use of Digital Signatures in Public Administration organized by the Catalan Certification Agency, CATCert, as the certification authority whose certificates can be used to access the greatest number of applications and services on the Internet.

8.5 Conclusion

Tele-government applications and services are emerging as a result of the technological, organizational and legal basis established by the Valencian Regional Government through the ACCV. These make certain aspects of the relationship between the public administration and citizens and companies faster and more effective.

These foundations, which will doubtlessly be enriched in the coming years with the start-up of new services, are being laid down in a way that allows them to be integrated with services provided by other Spanish and EU administrations for the common good.

The development of a common legal framework constitutes a first step towards the interoperability of systems and applications, but it must go further as far as cooperation between administrations is concerned, to achieve the reusability of applications and the establishment of common certification policies ensuring real recognition of digital certificates.

9 Identity Management for an Insurance Company

Jürgen Lorek

The Generali (Switzerland) Holding Company unites the business activities of Generali Insurance of Persons and Fortuna Life Insurance Company Ltd. Vaduz in the life sector and those of Generali General Insurance and Fortuna Legal Protection Company in the non-life sector. The company employs some 2,000 people in Zurich and Geneva. The parent company, Assicurazioni Generali, Italy's leading insurance company, directly or indirectly controls 626 companies worldwide. The Generali Group holds fourth place in Europe and ranks among the ten largest operators at world level in terms of assets under management. It is the third largest European insurer in the life sector.

9.1 The Starting Point

The situation in 2001 is as follows: Generali Group Switzerland is the product of a series of mergers and acquisitions that have assembled a number of formerly independent Swiss insurance companies under one roof. The formation of the new Group has provided an opportunity to consolidate operations on a reduced set of standard platforms, and the rationalization effort has been implemented successfully. The merger has also brought rapid growth in the number of IT users – there are now some 2,000 employees, each of whom requires access to a variety of services, data and applications running on a variety of platforms throughout the Group. The range stretches here from established, high-availability applications on the basis of hierarchical databases through to modern client/server applications on the basis of relational databases.

The Generali applications are predominantly proprietary developments, which were developed primarily in the past in the host area (Bull and AS/400). Current proprietary developments are based on the client/server architecture. Oracle is the relational database used, which is operated under Sun Solaris. Generali uses standard software extensively in the area of infrastructure and office automation. The internal network is operated under Microsoft Windows.

Because of the heterogeneous system landscape, numerous authorization solutions administered in isolation existed before a central security solution was deployed. The overall administration processes were therefore unwieldy as a result: Numerous different areas were involved in the individual processes with the result that correspondingly long process throughput times were the norm. In addition, the quality of the permissions assigned could have been improved on in some cases. Some systems, for example, contained user accounts that were assigned to employees who had already left the company.

Generally speaking the situation at this point in time at Generali Group is as follows: IT resource provisioning is performed manually. Each user is assigned, using printed paper forms, a set of access rights and permissions to a specific configuration of systems and resources that reflect his or her responsibilities. The forms are circulated from one department to the next, accumulating signatures authorizing varying degrees and types of access to different resources; these permissions are subsequently implemented by the relevant system administrator. Similar procedures are followed when employees change jobs (new responsibilities bring a new set of permissions) and when an employee leaves the company. Historically, manual right assignment has worked well enough, but with today's increasingly complex IT environments, it has become costly, time-consuming and subject to frequent errors. Although management had long been aware of the risks and attendant costs of the legacy provisioning system, previous attempts to deal with the problem had failed.

The deployment of a central authorization system should lead to a series of improvements:

- Increased availability and productivity: The use of a central, standard administration solution reduces the manual administration overhead and therefore increases productivity. Furthermore, the use of a high-quality infrastructure solution assures the availability and quality of the system landscape.

- Lower administration and operating costs: The increased productivity as a result of more effective and more efficient system usage in operative day-to-day business allows a reduction in administration and operating costs.

- Added security, convenience and trust: The use of roles as a central rights construct enables the transparent and reproducible assignment of permissions. This added security increases the trust of employees and customers in day-to-day business.

- Reduced costs through consolidation of heterogeneous services: By deploying a central administration tool, both administration components and administration processes can be consolidated, simplified and standardized.

- Competitive strategy owing to service differentiation: The fast and secure processing of business transactions is a key factor in competition especially in the insurance sector. The substantial improvement in the security of applications and systems thereby contributes directly to the success of the company.

Let's assume the following use case as a target scenario:

It's Rita X's first day on the job with Generali Group Switzerland and a Human Resources colleague is filling in the on-screen form with Rita's name, address, salary, start date, position, responsibilities, department as well as other relevant information. She's been hired into the Legal Protection Insurance division and her new job comes with a clear set of functional responsibilities requiring secure access to a broad set of

IT resources. As the session comes to a close, the HR manager executes one final mouse-click, smiles and sends Rita off to her new office.

A few minutes later, Rita has already powered up her PC, logged on to the office LAN, checked out the company Intranet, opened up her e-mail and replied to a message from her new boss inviting her to a meeting – now. The boss knocks on the door and the two of them spend the rest of the day going over her new responsibilities. She finds that she has already been assigned all the necessary access rights and permissions for all of the IT systems, applications and services she will need to do her job. A single password is sufficient to unlock the right doors to the right resources, so Rita is free to concentrate on the business at hand – right from day one.

The section below describes the identity management project that has been executed to turn the scenario described above into reality.

9.2 Project Setup and Goals

The project for deploying a central user administration solution was divided into a number of sub-projects. The sub-project "Organization" described the basic conceptual topic area, the deployment and integration of the authorization tool as well as the connection of this system to the HR and partner systems. The sub-project "Sun Solaris" was responsible for integrating the Solaris user administration, the Oracle user administration and the Oracle application administration. The working group "Windows" dealt with the connection of the Windows user administration, which is based on the Active Directory Services. Other aspects that were addressed in the sub-projects included, for example, the integration of the SAP system and the connection of the legacy systems.

The project pursued the following key objectives:

- Central and automated user administration. The solution being developed for user administration was to be administered centrally. In addition, the administration processes were to be extensively automated.

- Comprehensive solution: The solution being developed was to supply all employees, both in-house and field staff, with permissions in the long term. In addition, all legacy IT systems belonging to Generali were to be integrated in the solution.

- Replacement of decentralized administration applications. The decentralized administration applications were to be replaced through the deployment of a central solution.

- Simplified authentication: The long-term aim was to deploy a solution for unique, integrated authentication (single sign-on). Authentication was to be standardized in the short term through the use of the same login information (user name and password): In this procedure, known as "consistency sign-on", a user can be authenticated for different applications using the same login information.

- Standard-based solution: The solution being implemented was to be based as far as possible on standards. In the area of role-based authorization, the RBAC standard in particular (cf. Section 14.2.5) was to be considered. The repository for storing the permissions and user information was to comply with the LDAP standard (cf. Section 14.2.1).

- Flexibly extensible solution: The solution developed was also to be extensible among other things to the project organization and customers of Generali, so that the permissions of all contract participants could be administered uniformly. Integration of the Generali web platform is essential here in particular.

The starting point was an object-oriented analysis and design on the basis of UML (Unified Modeling Language) with respect to the Generali Group Switzerland's organizational structure and business processes.

The choice was made to focus initially on the Legal Protection division, which offers legal costs insurance. Some 55 users required differentiated access to a range of IT resources and services: sales administration, contract management and damage assessment systems (all running under Oracle), along with Microsoft ADS/Exchange.

A great deal of preparatory work had gone into the description of specific job functions and their definition in terms of roles. Each position in the organization had been assigned a corresponding role or set of roles, depending on the responsibilities and required competencies specified in each job description. Each role was assigned one of four hierarchical levels ranging from beginner through intermediate, expert and manager. Each role and level corresponded to a specific set of permissions, and each was defined as a set of access rights to a range of disparate resources.

9.3 The New Solution

The processes of the new central user administration solution are based especially on the interaction of the authorization tool Siemens DirXmetaRole and the HR system LOGA (cf. Figure 9.1). In order to automate the assignment of permissions, central information has to be recorded initially in the two tools. On one hand, the organization of the enterprise must be represented. Roles are created for this purpose in the authorization tool, to which system and application-specific permissions must be assigned. On the other hand, the positions specified in the HR system have to be exported to DirXmetaRole. The roles are imported as positions in LOGA into the system-specific repository. The system offers the possibility to keep a history of the roles or positions. This allows transparency at all times as to which employee holds which role at a given time.

Once the basic information regarding organization and permissions has been incorporated into the systems, the users can be assigned roles (cf. Figure 9.2). A HR employee records the personal details of the employee including the position held and also the length of time for which the position is assigned. The information entered is then copied to the authorization tool DirXmetaRole. The authorization tool creates the permissions for the employee fully automatically in the systems and applications of Generali. The role specification containing the permissions to be assigned, which is stored in the tool, is drawn on here.

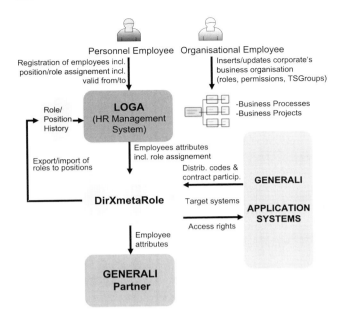

Figure 9.1
Concept of operational
procedures

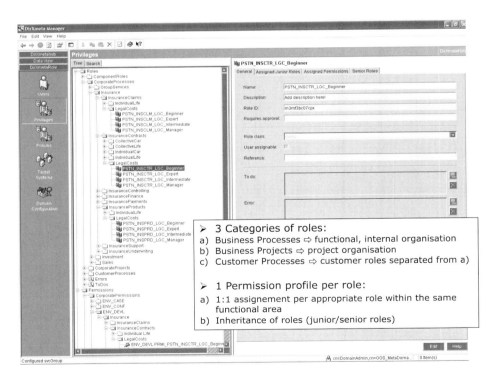

Figure 9.2 Overview of Business Roles

Generali subdivides its roles into three categories. Roles in the category "Business Processes", such as "Individual Life", include the permissions to be assigned in the framework of the internal organization. By aligning roles to processes, roles remain largely unchanged in the event that the company organization structure has to be reorganized. Roles in the category "Business Projects" include rights that are required in the framework of project organization of project employees. The category "Customer Processes" contains the customer roles that are administered separately from the internal organization.

The roles in the category "Business Processes" have a four-tier role profile. Roles of type "Beginner" contain the basis permissions of a group. Roles of type "Intermediate" include additional permissions. Specialists in a group are assigned the corresponding "Expert" role. Management employees are assigned the role "Manager".

A clearly defined inheritance concept defines which permissions of a role may be inherited by the next higher level (cf. Figure 9.3). "Junior Roles" are roles from which a role inherits permissions. "Senior Roles" roles are the roles that a role inherits.

A role comprises permissions. The permissions themselves contain groups. These groups correspond to permission bundles, such as roles in Oracle, which exist in the systems and applications of the enterprise. The individual system, which comprises one or more groups, is referred to as the target system. Three different types of permissions are distinguished by Generali: Permissions contain either rights for the production, test or development environment. Integration of additional environments, such as the preproduction platform, is possible.

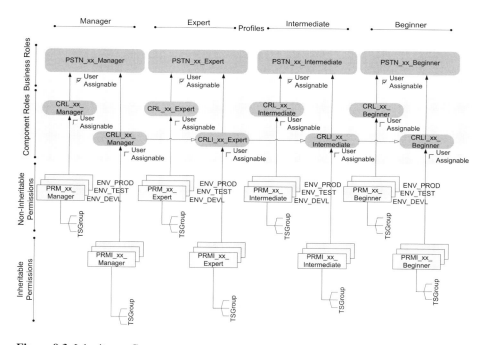

Figure 9.3 Inheritance Concept

In the area of authentication, Generali relies on the synchronization of passwords. If a password is changed by a user or an administrator, this change is recorded by a corresponding component (password listener), encrypted and propagated to the target systems Oracle and Unix. The passwords exist in encrypted form in the Active Directory as well as in the LDAP directory used.

9.4 Success Factors

The intensive conceptual preparations were a key success factor for the project. Before selecting the authorization tool, a tool-independent solution concept was created on the basis of "business models". This provided a concrete, high-quality basis for discussion for assessing the solution before the actual implementation. It was therefore possible to discuss advantages and disadvantages of solution variants or individual solution aspects at a very early stage of the project, for example with representatives of the review team or the special department. Likewise of key importance was the subsequent transmission of the elaborated, conceptual solution approaches to the selected authorization tool.

A further decisive factor was the cooperation with the special department. The elaborated roles with their permissions have to be decided in cooperation with the special department units, because these are the people who best know the business processes they have processed and therefore can judge which permissions are actually required by which employees. It was therefore essential to convince the group leaders of the advantage of the solution being developed so that the individual departments make their contribution to the successful implementation of the system.

Backward compatibility of the deployed solution was a further important success factor. The existing permission structures of the client/server systems were embedded without modifications in the new solution. This allowed the smooth operation of the existing systems to be guaranteed.

9.5 Conclusion

Today when a person is hired and assigned a role, or when role assignments change, all that is required from the HR manager is to check a box on screen. The identity management component (Siemens DirXmetaRole) reads the status of all user-to-role assignments – enabled, added or deleted – and the result is automatically synchronized with the relevant database applications – the entire legacy system running under Oracle, Sun Solaris, Microsoft Windows and Exchange. So the whole complexity of the paper-based, manual process in place prior to the project has been reduced to a single mouse-click.

An encrypted password synchronization system has also been put in place: a single user password unlocks access to all systems and a password change made while working on one system is automatically replicated across the entire resource base.

The identity and access management solution has been in production in the Legal Protection division since June of 2004. Subsequently the solution has been rolled out to the rest of Generali Group Switzerland's two thousand employees. Eventually, automated rights assignment will be extended to independent insurance brokers and other stakeholders requiring access to General Group systems. In the meantime, integration of remaining non-core applications continues (SAP will be brought in, legacy mainframe applications will not), and the benefits have begun to make themselves felt – significantly lower administration costs, near-perfect accuracy in terms of moves, adds and changes in rights assignment; greater confidence in the security of the IT environment and in the company's ability to satisfy evolving regulatory requirements.

10 Infosec Management in a Global Enterprise

Reinhard Schöpf

10.1 Introduction and Motivation

Founded more than 150 years ago and headquartered in Berlin and Munich, Siemens has offices or subsidiaries in 190 countries and is one of the world's largest electrical engineering and electronics companies. Siemens has more than 400,000 employees and offers products, solutions and services spanning the fields of information and communications, automation and control, power, transportation, medical and lighting.

Within Siemens, the value of information and the necessity for measures to enhance information security was recognized at an early stage. The corporate computer centers in particular have long boasted the very highest security standards. In the realm of decentralized systems though, maintaining such levels of security is a steady challenge.

Challenges

In the wake of technical advances, information systems and data media have penetrated the workplace directly and are thus less well protected than is the case within "sealed-off" computer centers. Most of these systems are linked to client-server systems via local networks and brought together on a global level by the Siemens Corporate Network. Challenges include:

- Inadequate protection of individual systems and subdivisions of this network (e.g. as a result of improper administration, either carried out negligently or by poorly-trained system support staff) may jeopardize the security of the entire network.
- On the other hand, internal networks have to be increasingly opened up to the outside world, for example for teleworkers or for business partners.
- The situation is often compounded by a lack of awareness of the problem on the part of management and employees, plus a poor level of knowledge about the threats and protective measures involved.

Thus, a program aimed at improving information security must apply especially to workstations, decentralized systems and their operators and users:

- Appropriate company-wide standards for the secure handling of information and systems are required.

- Management, employees and managers of information systems and networks must be apprised of the value of information, so that they treat documentation and systems with due care and make use of the available protective mechanisms.

- Appropriate measures must be drawn up to prevent the loss and corruption of data and to guarantee the smooth flow of information.

The introduction of such measures undoubtedly is not for free. If, however, one considers the value of the internal information base and the dependence of today's business processes on information technology and communications technology, then such an "insurance premium" is a small price to pay compared with the possible material and non-material damage involved.

Opportunities

While the original motivation for establishing an Infosec management program is often security enhancements, appropriate solutions also offer substantial potential for cost savings and for creating new business opportunities. For example, advanced information technologies are increasingly being used to improve the effectiveness of business processes between partners. Business transactions are processed over public networks without the need for partners to be there 'in person'. This trend exists in the business-to-business (B2B), business-to-government (B2G) and business-to-consumer (B2C) environments as well as in the context of enterprise-internal activities and communications.

Siemens wanted to take advantage of this potential and therefore made the move to digital certificates and PKI as well as smart cards and identity management.

10.2 The Siemens PKI

Siemens started its PKI project in 1998. Today, the Siemens PKI has more than 260,000 participants and is one of the largest private PKI implementations worldwide. Via the deployment of public key cryptography, the Siemens PKI serves to enable fully-electronic and reliable business processes and to improve IT security within the company. Each user is assigned a pair of cryptographic keys. Starting with functions such as encryption and digital signatures for e-mail and strong authentication for portals and corporate applications, this keying material opens up to the user the level of IT security required for many business processes, in particular the confidentiality and integrity of information and the binding nature of transactions.

The basis of any PKI is public key cryptography where users own a secret "private key" and a publicly known "public key" (for details see Chapter 12). Digital certificates guarantee the assignment of public keys and correct ownership of key pairs. In the case of the first version of the Siemens PKI ("PKI 1"), keying material and certificates are generated by a corporate Trust Center and distributed to users via Local Registration Authorities (LRAs), which are responsible for verifying the identity of the receivers. There are currently 115 LRAs in 45 countries worldwide. The private keys

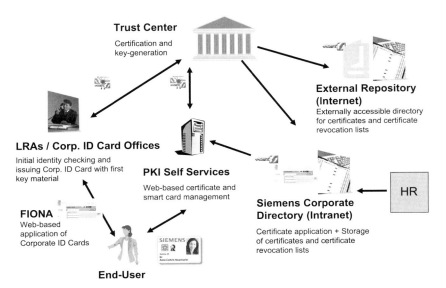

Figure 10.1 Siemens PKI: Overview

are issued on the Siemens Corporate ID Card (a smart card) or in the form of a "soft PSE"[1] on floppy disk. The digital certificates are published in the corporate directory.

Together with PKI, e-mail encryption and digital signing were rolled out company-wide in order to enable confidential communications and non-repudiation. To promote compatibility with other PKIs, Siemens is a member of the European Bridge Certification Authority (Bridge-CA).

Figure 10.1 provides an overview of the Siemens PKI.

Certificates

Two types of certificate are used within Siemens. The mainline corresponds to X.509 type certificates, which are issued by default. The X.509 Standard Version 3 (X.509v3) describes the exact format and data structure of a digital certificate [X509]. X.509 was developed in response to the demand for a facility to exchange certificates between users within a PKI. These certificates are used in conjunction with the e-mail encryption standard S/MIME.

Optionally, users can apply for certificates of a PGP (Pretty Good Privacy) type. In this case, the validation of certificates cannot be handled as effectively as in a hierarchically structured system such as X.509.

---

[1] Personal Security Environment

Personal Security Environment

A Personal Security Environment (PSE) includes the key material (private and public key) and the certificate for the user, together with other control information. The certificate is therefore permanently linked to the public key. A PSE is only issued if the owner proves his or her identity clearly.

A PSE can be issued on a smart card (hard PSE) or as file (soft PSE) on a storage medium. PGP certificates are only available as soft PSE.

To protect the PSE, a user PIN is issued, which is necessary to access the data within the PSE. This PIN can be changed by the user. For security reasons, a smart card is blocked if the user enters an incorrect PIN three times. Additionally, a master PIN ("PUK") is issued with the smart card, which cannot be changed. The master PIN allows for privileged functions such as unblocking a blocked smart card.

Local Registration Authorities and Trust Center

Local Registration Authorities (LRAs) are decentralized organizational units in close proximity to the users. They serve as a link between the users and the Trust Center. LRAs, for example, accept the application for a certificate and forward it to the Trust Center. In the opposite direction they check the identity of the applicant and hand over the PSE to the user.

The Siemens Trust Center provides services for operating the corporate Public Key Infrastructure. These include:

- Generation and archiving of key pairs
- Creation of user certificates
- Creation of server certificates
- Renewal of existing keys with certificates
- Revocation of certificates.

Upon request by an LRA, the Trust Center generates the cryptographic keying material (asymmetric key pairs, certificates) and the corresponding PSE and returns it to the LRA. The Trust Center CA signs all the certificates issued with a CA private key. Applications can refer to the signature on the CA certificate to determine whether a message or document comes from a trustworthy source.

As soon as a PSE is generated for a user, the PIN required to activate the PSE is sent to the applicant. As a standard procedure, the Trust Center archives all encryption keys. This is done by storing (in an especially secured environment) all user data, including the key pair, which is necessary for repeated PSE creation and delivery. A user-related key history can be established in this way.

Server Registration Authority

The mission of the Siemens Server Registration Authority (ServerRA) is the world-wide central procurement of certificates for servers. These certificates allow browser-

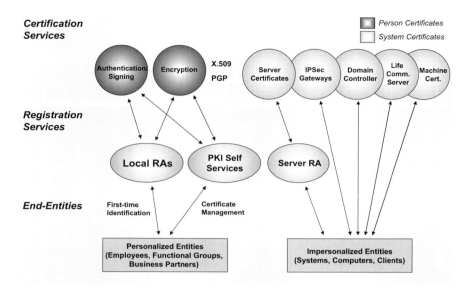

Figure 10.2 Services of the Siemens PKI

independent strong encryption of the data transmission and secure authentication of servers. The ServerRA provides the following services:

- Domain validation
- Order process for server certificates
- Certificate management processes.

In essence, the Siemens ServerRA acts as a local Registration Authority, which approves or rejects certificate requests according to the infosec guidelines and therewith provides the interface between Operating Units and the Certification Authority.

Figure 10.2 shows the different registration and certification services available through the Siemens PKI.

Evolution of the Siemens PKI

A second phase of the PKI project started at the end of 2000. "PKI 2" was introduced in March 2004 and replaced "PKI 1". Focus points of PKI 2 include:

- Secure electronic business processes
  - Support for authentication applications and electronic signatures
  - Secure communication and electronic transactions with business partners
  - Improvement of external recognition of the Siemens PKI and compatibility with other PKIs
- Simplification of PKI processes
  - Web-enabling of the processes for applying and managing certificates

PKI 2 delivers trust services corresponding to state-of-the-art technology, which is expected and required for secure electronic business processes by business partners.

The X.509 multipurpose certificates from PKI 1 are replaced by two application-specific certificates, one for encryption and one for authentication and signing. The PSEs are issued on the Siemens Corporate ID Card only (see below). The private keys are securely generated, stored and operated within the smart card crypto-processor of the Corporate ID Card.

The smart card interface standards Crypto-API (Microsoft) and PKCS#11 are supported by all current PKI applications and allow for easy integration of corporate ID cards and Siemens certificates in many applications.

Certificate Revocation Lists (CRLs) are used for checking the revocation status of certificates. Siemens PKI certificates and CRLs are published in an external repository (i.e. in the Internet), so that business partners have access to our certificates (for example for sending encrypted e-mails to Siemens employees) and can check their revocation status online.

In order to provide arbitrary business partners (e.g. clients) with Siemens PKI certificates, a separate certification service will be established.

"PKI Self Services" clearly simplify the PKI processes by offering web-based management of certificates from the workplace (e.g. regular re-keying).

PKI policies are prepared in accordance with the current standards, Certification Practice Statement (CPS) and Certificate Policy (CP) [RFC3647].

PGP is supported in PKI 2 via soft PSE as hitherto.

In addition to the certification services for persons, dedicated certification services for IPSec-gateways, domain controllers and client-machine certificates were built-up.

Applications

The use of asymmetric cryptography is opening up the potential for handling business processes using advanced information technology.

In a first phase, encryption of e-mail was implemented to protect internal communication over open networks. Building on the resulting infrastructure and the experience gained in this project, additional applications include secure web access with strong client/server authentication, encryption of stored data and the use of digital signatures for documents and workflows or to ensure the liability of transactions.

The Siemens PKI currently supports the following fields of application:

- E-mail encryption/signing (S/MIME and PGP)
- File/volume encryption
- Single-sign-on for web-applications
- SSL client-server authentication
- Windows PC/domain-login

- SAP R3
- Document signing
  - PDF- and Word-documents
- Web-signing
- Network security/access
  - Remote LAN Access, WLAN, IPSec, 802.1x

PKI Self Services

With the start of PKI 2, users of Siemens PKI are offered two ways of handling their requests for issuing keying material and certificates, key updates or certificate revocation.

In any event, the initial application for a Corporate ID Card with certificates must be made via the Local Registration Authorities. All further actions can be performed either using an LRA or in a web-based dialog via the PKI Self Services.

The "PKI Self Services" were implemented to allow easy and fast management of keying material and certificates stored on the Corporate ID Card. PKI Self Services is a web-based tool allowing employees who own a Corporate ID Card with certificates to self-administer their certificates from their workplace, including

- Re-keying of expiring certificates,
- Recovery of old encryption certificates,
- Revocation of certificates,
- Application of PGP certificates, and
- Migration from PKI 1 to PKI 2.

For login to the PKI Self Services a valid certificate is needed.

10.3 The Siemens Corporate ID Card

In addition to classical functions such as employee name, picture and magnetic stripe, the Siemens Corporate ID Card offers a contact-free Mifare chip for physical access control and a crypto chip for PKI keying material and cryptographic processing.

In PKI 1, the PKI keying material was stored in a soft PSE or on the crypto chip of the Corporate ID Card. The key management concept allowed for the private key being temporary accessible in plain text by a PKI application using this key. Consequently, disclosure of keys through manipulated code or Trojan horses was a potential risk.

PKI 2 eliminates this risk and makes full use of smart card technology. The crypto-processor function of the Corporate ID Card is used heavily in PKI 2, i.e. cryptographic operations using private keys are performed exclusively on the crypto chip and these keys never leave the chip. Keying material for authentication and signing purposes is even generated on the crypto chip.

Fields of application that require the use of smart cards include the following:

- Smart card domain login: Windows offers an integrated PKI-based domain login, which works exclusively with smart cards and replaces password login.
- Smart card based login to SAP R3 HR (in Germany)
- Strong authentication
- Electronic signatures.

Access to Intranet data or applications from the Internet or unrestricted access to portals requires strong authentication based on smart cards. PKI enables standardized and system-wide (domain, Web, SAP, ...) authentication and uses this as a basis for broad Identity & Access Management (IAM). A compromised private key provides an intruder with access to all resources assigned to this identity. Therefore, storing keys within a soft PSE is not sufficient.

A soft PSE is also generally considered to be inadequate for signature applications, because the private key, as in the case of an ordinary signature, represents the signing person (legally binding) and therefore must be adequately secured. In signature applications the level of security is essential for the acceptance of a user to apply electronic signatures and to save costs in this way.

The "Signaturbündnis", a public-private initiative of the German government, follows the aim to define standardized and compatible infrastructure standards for the application of electronic signatures. Thereby smart cards are generally required.

The law in the European Union distinguishes between "qualified" and "advanced" electronic signatures. Qualified signatures are considered to equal handwritten signatures but due to elevated organizational requirements are still rarely employed. The Siemens PKI supports advanced signatures, which are sufficient for most applications.

PKI 2 is compliant to the "Signaturbündnis". The security level is comparable to that required for qualified signatures.

Figure 10.3 presents an overview of the the Siemens Corporate ID card concept.

10.4 The Business Case

The Siemens PKI offers excellent potential for avoiding and saving costs and for creating new business opportunities. An efficient security infrastructure has been built-up thanks to more than 260,000 participants and many supported applications.

The potential of the Siemens PKI is exploited in many ways, numerous applications are supported and PKI is increasingly utilized in business processes. A quantitative statement on the overall business case of a PKI is difficult however. Adequate methods of return on invest (ROI) calculation and reference calculations are missing; sample calculations usually only relate to the ROI of a specific PKI application. Nevertheless, it is attempted below to evaluate several example business cases of the Siemens PKI. It must be noted that statistical comparisons are only available conditionally.

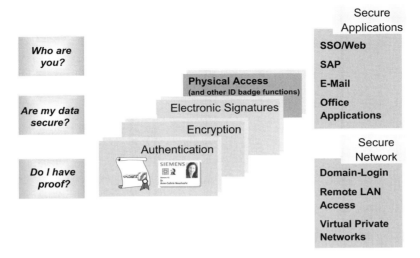

Figure 10.3 The Corporate ID Card

The PKI business case basically consists of the three main elements, Electronic Identities, Electronic Signatures and Increase of Security.

10.4.1 Electronic Identities

An important business case of the Siemens PKI is realized by the deployment of an enterprise-wide Identity & Access Management (IAM) solution, which is strongly based on PKI authentication.

Authorization schemes based on electronic identities allow standardized and application independent user management (see also Chapter 5). They enable so-called single sign-on (SSO) and form a basis for portal solutions. Employees and business partners can be authenticated uniformly and their access rights managed flexibly, regardless of the access network (e.g. Intranet or Internet). A reduced number of authentication requests are expected to improve user acceptance externally and internally. On the other hand, the costs for implementation and maintenance of otherwise required application-specific user management systems will be reduced significantly. An important factor that can be easily quantified is the reduction of helpdesk costs due to a smaller number of user accounts and passwords.

Identity & Access Management solutions require secure and reliable authentication of the person represented by an electronic identity. Access to internal data from the external world, in particular, requires strong authentication that can hardly be achieved with password schemes. Note that identity theft would allow access to all resources associated with that identity.

Example 1: Reduction of Helpdesk Costs

Use of PKI-based authentication reduces the helpdesk costs for an enterprise. The Gartner Group states that about 20 percent of all requests a helpdesk receives relate to problems with passwords, which causes average costs of about €106 per employee and year. Experience of other companies shows that the number of password-related helpdesk calls can be reduced by 40 percent by employing PKI and smart cards.

Applying these findings to the situation at Siemens where there are some 260,000 PKI users results in potential savings of about €11 million per year. In addition, the reduced time required by employees to solve such problems is noteworthy.

Example 2: Cost Effective Remote LAN Access

Remote LAN Access (RLA) requires strong user authentication, which is realized in many cases through hardware tokens and one-time-password mechanisms. Typical costs for such a solution are about €15 per user per year. Annual savings of up to €750,000 can be made by using PKI-based authentication for some 50.000 users of RLA.

10.4.2 Digital Signatures

Digital signatures allow documents to be signed electronically in a legally binding way. This enables complete electronic processes, which in turn leads to costs savings through process optimization, electronic archiving, elimination of transportation costs, reduced cycle times and greater flexibility as well as localization independence. Acceptance of electronic processes by users will also increase through the avoidance of media interrupts.

Legal regulations and compliance requirements can also be met with digital signatures. For example, the Siemens healthcare division MED uses digital signatures within its quality assurance and documentation processes in order to meet requirements set out by the US Health Office (Food and Drug Administration – FDA).

Example 3: Digital Signing of Documents

Numerous processes exist within an enterprise, in which documents have to be signed with typically two or more signatures. Apart from the signing parties, there are other persons involved in preparing, looking through and controlling these documents.

The following conservative calculation assumes electronic workflows (preparation, distribution and archiving) of one million documents to be signed per year. On average, such a document contains more than 5 pages and three people are involved in processing it.

The costs of printing or copying one document are estimated at €0.90. If we assume that the number of required copies can be reduced from three to one, savings per document amount to €1.80. In addition, the costs of distribution and postage of documents can be reduced through electronic distribution, according to an OECD study, from about €2.75 to €0.75 per recipient. This results in additional savings of €6.00

per document. Finally, €0.40 per page can be saved through complete electronic archive processing, which amounts to savings of €2.00 per document.

The total savings of €9.80 per document result in overall savings for one million documents of about ten million Euro per year. Studies conducted in different Siemens groups for specific areas of application strongly support these findings.

10.4.3 Increase of Security

As a corporate-wide security infrastructure, which can be integrated in applications independently of systems, a PKI provides security through encryption, data integrity and authentication.

Thanks to encryption, confidential information can be protected and secure communication can be assured. At the same time, encryption also enables the electronic distribution of confidential data, which otherwise must be distributed in paper format. Encryption thereby also enables process optimization and cost reduction. Examples are the distribution of the Siemens salary statements per encrypted e-mail or credit card information in the Siemens TravelNet via secure http.

Integration and authentication of data can be secured with digital signatures. Information disclosed by Siemens to the public or to business partners and which it receives from them can be protected in this way from manipulation or misuse, which is also in the interest of the corporate reputation.

The PKI also offers strong authentication of persons and machines when accessing Siemens resources. In particular, it is possible to protect those applications for which a password is not sufficient, for example unrestricted access to portals, access to Extranet, Remote LAN Access and Virtual Private Networks.

Example 4: Reduced Losses by Increase of Security

According to a study by the Computer Security Institute (CSI) and the FBI, which investigated 503 companies, losses detected due to insufficient IT security amount on average to €176 per employee per year [CSI02]. Recalculating this for Siemens with about 430,000 employees, such losses would amount to €75 million a year.

Actual losses are estimated to be substantially higher but are extremely hard to quantify. The loss of a single large contract due to industrial espionage could already exceed the said €75 million. The University of California in Davis estimates IT security related losses to be up to 5.7 percent of turnover, what would mean €4.7 billion for Siemens.

85 percent of the losses considered in the CSI study happen to be in areas that can be protected by PKI-based applications. Assuming that only 50 percent of these losses can be avoided, a conservative calculation based on the CSI findings already results in potential savings of €31.5 million through the consequent use of the Siemens PKI.

10.5 Benchmarking

Siemens and EEMA (European Forum for Electronic Business[1]) have conducted benchmarking in relation to PKI implementations [EEMA04]. A total of 23 companies took part in the benchmarking, of which 17 described themselves as international or multinational corporations, and of which 12 employ more than 30,000 people.

Of the 18 investigated companies that stated the scope of their certificate rollout, ten plan to equip 100 percent of their employees (PC users) with certificates, while an additional three plan a coverage of about 66 percent. Almost all of these companies distribute certificates generated by their own Certification Authority (CA), only two roll out certificates of an external CA, two others distribute both types of certificates. The majority of companies have opted for smart cards as key bearing media despite the additional costs for cards and card readers.

Three companies, among them Siemens, plan to issue 100,000 certificates or more. At the time of the study, this aim was achieved by up to 40-60 percent. The scope of rollout plans is also represented in the estimation of 75 percent of participating companies that PKI is a strategic condition for wide-scale realization of electronic business processes.

All companies participating in the benchmarking show high activity through realization of PKI-based applications (see Figure 10.4). The application portfolio of Siemens covers the most fields, with applications already realized in the most important areas.

The survey shows that PKI, despite the critique expressed after the PKI hype in 1998, is still of great importance as a security infrastructure and business enabler. PKI follows the natural technology lifecycle and is now in its establishing phase. The majority of the investigated companies follow a strategy similar to that of Siemens, with an own Trust Center, company-wide PKI rollout, smart cards as key bearing media and consistent development of application areas.

10.6 Conclusion

The dependence of business processes on information and communications technology continues to grow. Since system downtime and lost or corrupted information directly impair productivity, everything must be done in order to further improve the availability of systems.

Enterprises will only be able to maintain or improve their competitive position if they prevent corporate know-how falling into the hands of unauthorized persons. Careless handling of information or inadequate protection against eavesdropping on internal networks may lead to an unintentional leaking of information. Increasingly, information brokers or industrial espionage outfits will attempt to get hold of internal informa-

---

[1] See https://www.eema.org/

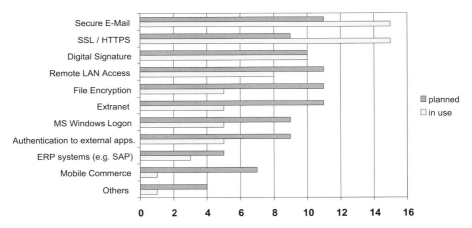

Figure 10.4 PKI Benchmarking

tion and pass on what they learn to competitors. The only solution to this lies in heightened awareness of the problem and the encryption of sensitive information and communication networks.

More and more data is leaving the premises of an enterprise. The "Virtual Office" and "Teleworking" require internal information systems and the data stored on them to be accessible from anywhere. Discussions involving participants at different locations increasingly make use of video-conferencing or other collaboration tools. Here too, it is essential to find secure solutions that ensure that the benefits of these technologies do not have to be paid for through the leaking of valuable know-how.

Information security measures and compliance with the appropriate instructions and guidelines also contribute significantly to the quality and efficiency of the processes, as evidenced by the numerous ISO 9000-certificated procedures and other quality standards. Information security will continue to grow in importance in the future as a result of further developments in information and communications technology.

Part III:
Technologies
and Standards

11 Cryptographic Techniques

Walter Fumy and Ute Rosenbaum

Cryptography is the discipline that embodies principles, means and techniques for the transformation of data in order to hide its information content, prevent its undetected modification or prevent its unauthorized use. This paper presents an introduction to the basic techniques available through this discipline and provides recommendations for the selection of appropriate techniques to meet specified security levels.

11.1 Goals of Cryptographic Techniques

Confidentiality of Data

In its more than 2500 years of history, cryptography was mainly used by military and secret services to keep secret data secret. Confidentiality was the main if not the only goal. Confidentiality means that only a predefined group is able to gain knowledge about the protected information.

How can confidentiality be achieved by cryptology? It is assumed that one cannot prevent others from reading the data. Imagine for example a broadcast network, for example a wireless LAN, where everybody can listen to all information being transmitted. The idea for solving this problem is to prevent others from *understanding* the data. To achieve this, cryptology offers *encryption techniques*. Encryption keeps the content of the data secret, but not the existence of the data.

Integrity and Authenticity of Data

With the advent of electronic data communication, additional threats arose. It became easier to manipulate data without leaving any traces. New goals of cryptology became methods to guarantee the *integrity* of data and the *authenticity* of data.

Data integrity means that it can be verified that data was not modified by someone who wasn't authorized to do so. Data authenticity means that it can be shown that the data was really sent by the given sender.

How can data integrity be achieved? Again, it isn't assumed that one can prevent attackers from modifying the data. This is a realistic assumption: think of data being sent over a network of different computers. Anybody having access to these computers could modify the information. By appending a *cryptographic check value* or *Message*

Authentication Code (MAC), it can be checked if the data was modified by someone not allowed to do so.

Note that in case a message was modified, a MAC doesn't provide means to reconstruct the original information. For this purpose, other techniques have to be applied, for example the data has to be re-transmitted.

The scenario for data authenticity is slightly different. In this case it is assumed that an attacker generates data with a falsified sender address. Again this cannot be prevented, but it can be detected using a MAC.

Non-Repudiation

In modern business applications, where data is only stored and processed electronically, *non-repudiation* mechanisms are one of the most important fields of application for cryptography.

Non-repudiation is the ability to provide evidence that an action or event has taken place, so that this event or action cannot be repudiated later. A number of different flavors of non-repudiation exist, for example it could mean that someone cannot deny having sent or received a message or originated a document.

Non-repudiation mechanisms have many applications, because they provide a means to prove something. This is required for instance to prove who originated a document, for example for revision purposes. Another area of application for non-repudiation mechanisms is to prove compliance with legal regulations.

The main cryptographic mechanism to achieve non-repudiation is the digital signature. A signature can only be generated by one person, but any recipient can verify the signature. Therefore, it can be unambiguously proven who signed a document.

11.1.1 Symmetric Algorithms

The cryptographic algorithms known from the beginnings of cryptology until the 1970s were mainly used to encrypt data in order to achieve confidentiality. All of these algorithms work with a secret parameter (key) that is used both in the encryption and decryption algorithm. Therefore, they are called symmetric algorithms.

If two people want to use a symmetric encryption algorithm to communicate securely, they have to proceed as follows: First, they have to agree upon a common secret key for the encryption algorithm they choose. Then, before sending the message, the sender encrypts the message using the secret key and the encryption algorithm and sends the resulting cipher text. The recipient, who gets the cipher text, decrypts it using the same secret key and the encryption algorithm and thus gets back the plain text.

Using symmetric encryption they can be sure that the message is not disclosed to others if:

- The encryption algorithm is secure, i.e. without knowing the key it isn't possible to decipher the message and

- The key is protected from illicit usage.

The second condition requires appropriate key management, which is a combination of technical and organizational functions.

Key Management

The prerequisite for using a symmetric encryption algorithm is that the keys are previously exchanged in a secret way. Therefore, we have to find methods for two communication partners to establish a common secret key.

Basic methods of exchanging keys are organizational: the communication partners meet each other and exchange the key directly or they use a trustworthy messenger. This could take place long before the keys are applied.

These organizational methods can be used to build up a hierarchical model with a central unit. The central unit exchanges a key with each member of a group using the organizational key exchange. When two members want to communicate secretly, the sender generates a symmetric key, sends this key encrypted to the central unit, which decrypts it and encrypts it again for the intended recipient. This key is then used for encryption. In this model, three entities have knowledge of the secret key: the communication partners and the central unit. While this seems to be a disadvantage, it can be tolerated in many scenarios with closed user groups.

The approach described is an example of encrypted key transport. Other methods will be explained in Section 11.3.

11.1.2 Asymmetric Algorithms

Symmetric key transport becomes a notable problem in open scenarios. The question therefore arose if it would be possible to encrypt data without having exchanged a secret key beforehand. Another problem discussed by cryptographers was the fundamental concept of digital signatures.

Both problems seem to be completely different but they can be solved using the same approach, asymmetric or public key crypto systems. The idea for such systems was first described in 1976 by Whitfield Diffie and Martin Hellman of Stanford University in their famous paper "New Directions in Cryptography" [DH76].

Principle

The idea of public key crypto systems is as follows: Each user gets two related keys: one key is called a public key, the other a private (or secret) key. As the names indicate, the public key can be made public and transmitted in plain text, whereas the private key must be kept private and secret. The keys are related, but for security reasons it has to be computationally infeasible to derive the private key from the public key.

For a public key encryption scheme, there has to be an algorithm that uses the public key to encipher the message and the private key to decipher it. For a signature scheme, there has to be an algorithm that takes the private key to generate a signature and the public key to verify that message and signature fit together.

Key Management

At first glance, public key crypto systems seem to solve all problems, especially the key management problem. The public key does not have to be kept secret, so it can be exchanged openly. But everyone who uses a public key has to be sure that the public key really belongs to the claimed person. In other words, the authenticity of public keys has to be guaranteed.

Different methods have been developed to achieve authenticity of keys. A simple organizational approach works as follows: the public key is exchanged a second time over a completely different channel than the first time and then the two values are compared. For instance, the public key could be printed on cards. More elegant, less work for everybody and more appropriate for enterprise environments is to use a so-called public key infrastructure (PKI) and certificates. This topic is addressed in detail in Chapter 12.

For an asymmetric encryption or signature scheme, the following requirements have to be fulfilled:

- The asymmetric algorithm has to be cryptographically strong, i.e. without knowing the private key it isn't possible to decipher or sign a message;
- The private key has to be protected from illicit usage and
- The public key has to be authentic, i.e. really belongs to the claimed entity.

Most asymmetric algorithms known today are based on one of two hard mathematical problems, the factorization problem and the discrete logarithm problem.

Integer Factorization

The integer factorization problem is easily explained. Given two large primes, it is relatively easy to compute their product; but given the product of two large primes, it is extremely difficult to find the two prime factors. The most prominent public key system based on the factorization problem is the RSA scheme [RSA78].

The Discrete Logarithm

Exponentiation is defined to a base g such that a number x is mapped onto g^x; the logarithm is the inverse function to the exponentiation. For applications in cryptography we look at finite groups, i.e. mathematical structures with a finite number of elements where a multiplication exists and an exponentiation function can be defined. Because of the finite number of values this is called a discrete exponentiation.

Discrete exponentiation is attractive for applications in cryptography because it provides a one-way function; if the parameters of the group are chosen carefully it is computationally infeasible to compute its inverse, the discrete logarithm.

Elliptic Curves

V. Miller [Mil86] and N. Koblitz [Kob87] independently proposed the use of elliptic curves to construct discrete logarithm-based crypto systems. Elliptic Curve crypto systems are attractive for cryptographers, because the known methods for computing elliptic curve discrete logarithms are much less efficient than those for conventional discrete logarithms. Therefore, to achieve the same level of security as in conventional discrete logarithm crypto systems, much shorter keys can be used.

11.1.3 Keyless Algorithms

Some applications of cryptography do not require keyed mechanisms. One example is the encryption of passwords to keep them confidential. For this application no decryption is needed: to verify a password it is also encrypted and compared with the stored value. Other applications make use of a "digital fingerprint" of a document. This "digital fingerprint" is a fixed-length value serving as a cryptographic check value.

One-Way Functions

A one-way function is a function whose function value can be easily computed, but is computationally infeasible to invert. One example already discussed in Section 11.3 is discrete exponentiation.

One-way functions can also be constructed using symmetric algorithms. For this a constant (and known) message is encrypted using the given data (e.g. the secret password) as a key.

Hash Functions

Hash functions yield a digital fingerprint. More formally, a hash function is a function that takes variably sized data as input and has a fixed size output called the hash value or message digest. When employed in cryptography, a hash function has to fulfill additional requirements: it has to be a one-way function and must be collision-free.

The one-way property of hash functions means that given a hash value, it is not feasible to find an input that yields this hash value. Hash functions map data of arbitrary length to data of a fixed length. Therefore, many different input values exist that are mapped onto the same hash value. A hash function is said to be *collision-free* if it is computationally infeasible to find two different input values that result in the same hash value.

For a strong hash function, the effort to find a collision simply depends on the length of the hash value. For a hash value of n bits, due to the birthday paradox[1], a collision can be found with about $2^{n/2}$ trials.

---

[1] The term "birthday paradox" stems from the somewhat surprising fact that in a group of 23 people the probability that any two of them share the same birthday is higher than 0.5.

11.2 Symmetric Encryption Algorithms

11.2.1 Stream and Block Ciphers

Symmetric encryption algorithms can be identified in the way they process the plain text for encryption.

Stream ciphers use the secret key to produce a stream of key symbols that is combined with the plain text using an invertible function, such as XOR, for encryption (see Figure 11.1). A symbol is a string of bits of a defined length that can be very small, for example 1 or 8 bits.

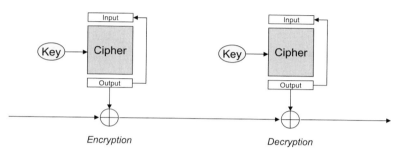

Figure 11.1 Stream Cipher

Using a stream cipher it is important never to use the same key stream to encrypt two different messages. If someone does, there is the danger that an interceptor will be able to deduce information about the plain text. XORing the two cipher texts will result in plain text XORed with plain text. Using basic techniques, such as letter frequency analysis, the two plain texts can be easily recovered. To prevent this attack, a unique initialization vector (IV) in addition to the key has to be used for each encryption process.

Block ciphers operate on blocks of plain text, i.e. strings of bits of a defined length, to yield cipher text blocks (see Figure 11.2). Each block is encrypted using the same key. The block size is typically at least 64 bits.

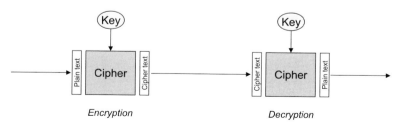

Figure 11.2 Block Cipher

There are many ways a block cipher can be used. These so-called modes of operation add additional properties to the underlying cipher. The most important modes are defined in ISO/IEC 10116 [ISO10116]. The basic mode described above is called Electronic Code Book (ECB) mode. It is used mainly for encryption of short data such as keys. Cipher Block Chaining (CBC) mode is normally used for encryption of bulk data. In CBC mode, each plain text block is XORed with the previous cipher text block and the result is encrypted. The first plain text block is XORed with an initialization vector (IV), which should be chosen randomly and can be transmitted in the clear. CBC mode conceals patterns in the plain text. Other modes are used to turn a block cipher into a stream cipher.

11.2.2 DES

The Data Encryption Standard (DES) was originally developed by IBM in 1975. In 1977, it was standardized by the U.S. National Bureau of Standards as FIPS 46 (Federal Information Processing Standards) [FIPS46]. The complete description of DES was published in the standard, such that everybody could implement and use this algorithm. However, the design criteria for DES have not been published.

DES is a block cipher operating on 64-bit blocks. The key length is 56 bits. Ever since DES was first published, it has been criticized for its short key size. Today it is widely agreed that 56-bit keys offer only marginal protection against a committed adversary. In 1999, a worldwide computing team utilized a network of nearly 100,000 PCs on the Internet and a specially designed supercomputer, the Electronic Frontier Foundation's (EFF) "Deep Crack," to break a DES cipher in 22 hours and 15 minutes.

11.2.3 Triple-DES

Over the past 20 years, researchers have proposed a number of potential replacements for DES, for example the financial services industry has developed a standard for triple-DES encryption. In triple-DES, each message block is encrypted with three successive DES operations rather than one, a construction that involves two or three different keys. In typical applications, triple-DES offers an effective key size of 112 bits. The main disadvantage of triple-DES is its relatively poor performance; furthermore, the block length is too small for some applications.

11.2.4 AES

The U.S. National Institute of Standards and Technology (NIST) has been working with industry and the cryptographic community since 1997 to develop a long-term successor for DES. The outcome of this process is the Advanced Encryption Standard (AES), published by NIST in 2001 as [FIPS197]. The AES specifies the Rijndael algorithm [DR00], a symmetric block cipher that can process data blocks of 128 bits using keys with lengths of 128, 192, or 256 bits, and referred to as "AES-128", "AES-192", and "AES-256" respectively. Rijndael was designed originally to handle additional block sizes and key lengths, however they have not been adopted in the AES standard.

There are more than 10^{20} times more AES-128 keys than DES keys. Assuming that one could build a machine that could recover a DES key in a second (i.e. try 2^{55} keys per second), then it would take that machine approximately 149 trillion years to crack a 128-bit AES key.[1]

AES is specified as a symmetric encryption algorithm for use in communication protocols, such as S/MIME, TLS and IPSec.

11.2.5 Other Symmetric Ciphers

There are many more symmetric encryption algorithms and standards.

- IDEA (International Data Encryption Algorithm) was designed in 1990 by X. Lai and J. Massey. IDEA is a 64-bit block cipher with 128-bit keys. The performance in software compares to the DES. IDEA has been used in PGP since the early versions.

- Ron Rivest has developed several ciphers named RCn where "RC" may stand for "Ron's Code" or "Rivest's Cipher." Most well-known is RC4, a stream cipher with variable key size and very good software performance. It was found that RC4 has some statistical weaknesses and needs careful key management for being secure. The algorithm is used in many products and communication protocols including S/MIME, SSL/TLS and IEEE 802.11 (WLAN encryption). RC6 is a block cipher based on RC5 [RFC2040] and developed to meet the requirements for AES candidates.

Table 11.1 Symmetric ciphers

Algorithm	Block Size (in bits)	Key Sizes (in bits)	Standards
DES	64	56	FIPS 46-3, withdrawn 1999
Triple DES	64	112, 168	FIPS 46-3 ISO/IEC 18033-3
IDEA	64	128	
RC4	stream cipher	variable	
RC6	128	variable	
CAST-128	64	128	RFC 2144 ISO/IEC 18033-3
MISTY1	64	128	RFC 2994 ISO/IEC 18033-3
Camellia	128	128, 192, 256	ISO/IEC 18033-3
AES	128	128, 192, 256	FIPS 197 ISO/IEC 18033-3

---

[1] The universe is believed to be less than 20 billion years old.

- CAST was originally invented by Carlisle Adams and Stafford Tavares. Several versions exist. CAST-128 is a 128-bit block cipher accepting keys of up to 128 bits [RFC2144]. CAST-256 accepts key sizes of up to 256 bits [RFC2612]. Both algorithms are not as high performant as Rjindeal. CAST-128 is used in PGP.

- MISTY1 is a 64-bit block cipher designed in 1995 by M. Matsui and others for Mitsubishi Electric with 128-bit keys and a variable number of internal operations. It runs quite fast on a variety on platforms.

- Camellia was developed jointly in 2000 by NTT and Mitsubishi Electric Corporation. It has many similarities to AES, which means that much of the analysis for AES is also applicable to Camellia. Camellia Cipher Suites have been specified for TLS [RFC4132].

Table 11.1 provides an overview of selected block ciphers and their standardization.

11.3 Asymmetric Encryption Algorithms

When using an asymmetric encryption algorithm in a communication scenario, the key exchange procedure is quite different from that of symmetric algorithms. Firstly, the intended recipient has to generate a key pair, keep the private key secret and publish the public key. If anybody wants to send him an encrypted message, the sender encrypts the message using the public key in combination with the asymmetric encryption algorithm and sends the resulting cipher text. The recipient decrypts the cipher text using the corresponding private key in combination with the asymmetric encryption algorithm.

A selection of asymmetric ciphers is standardized in ISO/IEC 18033-2 [ISO18033b]. As an example we describe encryption based on the RSA algorithm.

11.3.1 RSA Encryption

In May 1977, Ronald Rivest, Adi Shamir and Leonard Adleman discovered how a simple piece of classical number theory could be used to construct the first public-key crypto system known as the RSA algorithm [RSA78].

The RSA algorithm is based on the difficulty of integer factorization. Key size is variable – which is typical for asymmetric schemes – and the algorithm therefore can be adapted to the security needs of the application. Recommendations for appropriate key sizes are discussed in Section 11.7.

Key generation for RSA involves the generation of two large primes and some computations using these numbers. The key generation process results in three numbers that form the key pair: an RSA number n, product of the two primes and two parameters e and d. The public key consists of e and n, the private key of d and n. Observing some restrictions, e can be chosen freely. Often the number 65537 (binary 10000000000000001) is taken, because operations using this public key are relatively fast.

Encryption using RSA consists of raising the message to the e-th power and reducing the result modulo n, i.e. dividing by n and taking the rest. *Decryption* is the same operation using the private key instead of the public key.

11.3.2 Hybrid Encryption

Asymmetric encryption has one drawback: it is relatively slow. Therefore, asymmetric techniques normally are not used for encrypting long messages but only for short ones, such as cryptographic keys.

With hybrid encryption, a random key for some symmetric encryption algorithm is generated and used to encrypt the message. This key is then encrypted using an asymmetric algorithm, for example RSA. The symmetric encrypted message along with the RSA-encrypted secret key is sent to the recipient. Upon receipt, s/he firstly uses his/her private RSA key to decrypt the encrypted secret key. Secondly, s/he decrypts the message with the symmetric algorithm.

11.4 Hash Functions

There are different ways to construct a cryptographic hash function. They can be built using block ciphers, using modular arithmetic methods or they can be constructed using dedicated designs. Developing a hash function of high quality is not an easy task. Feasible methods have been found to construct collisions for several hash function proposals, which limit their range of application.

Hash functions based on a block cipher are specified in ISO/IEC 10118-2 [ISO10118b]. This international standard describes four such constructions.

In the past years, however, designers have been focusing on dedicated hash functions. Examples include:

- Ronald Rivest developed the hash functions MD2 in 1989 [RFC1319], MD4 in 1990 [Riv90] and MD5 in 1991 [RFC1321]. Today, flaws are known for all of them [Dob98], [WY05], however the basic design principles of MD4 can still be found in many new hash function designs. In particular, MD5 has been employed in a wide variety of security applications and is also commonly used to check the integrity of files.

- SHA-1 is a hash function with a 160-bit hash value developed by NIST in 1994 [FIPS180], especially for use in combination with the signature algorithm DSA (see Section 11.6). SHA-1 replaced the originally published SHA to correct a flaw. SHA-1 produces a 160-bit digest from a message with a maximum size of 2^{64} bits, and is based on principles similar to those used in the design of MD5. In 2005, Chinese cryptologists published theoretical results about collision search attacks that lower the complexity required for finding a collision in SHA-1 to 2^{63} [WYY05]. While still not a practically feasible attack, we recommend to be cautious with new deployments of SHA-1, in particular since it cannot be excluded that these attacks will be improved in the near future.

Table 11.2 Hash functions

Algorithm	Block Size (bits)	Message Digest Size (bits)	Standards
Hash functions using a n-bit block cipher	*n / 4n / 3n*	$\leq n$ / 2n / 3n	ISO/IEC 10118-2
MD5	512	128	RFC 1321
SHA-1	512	160	FIPS 180 ISO/IEC 10118-3
SHA-224 / SHA-256	512	224 / 256	FIPS 180-2 ISO/IEC 10118-3
SHA-384 / SHA-512	1024	384 / 512	FIPS 180-2 ISO/IEC 10118-3
RIPEMD-128 / RIPEMD-160	512	128 / 160	ISO/IEC 10118-3
Whirlpool	512	512	ISO/IEC 10118-3

- NIST has specified four additional hash functions under the label SHA. These are named after their digest lengths SHA-256, SHA-384, and SHA-512 and were published in 2002 in FIPS 180-2, which also includes SHA-1. In 2004, an additional variant, SHA-224, which was defined to match the key length of two-key triple DES, was standardized.
- In the framework of the EU project RIPE (Race Integrity Primitives Evaluation), a hash function called RIPEMD was designed based on the principles of MD4. An improved version RIPEMD-160 was published in 1996 [DBP96].
- Whirlpool, a hash function named after a galaxy, was developed by V. Rijmen and P. Barreto [BR00]. Whirlpool is a dedicated hash function based on a substantially modified version of the AES encryption algorithm.

Table 11.2 provides an overview of selected hash functions and their standardization.

11.5 Message Authentication Codes (MAC)

A cryptographic Message Authentication Code (MAC) is a short check value used to authenticate a message. As input, a MAC algorithm accepts a secret key and an arbitrary-length message to be authenticated and outputs a MAC. The MAC value protects both the integrity and authenticity of the message by allowing verifiers (who also need to possess the secret key) to detect any alterations to the message content.

Unlike digital signatures (see Section 11.6), MACs are calculated and verified using a shared secret key. Therefore, a MAC cannot be verified by a third party not in possession of the key.

MAC algorithms can be constructed from other cryptographic primitives, such as hash functions (as in the case of HMAC) or from block ciphers (e.g. CBC-MAC [ISO9797a]). The HMAC construction was first published in 1996 by Mihir Bellare, Ran Canetti and Hugo Krawczyk. FIPS 198 as well as ISO/IEC 9797-2 generalize and standardize the use of HMACs [FIPS198], [ISO9797b]. HMACs utilizing SHA-1 (in short HMAC-SHA-1) and MD5 (HMAC-MD5) are used, for example, within the IPSec and TLS protocols.

11.6 Digital Signatures

An essential prerequisite for electronic commerce is an electronic substitute for the handwritten signature as a means of non-repudiation. To this end, a function is required with the property that only the signer can generate the signature, but anybody can verify the signature and the signer cannot deny having signed this message.

Digital signature algorithms are typically based on public-key cryptography. To sign a message, the private key is applied to the message to generate the signature. Using the public key, anybody can verify if the signature is valid. Because only the signer has the private key only s/he can produce the signature and cannot deny having signed the message.

For efficiency reasons, a hash function is classically applied to the message before signing. This makes the signature short and saves computing power since hashing is generally much faster than signing. However, if the hash function is insecure (for example, if it is possible to generate collisions), then it might be feasible to forge digital signatures.

A substantial number of digital signature schemes have been proposed. Today, three families of public-key crypto systems are established in the marketplace:

- Prominent examples of integer factorization based schemes include the RSA digital signature scheme [RSA78] and the Rabin-Williams scheme.
- Examples of discrete logarithm-based systems include NIST's Digital Signature Algorithm (DSA) [FIPS186] and Nyberg-Rueppel signatures [NR93].
- Elliptic Curve-based systems are analogous to discrete logarithm schemes; examples include the EC-DSA scheme and the EC-NR scheme [ISO15946]. The primary advantage of elliptic curve crypto systems is their cryptographic strength relative to the required parameter size, i.e. elliptic curves offer more security per bit.

11.6.1 RSA Signatures

The RSA algorithm can be used for encryption as well as for generating and verifying digital signatures. Generally speaking, the mechanisms are the same; the main difference is the reverse usage of public and private keys.

In principle, an RSA signature works as follows. Signature generation for a message is based on an exponentiation using the private key. To verify the signature, the message is first recovered using an exponentiation with the public key. The recovered message is then compared to the original message. If neither message nor signature has been modified and the message was signed with the corresponding private key, the values will match.

For reasons of efficiency and to counter certain signature forgery attacks, the message is typically hashed for signing, padded and formatted prior to applying the RSA algorithm. RSA-based signature schemes providing message recovery are standardized in [ISO9796b], while classical schemes utilizing a hash function are standardized in [ISO14888b].

11.6.2 Discrete Logarithm-Based Signatures

In the case of discrete logarithm-based schemes, encryption and digital signatures work rather differently. Discrete logarithm-based signature schemes providing message recovery are standardized in [ISO9796c], while classical schemes utilizing a hash function are standardized in [ISO14888c]. The most prominent example is the Digital Signature Algorithm (DSA) developed by NIST.

The DSA is based on a scheme originally proposed by Taher El Gamal [ElG85] and was standardized as Digital Signature Standard (DSS) [FIPS186].

11.6.3 Elliptic Curve-Based Signatures

From the encryption, signature and key agreement schemes utilizing the discrete logarithm problem, analog schemes can be constructed that are based on the elliptic curve discrete logarithm. These schemes typically are denoted by the prefix "EC", for example EC-DH (elliptic curve based Diffie-Hellman key establishment [ISO15946c]) or EC-DSA (elliptic curve based DSA variant).

Various signature schemes based on elliptic curves have been proposed. As for normal discrete logarithm signature schemes, there are schemes with and without message recovery. Elliptic Curve-based signature schemes providing message recovery such as EC-NR are standardized in [ISO15946d], while classical schemes utilizing a hash function (e.g. EC-DSA, EC-GDSA and EC-KCDSA) are standardized in [ISO15946b].

11.7 Algorithm and Parameter Recommendations

Security is a process, rather than a state. In particular, the field of cryptology is constantly advancing – major breakthroughs in cryptanalysis may occur at any time. Therefore, recommendations for the use of cryptographic algorithms, keying material (e.g. key sizes), and other parameters need to be reviewed and updated on a regular basis.

One fundamental way for a third party to crack a cipher where the algorithm is known but the key is not is to mount a "brute-force" attack using computers or specially optimized hardware to try every possible key until the message is decrypted. Finding a key gives the attacker access to all messages enciphered under the same key. If the only (known) way to decrypt a cipher text is to try every possible key, then longer keys offer stronger protection.

Security objectives in enterprise security systems closely coupled to cryptographic techniques include data confidentiality, data integrity and non-repudiation. The *target security level* determines quantitatively to what extent these objectives need to be met. In general, the required security level is based on a threat and risk assessment of the IT system, discussing issues such as

- What is the lifetime and/or the value of the assets to be protected?
- How long into the future does the security level need to persist?
- What is the attack model, i.e. who is the attacker and what resources does s/he have?
- How will these resources evolve and what cryptanalytic progress is expected to occur during the lifetime of the protected assets?

A common approach (for a classic example see [LV01]) is to analyze the current state-of-the-art concerning cryptanalysis, make assumptions about the advancement of resources available for an attack, and from there extrapolate algorithm and key size recommendations to match different security levels.

The central question usually is how long it will take an attacker to "break" the security mechanism and what resources s/he needs in order to have a reasonable chance of success. For obvious reasons, the security level needs to ensure that the cost of breaking a system is significantly higher than the value of the protected assets. On the other hand, if information needs only to remain secret for a few hours, a break of the system requiring an attack effort of a few weeks might be acceptable.

11.7.1 Security Levels and Moore's Law

The computing power available to an attacker strongly depends on the type of adversary and ranges from the "hacker" without any significant budget dedicated to his/her attacks to the intelligence agency with a multi-million dollar budget (cf. Table 11.3 [ECR05]).

To estimate how the computing power available to attackers may change over time, *Moore's law* is typically used. Moore's law states that the density of components per integrated circuit doubles every 18 months, which is interpreted as the computing power per chip doubles every 18 months.[1]

Based on Moore's law and the steady growth of the Internet, it is safe to assume that the computing power available for attacks doubles every 12 months, which can be

---

[1] There is some skepticism as to whether this law will hold much longer because new technologies will eventually have to be developed to keep up with it.

interpreted as a steady loss of cryptographic strength. Under this assumption, the following conclusions hold:

- Symmetric ciphers "lose" 1 bit of security per year;
- Hash functions and Elliptic Curve-based schemes "lose" 2 bits of security per year; and
- RSA schemes "lose" about 20 to 30 bits of security per year.

In addition, unanticipated advances in cryptanalysis may occur.

11.7.2 Cryptanalysis

The ultimate goal of cryptanalysis is to find weaknesses in cryptographic techniques. A wide variety of cryptanalytic attacks are known and they can be classified in several ways. One distinction concerns what an attacker is able to know and do in order to learn secret information. Specific scenarios include cipher text only attacks, known plain text attacks and chosen plain text attacks.

General methods for attacking symmetric encryption algorithms include linear cryptanalysis and differential cryptanalysis. When the security of an algorithm rests on hard mathematical problems, as is usually the case in public key cryptography, techniques for tasks such as factoring turn into potential tools for cryptanalysis.

Pure cryptanalysis exploits weaknesses in the algorithms themselves, while other attacks are based upon properties of the implementation of algorithms, known as side-channel attacks. For example, if a cryptanalyst has access to the amount of time or the amount of energy an algorithm took for an operation, s/he may be able to use this information to break a cipher that is otherwise resistant to cryptanalysis. Examples of this class of attack are timing attacks and differential power analysis (DPA).

Cryptanalysis is in general regarded as being successful and the attacked algorithm labeled "broken" when an attack needs fewer computational operations than brute force would take. Note that such a "broken" algorithm may still provide sufficient security if the resources required for the attack are nevertheless beyond the capabilities of the attacker.

11.7.3 Quantum Cryptanalysis

Quantum computing is a relatively new field that has developed with the increased understanding of quantum mechanics. Quantum computing promises computing devices that are exponentially faster than conventional computers, at least for certain problems. The story of quantum computing started in the 1980s with the publication of a theoretical paper that first described a universal quantum computer [Deu85].

In a classical computer, a bit has a discrete range and can represent either a zero or a one – consequently a register composed of L physical bits can be in one out of 2^L possible states. In a quantum computer, a quantum register composed of L quantum bits (or *qubits*) can store in a given moment of time all 2^L values in a quantum superposition, i.e. at once. Because of superposition, a quantum computer can in one computational step perform the same operation on 2^L different numbers encoded in L qubits. In order to accomplish the same task, a classical computer has to repeat the same computation 2^L times or has to employ 2^L processors working in parallel. Therefore, quantum computers promise an enormous gain in the use of the computational resources of time and memory.

Several of the unique features of quantum computers have applications for cryptography. In 1994, Peter Shor published a quantum algorithm that, in theory, can very efficiently factor large integers or compute discrete logarithms [Sho94]. Shor's algorithm runs in polynomial-time. Another quantum algorithm published by Lov Grover achieves searching an unsorted list of N items in only about sqrt(N) steps [Gro96]. An important application of this algorithm is the cryptanalysis of symmetric ciphers, such as DES or AES. Grover's algorithm can be used for speeding up exhaustive key searches – however its running time is still exponential.

How a quantum computer could be built is known in principle. However, as the number of quantum logic gates in a network increases, one quickly runs into serious practical problems. One main reason is a phenomenon called quantum decoherence, which is due to the influence of the outside environment on a quantum computer. Therefore, the development of practical quantum computers still remains an open question. In the unlikely event that a sufficiently large quantum computer can be built, public-key cryptography may have to be abandoned, and key sizes may have to be doubled for symmetric crypto systems.

11.7.4 Key Size Recommendations

This section provides recommendations for selecting cryptographic algorithms and key sizes to match specified security objectives. Note that the recommendations below reflect state-of-the-art in public knowledge at the time of writing.

Symmetric Key Sizes

For symmetric cryptographic techniques, key size recommendations are relatively straightforward. Assuming that the cryptographic algorithm as such cannot be broken for the lifetime of the protected data, the only attack method is an exhaustive key search, whose success rate only depends on the size of the key space and the amount of computing power available to the attacker.

If one defines minimum security as maintaining confidentiality for at least several months, this results in the minimum key size recommendations for various attack models as shown in Table 11.3 [ECR05].

Today, a security level of about 80 bits appears to be the smallest general-purpose level as it provides sufficient protection against reasonable attack scenarios. Lower security levels are in general not recommended for confidentiality protection. In particular, 56-bit DES keys offer only marginal protection relative to any type of attacker. Nevertheless, applications exist where even lower security levels (e.g. 32-bit keys) may be appropriate if some security is to be provided at all, for example for integrity tags.

Table 11.3 Minimum symmetric key size in various scenarios

Adversary	Budget	Hardware	Min Key Size
Hacker	0	PC	51
	$300	PCs / FPGA[1]	56
Small organization	$10k	PCs / FPGA	62
Medium organization	$300k	PCs / FPGA	66
Large organization	$10M	FPGA / ASIC[2]	76
Intelligence agency	$300M	ASIC	81

[1] Field Programmable Gate Array, a programmable semiconductor device that can be reprogrammed after it is manufactured, rather than having its programming fixed during manufacturing.

[2] Application-Specific Integrated Circuit, an IC customized for a particular use, rather than intended for general-purpose use.

Hash Functions

For a hash function to match the security level given by any symmetric key size, one simply applies a factor of two to obtain the corresponding hash code length.

Asymmetric Key Sizes

To convert a given (symmetric key) security level into an equivalent asymmetric key size is more complicated and details are beyond the scope of this paper. Based on assessments made as of today, Table 11.4 summarizes equivalence guidelines for symmetric ciphers, hash functions and digital signature algorithms [ECR05].

According to current knowledge, the difficulty of solving the discrete logarithm problem in prime order fields of size 2^n is, up to constants, asymptotically equivalent to

Table 11.4 Commensurate security levels

Symmetric Cipher	Hash Function	RSA Scheme	Elliptic Curve
48	96	480	96
56	112	640	112
64	128	816	128
80	160	1.248	160
112	224	2.432	224
128	256	3.248	256
192	384	7.936	384
256	512	15.424	512

Table 11.5 RSA Signature key lifetimes [Wei04]

Key size	512	640	1024
Lifetime	1 hour	4 days	1 year

that of breaking n-bit RSA. In practice though, the discrete logarithm problem is noticeably harder to solve. On the other hand, in standardized algorithms the discrete logarithm problem often applies to a smaller subgroup, and in this case the size of the subgroup is also of relevance. According to the generic attacks that also apply to elliptic curve systems, in this situation the symmetric key equivalent is theoretically half the bit-size of said subgroup. In essence, field size recommendations for today's commonly deployed discrete logarithm systems equal RSA key size recommendations and subfield size recommendations equal elliptic curve (and hash function) recommendations.

The above RSA key size recommendations from [ECR05] are slightly more conservative than those found in an equivalence table published by NIST [NIS01] which states that 80-bit symmetric keys correspond to 1024-bit RSA. IETF recommendation RFC 3766 advocates that an 80-bit symmetric key is equivalent to 1228-bit RSA and 148-bit discrete logarithm subgroups [RFC3766].

The IETF has also drafted recommendations for the lifetime of (short) RSA signatures [Wei04]. The values given in Table 11.5 are based on a 100-fold security margin, for example 512-bit RSA keys are assumed to require an attack effort of 5 days.

Figure 11.3 shows some of the latest integer factoring records, which relate closely to key size recommendations for RSA. At the time of writing, the record was the 200-digit (663-bit) number RSA-200, which was factored in May 2005. The previous record was a 174-digit number factored in December 2003. The chart suggests that 1024-bit RSA can be factored in less than 10 years. Consequently, to provide suffi-

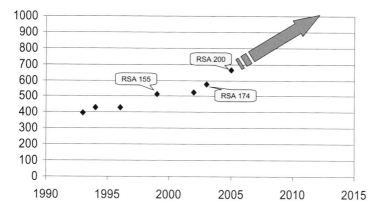

Figure 11.3 Factoring records (1993 – 2005)

cient protection against forgery of digital signatures, RSA key size recommendations of 2048 bits (and elliptic curve parameters of 224 bits) will become common in the near future.

11.8 Conclusion

In the area of cryptography, many alternative techniques have been proposed, each presenting its own advantages, such as performance, code size, key size, patent coverage or standardization. Public-key cryptography, in particular, has shown itself to be an extremely valuable tool for the design and implementation of scaleable secure systems. Due to the substantial computational overhead associated with public-key algorithms, security architectures typically utilize symmetric cryptographic mechanisms for bulk encryption and integrity protection, and public-key techniques for key establishment, digital signatures and non-repudiation services.

Cryptography is a well established technology today; many specific algorithms and techniques have been standardized. However, technology development never stands still. Attacks and attack tools will continue to advance, as will cryptographic technologies and other security controls. In the area of cryptography, technology development tends to be not linear, but to go in leaps. Also, disruptive technological innovation may occur, for example due to unanticipated advances in hardware design and algorithms or in quantum computing.

On the other hand, such innovation can often in turn be exploited for cryptographic purposes. Quantum mechanics, for example, can be utilized for the establishment of shared secrets over an insecure channel. This technology is referred to as *quantum cryptography* [BBB92] [Bra93]. Photons have a polarization, which can be measured in any basis consisting of two orthogonal directions. If a photon's polarization is read twice in the same basis, the polarization will be read correctly and will remain unchanged. If it is read in two different bases, a random result will be obtained in the second basis and the polarization will be changed randomly. Quantum key establishment protocols have been designed based on this observation. These protocols enjoy the property that their security is based on the fundamental laws of quantum mechanics, rather than on computational assumptions.

12 Public Key Infrastructure (PKI)

Michael Munzert

12.1 Motivation

Developments in the field of information security are moving towards the more wide-spread use of public key cryptography (see Chapter 11). This technology enables scalable security of communication and information exchange.

In general, the use of cryptographic protection for communication in distributed environments demands the authenticity of the keying associations involved. In terms of public key schemes, this means that relying parties need to have an authentic binding of public keys to communication partners (holding the corresponding private key). Since public key schemes do not require secrecy for the keys held by the relying party, the authenticity assurance can be performed in another way as for symmetric schemes.

Major challenges for the use of public key cryptography include the secure generation of private keys, the authentic distribution of public keys, as well as the management of these keys. The first applications using public key technology often resolved these problems by designing their own solutions, which were only useful for this specific application, for example a VPN (see Chapter 3). As more and more applications and business processes became public key aware, the need for a common solution became clear. Typical applications that can make use of services offered by a PKI include secure mail (e.g. S/MIME), digital signing of documents and secure communication with web servers (e.g. SSL/TLS with client and/or sever authentication).

The "I" in PKI

In the same way that electric power infrastructures with their power grids enable us to operate manifold electronic equipment on a needs-must basis, the public key infrastructure aims to be a pervasive security infrastructure for public key-enabled applications and services.

Benefits of a Common Infrastructure

The fundamental benefits of operating a single infrastructure for managing private and public keys instead of having several solutions for different public key-aware applications are obvious:

- Cost savings: although the expense of setting up a common PKI that can be used by multiple applications and services will be higher than for a single application, overall the expense will be less than that required to operate separate security infrastructures for each application.

- Interoperability: uniform solutions simplify the interoperability of applications within an enterprise as all applications access and use this infrastructure in an identical manner. Moreover, if the security infrastructure is based on open, international standards, there is a higher chance of even achieving interoperability between enterprises or domains.

- Enforcement of security policies: it is much easier to enforce a consistent security policy in a single security infrastructure than in a scenario where every application uses its own security infrastructure.

- Choice of provider: by opting for a common infrastructure, the security infrastructure can be put to tender and a suitable provider chosen for the PKI. This can be a particular group within the organization or can even be selected from a list of external candidates.

Certificates

As already mentioned, one of the challenges of public key cryptography is the authentic distribution of public keys. In addition, the public key has to be linked to entity information (information about the owner of the key) such as name, pseudonym or identification number (ID) and to the issuer. To achieve this, a data structure called a "certificate" is defined and used. Therefore, before discussing the components of a PKI and their interactions, we will introduce and describe the design and role of a certificate.

12.2 Certificates

A certificate can be regarded as a digital ID card or passport with the additional feature that it contains the public key or a link to a public key. Similar to an ID card, a certificate in the digital world should at least contain information about:

- The public key
- The owner (subject name)
- The validity
- The issuer of the certificate
- The signature algorithm (used to protect the data structure)
- The signature itself (verifying the certificate data).

In addition, a certificate may contain information about:

- The usage of the key material (e.g. whether it can be used for digital signatures or for encryption)
- Possibly further information.

Apart from the fact that ID cards have to be signed and issued by an authority, certificates are digitally signed by the issuer, the so-called *certification authority* (CA). This signature binds together all information included in the data structure. It also means, however, that the relying party, which validates the certificate for example within a signature verification process of a document, must trust that the CA only signs and issues correct certificates, i.e. that the CA has verified the data within the certificate. On the other hand, the technical means must be in place to establish a trust relation between the PKI users and the CA. This can be done by securely (authentically) distributing the public key of the CA to the PKI users. This public key is usually distributed in the form of a so-called *self-signed certificate*. This means that the certificate is signed using the private key (instead of using an independent one) that corresponds to the public key included in the certificate. Note that the establishment of the trust relation between the CA and the PKI users is the basis for all security services that are based on certificates and corresponding keys. Also note that the subject name must be unique within the domain of a CA to allow unambiguous identification of the certificate holders.

Types of Certificates

It is important to note that there are different types of certificates. The most popular types are

- *Public key certificates or identity certificates* and
- *Attribute certificates.*

Identity certificates are the same as ID cards. Their main purpose is to bind the identity of a key owner and his/her public key together.

In contrast, attribute certificates aim to bind attributes, which are related to privileges and permissions, to an entity. The entity may be identified through "pointers" to the associated public key certificate.

Certificate Standards

Data formats for certificates have been standardized by different standardization organizations. The basis for the most popular certificates is the X.509 standard specified by ISO/ITU [X509]. This standard has been used and profiled by the PKIX working group within the IETF to specify today's most widely used certificates. RFC 3280 defines a (identity) certificate profile based on X.509 (version 3) for use in the Internet [RFC3280], and RFC 3281 defines attribute certificates that can be used in Internet protocols [RFC3280]. The former are typically used in enterprise PKIs or in PKIs built for government applications or other large user groups (e.g. health applications).

In addition to the PKIX certificate standards, the IETF has defined an alternative certificate standard, which does not conform to X.509: OpenPGP (Pretty Good Privacy) [RFC2440]. This standard assumes a totally different trust model, the so-called *web of trust*. Namely, there is no single certification authority that the users trust, rather every PKI user (in principle) can act as a certification authority. The OpenPGP model has gained only limited dissemination within corporate and government PKIs.

In contrast to the IETF PKIX working group, a separate IETF working group has produced a number of technical and information documents with the aim of addressing a simpler public key infrastructure for the Internet, referred to as the *Simple Public Key Infrastructure* (SPKI). However, the IETF concluded this work and, due to absence of market demands, PKI vendors are not likely to support this different certificate syntax within their products.

The standards defined by the IETF have been designed mainly for the Internet and do not take specific requirements into account, such as requirements from wireless applications and their limited bandwidth. OMA[1] has therefore defined special purpose wireless PKI (WPKI) certificates, which are not interoperable with the PKIX standards. Although a broader use of wireless certificates has been expected for years, it is unclear whether a large scale roll-out of these certificates will take place in the near future due to the limited dissemination of PKI-enabled wireless applications and the fact that the "bandwidth" argument is becoming less important.

Certificate Lifecycle

Because certificates are a basis for distributing public keys, the PKI must support all states of the lifecycle of certificates (see Figure 12.1):

- Certificate creation: The first step after the information about the owner has been validated is the generation of the certificate by the so-called certification authority (CA) by signing the data structure including public key, entity information and information about the issuer.

- Certificate distribution: there are two approaches to distributing certificates. The first is the pull approach, where the certificate has to be fetched by the relying party. An example of an application using this approach is S/MIME encryption. The second is the push approach, where the certificate owner takes on the task of distributing the certificate, for example within the data structure or within the protocol. Examples of applications that adopt the latter approach are SSL/TLS, digital signatures according to PKCS#7[2] [PKCS] and XML signature [XMLSig].

- Certificate usage: Certificates can be used within the PKI enabled application once they have been distributed. For example, the public key may be used for encryption purposes, or the certificate may be validated (see also *certificate validation* below) to ensure data origin authentication or non-repudiation. However, the certificate must be validated before using the public key included in the certificate.

- Certificate renewal: if the certificate contains a validity attribute, the certificate has to be renewed once it has expired. However, certificates without an explicit validity period usually also have an implicit validity. In this case, the PKI must support re-issuing of certificates.

- Certificate revocation: if the private key has been compromised, the PKI must support the revocation of certificates in order to minimize the consequences.

---

[1] http://www.openmobilealliance.org/

[2] Public Key Cryptography Standards (PKCS) are developed and published by RSA Laboratories, see http://www.rsasecurity.com/rsalabs/.

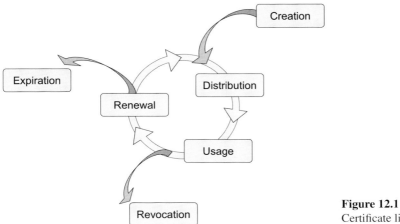

Figure 12.1
Certificate lifecycle

- Certificate expiry: although exceeding the validity period means that the private key will no longer be accepted, the PKI must implement actions to ensure, for example, that past document signatures can be verified in the future as well.

Certificate Validation

Before accepting or using a public key, the certificate should be correctly validated. This validation process consists of the following steps:

- Signature validation: the signature of the certificate is checked to ensure that the certificate has been signed by a trusted authority and that it has not been altered. To do this, the public key of the certification authority has to be transmitted in a secure way to the entity performing the validation process (see also PKI and Authentication).
- Validation of the validity period: the validity period of the certificate is checked to ensure that the corresponding key material is still valid.
- Revocation check: this is necessary to ensure that the certificate has not been revoked before the end of the validity period.
- Last but not least, the *subject name* of the certificate should be checked against the expected name of the communicating party.

12.3 Users, Services and Components of a PKI

12.3.1 PKI Users

On one hand, there is the *certificate holder*, who is the owner of the certificate including the public key and also the owner of the corresponding private key. The certificate holder can be a person or a company (legal person) but also a machine, for example a web server or a VPN gateway. On the other hand, there is the *relying party*, who relies on the certificate information, for example on the name of the certificate holder. The relying party can be a person or a machine as well.

Both certificate holder and relying party use the services offered by the PKI.

12.3.2 PKI Services

We describe the PKI services that can be found in a typical implementation below. However, variants are of course possible depending on the requirements of the public key-enabled applications for which the PKI is built.

Provision of Certificates

As already described in the certificate lifecycle section, there are two approaches to how certificates can be provided: the push approach and the pull approach (see above: certificate distribution). In the case of the pull approach, for example SMIME encryption, certificates are typically provided by the security infrastructure. This is usually realized by repositories that can be accessed using the *LDAP* protocol.

Certificate Revocation

In the case of a key compromise, for example, the certificate holder must have the possibility to revoke her/his certificate. Typical enterprise implementations of this service comprise realizations via "hotline" or web server (PKI portal / PKI self service), where users can revoke their certificates for example by presenting an individual revocation password.

Provision of Certificate Status

The validity of the certificate is required during the certificate validation process. This is usually realized by either distributing so-called *certificate revocation lists (CRLs)*, which contain the list of revoked certificates signed by an authority, or by a *certificate online service*, which provides the status of a specific certificate on request.

Certificate Renewal / Key Renewal

To enable continuous usage of PKI-enabled applications, certificates have to be renewed before they expire. This can be done by issuing a new certificate (and retaining the private and public keys) or by generating new keys and issuing a new certificate. Provided that the keys are still valid (and have not been revoked) they can be used to establish a secure channel, for example with a PKI portal (implementing a self service), which even can be used to securely issue a centrally generated private key (see also *Key Backup and Key Recovery* and *Key Generation*).

Key Backup and Key Recovery

If private keys are used for long-term encryption, for example of documents within an enterprise, it will be necessary for the enterprise to be able to decrypt employee-specific encrypted documents if necessary. Encryption of data is usually performed by a hybrid encryption process. In other words, the data is encrypted with a symmetric algorithm and the symmetric key is encrypted with the public key. Although the primary goal is to achieve data recovery, one possibility is that the private keys used for encryption are backed up by the enterprise. Should the enterprise need to decrypt some documents, the key may be recovered and the data can be decrypted. Note that this is an optional service.

Key Generation

In the key backup scenario described above, one possibility is for the public key pairs (for encryption purposes) to be generated by a key generation service and not by the certificate holders themselves. There may be other requirements, however, which call for implementing such a service, for example if the quality of the key generation process is to be monitored.

In addition to the PKI services described above, there are additional services that may be implemented in advanced PKIs:

Secure Time Stamping

A secure time stamping service links a trusted time with some data by signing both. Similar to the signing of a certificate, the signing of the time stamp must be performed by a trusted authority. This service is needed especially in order to achieve non-repudiation (of origin), because otherwise a sender of a signed message may claim that the data has been signed with a revoked key.

Notarization Service

This service certifies that data that has been presented to this service is "correct". The meaning of "correct" thereby depends on the data or the application. For example, if the data to be certified is a digital signature, the notarization service may certify that the signature is valid.

Certificate Validation Service

The certificate validation service can be seen as a special kind of notarization service by certifying that a presented certificate is correct and valid. This task is not very difficult in cases where there is a flat key hierarchy, i.e. if all public keys are signed by one trusted CA. However, if the key hierarchy is more complex, for example if there is a hierarchy of CAs and there are multiple trust domains, then the certificate validation process may become rather tricky.

12.3.3 PKI Components

The PKIX model (see Figure 12.2), described in more detail in [RFC3280], provides a good overview of the interactions between the infrastructure components (CA, RA and repository) and the PKI users (end entities).

The components of a PKI are described in more detail in the next section.

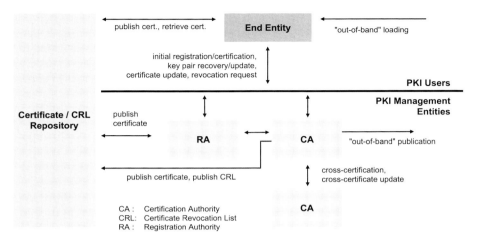

Figure 12.2 PKIX Model

Certification Authority (CA)

The core element of every PKI is the certification entity, which digitally signs a clearly-defined set of technical and tested organizational data, thereby creating the certificate that can be used in a whole range of applications. Access to this component is usually secured with different technical and organizational measures.

There may be logical CAs for different purposes within a PKI, for example there may be different CAs for different user populations, or different CAs for different types of keys for example for user signature keys, user encryption keys, server keys, etc.

Registration Authority (RA)

When issuing certificates, the details relating to the person or instance for which a certificate is to be issued must be checked.

Certificates can of course be requested very quickly over the Internet via "commercial CAs", which only require a current e-mail address. Depending on what the certificates are to be used for, i.e. what level of trust the certificates are to provide, the time involved in making the necessary checks, which must precede the issuing of a certificate, increases proportionately.

If a certificate is to be generated for a person, the personal details should be checked against an existing database for correctness and plausibility. When generating a certificate for the first time, the correct identity of the applicant should also be verified by providing a suitable means of identification.

When creating certificates for servers, a verification instance should be provided that verifies the applicant's details. Wherever possible, these procedures should be completely automated. Large organizations very often have a suitable electronic communications directory in place, which is ideal for automatic data coordination.

Interfaces with such a directory should therefore be set up for correctly issuing key material, in order also to exclude errors when generating certificates (e.g. slight differences in name spellings) right from the start.

RAs are the link between the central components in a PKI and the PKI user. Ideally, these components will run fully automatically.

Suitable means of communication should be established between the RA and the other PKI components. Of particular importance is the link to the CA and the Trust Center (see below). In this situation, all data must be transmitted in encrypted form. RAs should be located near to the user, so that the key material can be collected or delivered in person. In many cases, a network of suitable contact locations is already in place. In businesses, this might be the department where staff passes or visitors' day passes are issued and administered. In the public sector, branch networks of any form would be eligible. It is important in this context to provide thorough basic training for the staff commissioned with these duties and a clear, constantly updated description of the issuing processes.

Key Generation (KG) and Key Archival (KA)

It is essential first of all to decide whether (and, if so, which) key pairs are to be generated directly on the user's client system. There is typically no need to generate key pairs envisaged for authentication or signature purposes not at the client side (provided that there is a "secure environment" such as a smart card), whereas key pairs used for encryption often are generated and archived centrally.

However, central key generation has the following advantages:

- Keys are generated in a secure environment with high-quality algorithms that are harder to manipulate since the corresponding system can be monitored more extensively.
- Storage for archiving is supported (useful for avoiding information loss through encryption within the company, for example).

The following issues are important in conjunction with key archiving:

- Special measures must be taken to protect the central TC key archive and it must be safeguarded against compromise by employing appropriate technical and organizational measures.
- The delivery of individual keys (e.g. to companies, since certain information must be made accessible again) must be protected against misuse (e.g. "4-eyes principle", limited number of people).

Repository

Certificates that have been generated and the blocking list for revoked certificates (Certificate Revocation List / CRL) are stored by the CA in a repository. Typically, this is implemented using directories. Access to this directory is generally via LDAP (light weight directory access protocol).

Trust Center (TC)

The term trust center has a number of different definitions associated with it. In its broadest sense, the term trust center encompasses the functions Certification Authority (CA), Key Generation (KG) and Key Archival (KA) described above, and all of the processes relating to their coordinated interplay. In a narrower sense, the term TC denotes the particular physical and organizational measures required for ensuring that the critical central hardware and software components of a PKI operate securely. The amount of work involved, be this constructional in nature or relating to processes within the TC, depends on what degree of security is required and whether, for example, certification is required to satisfy digital signature policies. In the first instance, it will thus be a question of recognizing and giving equal status under the law to digitally signed documents or transactions in cases of legal dispute.

Private Security Environment (PSE)

The private security environment is the component where the private key of the certificate holder and other PKI related data, for example the self-signed certificate of the trusted CA, can be stored securely. Examples how such PSE can be realized are PKCS#12 modules on Windows clients, Java key stores and smart cards.

12.3.4 Communication between PKI Components, PKI Users and PKI Services

In addition to certificate and CRL profiles, the PKIX and other security working groups within the IETF have defined a set of additional standards defining formats, operational and management protocols. These standards can be used within a PKI for communication between PKI components, services and users, for example

- RFC 2510: Internet X.509 Public Key Infrastructure – Certificate Management Protocols
- RFC 2511: Internet X.509 Certificate Request Message Format
- RFC 2560: X.509 Internet Public Key Infrastructure Online Certificate Status Protocol – OCSP
- RFC 2797: Certificate Management Messages over CMS
- RFC 3161: Internet X.509 Public Key Infrastructure Time-Stamp Protocol (TSP)
- RFC 3852: Cryptographic Message Syntax (CMS)

For further information, see http://www.ietf.org/.

In conjunction with the W3C recommendations for XML Signature [XMLSig] and XML Encryption [XMLEnc], the World Wide Web Consortium (W3C) also specified protocols for distributing and registering public keys: the XML Key Management Specification (XKMS) [XKMS]. XKMS is designed to simplify the integration of PKI and certificates with all kinds of applications by allowing PKI functions, such as certificate processing and revocation status-checking, to be outsourced to external services. XKMS offers the possibility that XKMS clients can concentrate on basic digital signature and verification operations as well as on the ability to manage private keys and thus can be unburdened from other PKI related tasks (e.g. certificate processing).

12.4 PKI and Authentication

It is important to note that the PKI itself (e.g. the certificate) does not provide authentication of a certificate holder, but can be used to achieve entity authentication. This is because an identity certificate binds information related to the key owner (and included in the certificate) to the public key. Therefore, the presentation of a certificate and its validation can only provide identification of the public key owner, provided the relying party trusts the certification authority.

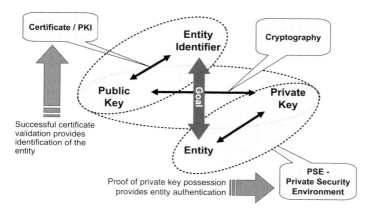

Figure 12.3 Coherence between PKI and authentication

To achieve entity authentication, for example within a security protocol, the certificate holder must prove its possession of the corresponding private key. The same is valid for data origin authentication: only the validation of the signature, which has been generated by applying the private key, allows the relying party to authenticate the source of this data (see Figure 12.3).

12.5 PKI Domains

12.5.1 Single Trust Domain

Single CA Domain

Up to now, we have only discussed the scenario where there is a single CA, which issues (non-CA) user certificates. This is the simplest PKI domain (Single CA), but one can imagine that it is also very limited. Such an architecture means that all users must trust a single CA and also that if the private key of the CA is compromised, all user certificates are compromised as well and the trusted CA key has to be distributed securely again. On the other hand, certificate validation is simple as well. The *certification path*, in other words the sequence of certificates starting with the user certificate and ending with the certificate of the trusted CA (which is self-signed and therefore has to be transmitted to the users in a secure way, e.g. in connection with registration or certification process), only consists of one real certificate, the user certificate (see Figure 12.4).

Hierarchical PKI Domain

A straightforward extension of the single CA hierarchy is to add another CA level. In other words, there is one CA (the top-level CA) that issues certificates for one or multiple subordinate CAs. These subordinate CAs issue certificates to the (non-CA) end users. This kind of extension is called *hierarchical PKI domain*. The distribution of tasks between the subordinate CAs, for example, can be performed with respect to geographical aspects or with respect to the purpose of the key material. One benefit of such an architecture is that the top level CA is only required to issue the CA certificates of the subordinate CAs and therefore does not need to be online. Often this top-level CA is implemented on a laptop, which is placed in a vault and can only be accessed under multiple controls. In the case of a subordinate CA key being compromised, the top-level CA can easily establish a new CA and only one CA key has to be revoked. The certification path consists of two real certificates, the user certificate and the certificate of the subordinate CA that issued the user certificate (signed by the top level CA).

Figure 12.4 illustrates single and hierarchical CA domains and the corresponding certification paths.

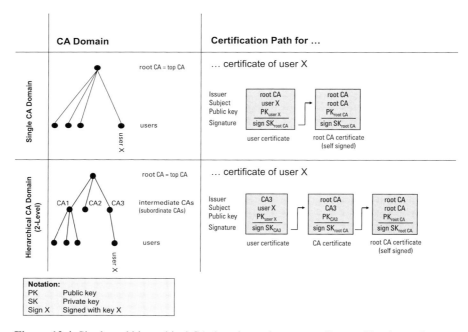

Figure 12.4 Single and hierarchical CA domains and corresponding certification paths

12.5.2 Combining Trust Domains

One important question is how trust can be extended from one PKI to another and vice versa. There are two major approaches that are briefly discussed below.

Cross-Certification

In the case of cross-certification, the linkage between two PKIs (X and Y) is performed by signing the CA public key of the other PKI domains and vice versa. This means CA X signs the public key of CA Y and vice versa. If a certificate of user A_X (X denotes, that A belongs to PKI X) has to be validated within PKI Y (assuming both PKIs are hierarchical with one subordinate CA and the cross-certification has been performed at the top-level), the certification path consists of the following real certificates (see Figure 12.5):

- The certificate of user A_X
- The certificate of CA_X (which issued the certificate of A_X)
- The cross-certificate of PKI X issued by the top level CA of PKI Y (which will be validated using the trusted top level public key).

Bridge CA

To reduce the administrative efforts necessary to cross-certify with many PKIs, a so-called bridge CA can be used to link to the other PKIs. Every PKI cross-certifies with the bridge by issuing a certificate for the bridge CA's public key and on the other

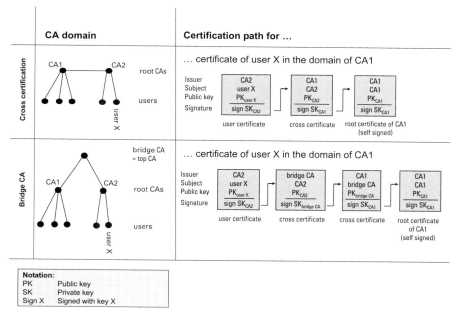

Figure 12.5 Cross-certification and bridge CA and corresponding certification paths

hand, the bridge CA issues certificates for all public keys of the top-level CAs (which are to be linked together). If a certificate of user A_X has to be validated within PKI Y (again assuming both PKIs are hierarchical with one subordinate CA and the cross-certification has been performed at the top-level), the certification path consists of the following real certificates:

- The certificate of user A_X
- The certificate of CA_X (which issued the certificate of A_X)
- The cross-certificate of PKI X issued by the bridge CA
- The certificate of the bridge CA issued by the top level CA of PKI Y (which again will be validated using the trusted top level public key).

Figure 12.5 illustrates the concepts of cross-certification and bridge CA domains and the corresponding certification paths.

12.6 Deployment Considerations – Essential Steps for Building up a PKI

Some of the tasks that enterprises are faced with when deciding to implement a PKI are discussed briefly below.

Definition of Requirements

Many questions have to be settled prior to implementing a PKI. Note that the following list is only a limited subset of the questions that should be answered during the requirements definition phase:

- Which public key-enabled applications are to be supported by the PKI?
- Which PKI functions and services are necessary: for example revocation (via CRLs or online), key backup, time stamps?
- Will it be a closed PKI (dedicated only for intra-enterprise communication) or will it be open (dedicated for inter-enterprise communication, for example dedicated to support establishment of secure business processes with partners)?
- Which certificate formats are to be supported (PKIX, PGP, ...)?
- What is the right PKI architecture?
- Which key management model is to be implemented (e.g. central or distributed key generation)?
- What type of PSE will be used (e.g. smart card)?
- How and where does the identification of the users take place for distributing key material (local or distributed RAs)?
- Will the PKI conform to signature laws or other directives?
- What are the performance requirements?

The more carefully the requirement analysis is performed, the greater the success of the PKI. Therefore, vendor-independent, PKI-experienced consultants often support this decision process.

Make or Buy

Once all requirements have been collected and analyzed, the decision has to be taken as to whether the infrastructure will be built up and operated by the enterprise or organization or whether a PKI provider will be chosen. There are different pros and cons that impact this decision and there are of course solutions where only a part of the PKI will be outsourced. The main advantage of an outsourced PKI provider is that the cost of the PKI can be calculated quite precisely. The main advantage of operating your own PKI is that the PKI can be tailored exactly to your requirements.

We assume below that the enterprise or organization has decided not to outsource the PKI. Within an outsourced PKI, most of the issues below will be determined by the PKI provider.

PKI policies – CP and CPS

In order to ensure the security of a PKI, some fundamental security needs must be addressed by the PKI owner. The key security requirements include:

- The key owner must keep his/her private key confidential.
- It must be impossible for unauthorized persons to use the private key of others.
- The integrity of public keys must be assured.
- The private key holder and the subject as part of the certificate must be identical, i.e. the initial authentication as part of the registration process must be strong.

How these requirements are addressed in a specific PKI implementation is documented in the *Certification Practice Statement (CPS)*. A CPS therefore mainly describes the procedures controlling how certificates are issued and administered within the framework of the PKI. In addition, it lists the obligations of the PKI users and typically also includes liability and legal aspects.

Another important document is the *Certificate Policy (CP):* The CP is a type of certificate usage regulation. The PKI typically defines certificate classes and the CP prescribes which certificates shall be used for what purpose.

Both documents are important for relying parties to assess the level of trust in a specific PKI. The IETF describes a framework or structure in [RFC3647], which aims to help writers of these documents and to make CP and CPS of different PKIs comparable.

PKI Design

Once all requirements have been evaluated (and the decision has been taken to implement the PKI), all necessary PKI processes have to be designed. This includes the processes supporting the certificate lifecycle as well as processes to maintain the PKI. For the latter, the requirements have to be evaluated periodically in order to detect a shift in the requirements at short notice.

In addition, the PKI architecture has to be defined. This includes the location and distribution of the PKI components that provide the PKI services as well as the definition of the CA hierarchy.

Creating, Operating and Maintaining the PKI

Last but not least, PKI components such as CA, RA, repository and additional PKI services (e.g. time stamp service) must be set up and the processes and the personnel for operating and maintaining the PKI have to be defined. All of these components and processes have to be integrated into the existing environment.

Another important aspect is the training and familiarization of all persons involved, the PKI users as well as the personnel operating and maintaining the PKI. In particular, providing information for users about the benefits of the PKI is a pre-requisite for acceptance and success of the PKI.

12.7 Conclusion

A public key infrastructure aims to be a pervasive security infrastructure for public key-enabled applications and services and is vital for using public key cryptography in large or dynamic systems. Therefore, PKIs allow us to build scalable solutions for secure communications. In addition, this infrastructure itself is implemented and delivered using public key concepts and techniques.

Numerous standards exist, which allow interoperable solutions to be realized for enterprises or within the public or government sector. Moreover, there are a couple of leading manufacturers offering very experienced software for PKIs. There are also leading manufacturers offering PKI-enabled applications. However, the integration of PKI services in these applications lags somewhat behind the opportunities offered by the PKI products.

In addition, a PKI is a complex system that is also highly dependent on its environment (organizational and technical), and one which in turn significantly influences its environment. A high level of experience, technical expertise and an overview of the product landscape is therefore an absolute necessity for making the right decisions in the PKI environment, in order to fully harness future opportunities in the fields of e-business, e-government and e-commerce.

13 Smart Card Technologies

Detlef Houdeau

Smart cards have been with us for over 20 years now. Since the 1970s, the history of smart cards has reflected steady advancements in chip capabilities and capacity, as well as a significant rise in the variety and number of applications.

This paper provides a brief introduction into the history of smart cards and presents the current state-of-the-art.

13.1 The Beginning

When Jürgen Dethloff and Helmut Gröttrup presented their patent for a plastic card with integrated circuit in 1968, few expected a triumphal procession of the intelligent memory card. The same happened in 1977 with the patent for the microprocessor card. The patent declaration was the technology response to a deficiency in banking cards and the abuse of cash points. This solution was easy to manipulate and the provider sustained substantial damages.

Back in 1974, the semiconductor division of Siemens AG successfully demonstrated in a model test that the chip thickness is reducible, that the chip can be accommodated in a conventional smart card body and even with a chip size of no greater than 25sq. mm, the risk of breakage over its lifetime does not represent a failure rate.

The first field trial test of a banking card took place in Blois, France in 1978. It took 8 years for the first serial production of the chip card to begin in France. France Telecom used an EPROM memory card to enable convenient public phone calls without the use of memory coins in the expectation that damage to public phone boxes would decrease.

A large-scale field trial test was started in Germany in 1986 by German Telecom, which looked at the use of chip cards as an alternative for the magnetic stripe card. The decision in favor of the prepaid chip card as a new medium was made in 1988. Since then, more than 3 billion prepaid phone cards have been produced and issued worldwide. The reason for such high quantities is because other countries followed the approach adopted by France and Germany.

The use of contact-based memory chip cards for access control and storage of cash values is possible on a broad scale. However, not all processes and applications are well suited to deal with an contact-based chip card. For example, tickets have to be checked very quickly in public transport. The use of contact-based chip cards is not practicable here – "touch and go" is what is needed in solutions of this kind.

In response to this challenge, the industry began at an early stage to develop contactless chip cards with a chip and an antenna (= inlay), which typical worked on 13.56 Mhz. A reader is required for this purpose, which sends power to the chip card Integrated Circuit (IC) for activation and then to start the data transmission between the reader and cards. Transmission must be both fast and secure. The checking of access authorization and, if necessary, the direct debiting of the fare must be performed in a few seconds.

The industry has developed ICs for this purpose, which have anti-collision stability. This means that if more than one card is in the active reader field, the reader can differentiate between the cards and proceed with communication for only one contactless card. One of the most popular products is marketed under the name Mifare™.

The first application came on stream in 1995, the frequent card from Lufthansa. The major take-up of the technology was in public transport in places like Seoul in Korea 1996, Moscow in Russia 1997 and Sao Paulo and Rio in Brazil and Shanghai in 1998. Europe followed with major cities like London, Moscow, Stockholm and others.

13.2 Application Segments for Smart Cards

Table 13.1 shows segmentation of the smart card (microprocessor card) market by application segment[1]. Corporate Security is the application segment showing the strongest growth rate of 72% per year.

Table 13.1 Smart card market 2004

Segment	Million of Units
Telecom	1050
Financial services / Retail / Loyalty	280
Pay TV	55
Government/ Healthcare	45
Transport	15
Corporate Security	12
Others	12
Total 2004	1469

[1] Source: www.eurosmart.com

The share of contact-based to contact-less microprocessor cards is:

- > 90 %   contact-based
- < 10 %   contact-less

13.3 Technology Drivers

13.3.1 Computing Power

Moore's law predicted that computing power would double about every two years. A similar situation exists in the area of smart cards with the microprocessor (controller). The current crypto-controller is 3 times faster than 5 years ago. Development activities in the semi-conductor area include:

- Ultra short transistor switching time
- Higher density
- High speed gain
- Parallel processing.

The short lifetime of products and continuous product development are the key factors for this market. Increasing computing power goes along with bigger memory sizes and additional security features as well as high-speed interfaces.

13.3.2 Memory Size

Developments here are similar to those for DRAM[1] in computers, i.e. the memory size doubles every 2 years. For example, the Health Card in 1995 in Germany needed 1 kbyte RAM. The national electronic ID card in 2002 in Italy needed 32 kbyte RAM. The new travel document with stored biometric face and fingerprint image data, which began being issued in many European countries in 2005, needs 64 kbyte RAM. This development can open up new application scenarios, like multi-application cards.

The main driver for higher memory sizes comes from the GSM/UMTS SIM[2] card market. More and more data, like private phone libraries, is stored on the SIM card.

A high-speed interface is required for writing (e.g. for personalization) and reading owing to the bigger memory size. The physical limitation, based on international standards, is outlined in Section 13.4.

---

[1] DRAM (Dynamic Random Access Memory) is a type of memory that stores each bit of data in a separate capacitor. As the capacitor leaks electrons, the memory must be refreshed periodically. Also, DRAM loses its data when the power supply is removed.

[2] Subscriber identity module (SIM) is an application running on a smart card. The SIM provides secure storage of the key identifying a mobile phone service subscriber, subscription information, preferences and text messages. The equivalence of a SIM in UMTS is called Universal Subscriber Identity Module (USIM).

State-of-the-art-controllers require:

- ROM (Read Only Memory)
- RAM (Random Access Memory)
- EEPROM (Electrical Erasable Read Only Memory)[1]

The ROM is the part of memory for the operating system and application, i.e. for the program and data. This memory works only in read mode. The RAM is the core for crypto calculation and for fast data processing. This memory works in read and write mode. The EEPROM is used for storing application programs and data.

Typical controller configurations are:

- 4k class: 256 byte RAM, 4kbyte EEPROM, 68kbyte ROM
- 8k class: 4kbyte RAM, 8kbyte EEPROM, 96kbyte ROM
- 16k class: 4kbyte RAM, 16kbyte EEPROM, 96kbyte ROM
- 32k class: 4kbyte RAM, 32kbyte EEPROM, 136kbyte ROM
- 64k class: 4kbyte RAM, 64kbyte EEPROM, 208kbyte ROM

13.3.3 Security on Silicon

Smart card security starts in the value chain with secure controllers. High-security products and production have been in demand since the inception of this market. The scenario with respect to threats changes every 3 to 4 years. The power attack was the dominant threat in 1999, while the light attack was the most frequently used method in 2003. A combination of both, the so-called hybrid attack, is expected to dominate in the future.

The counter-measures from the semiconductor industry are keeping pace with the threats. The current crypto controller typically contains 50 security features. Compared to this, the European banknote today only has 28 security features.

The security concept for crypto controllers is subdivided into:

- Electrical security, for example for encryption/decryption
- Operation state monitoring for attack protection.

Electrical security contains the elements true random number generator (RNG), dual key triple Data Encryption Standard (DES, cf. Chapter 11) and an elliptic curve calculator (ECC, cf. Chapter 11) and accelerator, combined with an advanced crypto engine.

The operation state monitoring mechanism offers a function whereby the chip goes into a secure reset state for any sensor alarm, like from low/high voltage sensors, frequency sensors, light sensors, temperature sensors, internal power on reset sensors and active shield sensors. These monitoring systems on the chip prevent unauthorized

---

[1] EEPROM such as Flash memory allow the ROM to be electrically erased ("flashed back to zero") and then written to. Writing to EEPROM is much slower than writing to RAM (Random Access Memory).

reading of data on the chip as well as reverse engineering of the chip design and functionality.

Overall the attacks on the hardware can be classified into three different groups:

- Manipulating attacks
- Observing attacks
- Semi-Invasive attacks.

Manipulating attacks try to modify the silicon chip itself. The smart card therefore has to be opened and the silicon chip accessed directly. A famous attack in this field is the so called probing/forcing attack. Using a microscope the attacker tries to contact the electrical lines on the chip with fine needles and read out or inject signals.

The *observing attack* monitors the behavior of the smart card very precisely. The power consumption or the timing of operations can be observed during normal operation without opening the cards. Famous examples of these side channel attacks are the power analysis or the timing analysis. The attacker checks the smart card performance with an oscilloscope.

Semi-invasive attacks use disturbances to induce faults in the smart card's program flow. Voltage transients, optical radiation, temperature changes or even alpha particles can be used by an attacker for this threat. In a cryptographic operation, a fault can lead to the compromising of the secret key. Also in a normal program flow at a point where a decision has to be made the fault can modify the operation to the attacker's advantage.

In addition to these hardware attacks, logical attacks can also be performed by an attacker. The attacker might try all combinations of a password, the so-called brute-force-attack, or might use non-permitted commands. The smart card operating system and application software therefore also has to be developed with a deep understanding of the different attack scenarios.

Security scrambled and optimized chip layouts counter physical chip manipulation. The controller has a memory encryption/decryption module for the RAM, ROM and EEPROM. This counters reverse engineering and power attacks. The ROM code, which is part of the operating system, is not visible due to implantation. The chip has low and high voltage sensors, frequency sensors and filters, light sensors, glitch sensors, temperature sensors, life tests sensors, internal power-on reset sensors and an active shield with automatic and user-controlled attack detection.

The main driver for this security technology comes from the pay-TV market, with the highest attack rate in the smart card market. The main market at the moment is North America. Semiconductor companies are following this market trend and are making security features mandatory for other applications, like banking cards.

13.4 Interface and Speed

Three major interfaces are currently used:

- Contact interface, according to international standard ISO/IEC 7816
- Contact-less interface, according to ISO/IEC 14443 and ISO/IEC 15693
- USB interface.

13.4.1 Contact Interface

The international standard ISO/IEC 7816 defines the pad location and the pinning for the contacts on the smart card [ISO7816]. Memory cards typically have 6 pins, while controller cards typically have 8 pins. The contacts come in more than 95% of cases with gold finish as anti-corrosion material. The layer must be flush with the surface of the card. The lifetime for long-life banking cards is limited with some 100,000 plug ins. The chip is mounted under the gold contacts in a thin housing with an overall thickness of 0.6 mm.

The speed of the data transaction between the card reader and card is limited to 115 kbps. The power and the clock for the chip is provided through the galvanic interface.

13.4.2 Contact-less Interface

The international standards ISO/IEC 14443 and ISO/IEC 15693 define the field energy, the frequency, the coding and the modulation [ISO1443], [ISO15693]. The position of the chip is not part of the standard. Contact-less cards contain the chip and the antenna in the centre layer of the card, which means that the components are not visible. The industry standard for the thickness of the inlay is around 450 to 500 microns. The antenna can have different formats and the chip position is arbitrary.

ISO/IEC 14443 defines a read distance of typically 10 cm, this is the so-called proximity. Three different data transaction speeds are allowed for this standard: 106 kbps, 212 kbps and 424 kbps. The following products are available on the market today:

- Memory cards with typically 1 kbyte EEPROM and
- Controller cards with typically 64 kbyte EEPROM.

ISO/IEC 14443 allow two types of modulation configuration, the amplitude shift key with 100% (ASK 100) and the amplitude shift key with 10% (ASK 10). ASK 100 is called ISO 14443 type A whereas ASK 10 is called ISO 14443 type B. Both types have different anti-collision mechanisms; type A uses bit anti-collision and type B uses slotted aloha anti-collision. These mechanisms are relevant for reading more than one card in the reader field. This is possible, for example, if there is more than one card in the purse.

The selection or decision in favor of type A and type B is variable. In practice today, for example, in the area of public transport systems, we have

- Type A: London, Moscow, Seoul, Sao Paulo, Rio de Janeiro, Stockholm
- Type B: Paris, Hong Kong, Tokyo, Beijing

ISO/IEC 15693 defines a read distance of typically 50-70 cm, this is the so-called vicinity. A single data transaction speed of 25 kbps is selected for this standard. Today for this standard only memory cards with typically 1kbyte EEPROM are available on the market

13.4.3 USB Interface

The Universal Serial Bus (USB) interface is used in cases where a card is plugged into a laptop or PC. The data transaction speed can be up to 120 Mbps. This is a much higher order of magnitude than the contact-based and contact-less interface.

13.5 Standards

Industry, customer and service providers need international standards for driving new products and new applications. The first smart card standard for contact-based interfaces was ISO 7816, which was frozen in 1986. In the time from 1994 to 2000, the main focus was to push the technical standards with ISO 14443. This time window was 1998 to 2001 for ISO 15693. These technical standards represent the basis for the application standards. The drive comes from the semi-conductor and reader device industry.

The application standards aim for a specific application field to describe the data structure, security architecture and information about the use cases. Examples of these application standards include:

- ICAO[1] 9303 for electronic passports
- ISO 18185 for electronic seals on containers [ISO18185]
- CEN / TC 224 specifications for European citizen cards
- ISO/IEC JTC1/SC17/WG 10 specifications for electronic driver licenses.

In some cases, governments or related organizations push a national or international regulation according to the application standards. Examples from the recent past include:

- EU regulation 2252 for electronic passports
- CSI regulation for containers with departure USA
- UTMS regulation for the next generation electronic driver licenses in Japan
- Ministry employee card in France (CAP Program)
- Government employee card in the USA (PIV Program).

The scope of these regulations is the roadmap for technical migration in tandem with the legal process.

---

[1] International Civil Aviation Organization, see www.icao.org.

13.6 Smart Card Production

Chips generally are produced in the form of wafers. Typical wafer sizes today are 8 inches. In the case of memory chips there are typically more than 20,000 dies on a single wafer, in the case of controller chips, we have quantities in the range between 2,000 and 4,000. Production is carried out in class 10,000 clean rooms[1]. Wafer thickness is around 925 microns when the electronic circuits are put in place. When this front-end process is complete, the wafers are ground to around 185 microns for contact-based chips and 150 microns for contact-less chips.

High-speed diamond grinding wheels are currently used for wafer dicing. The blade thickness of the grinding wheel is around 25 to 30 microns, the dicing street is around 60 to 80 microns.

The next step is to pick up the die and mount it on the module substrate, contacted with the module and protected with a globe top or mould resin.

- For contact-based modules, the substrate is configured as double track and endless. The module is on a reel. One reel typically contains 20,000 modules. The reel is then placed in the delivery box.
- For contact-less chip cards, the inlays have to be assembled after mounting in the package. These inlays are produced in sheet format. The size and pitch of the format are defined by the card lamination process step. Industry standard formats are 3 x 6, 3 x 7 and 3 x 8 inlays per sheet. The process involves punching out the contact-less module, producing the wire antenna, contacting the module on the antenna and testing the inlay. The sheet comes in a flat box for delivery.

The first production step for low-cost cards is the injection mould card body without surface print. The main applications for this process are prepaid telephone cards and SIM cards. Card producers buy this part from the vendor, mount the module (called implanting), and then perform the electronic and optical personalization of the card. Card material typically is ABS.

Long-life cards like banking or electronic ID cards are multi-layer lamination cards with 6 layers. Two of these are core layers (white), with 2 printed layers on top and bottom, each 100 microns thick. There are also two transparent protection layers (outermost layers) with a thickness of 50 microns. The layer structure is symmetrical. This is important to have a flat high-quality card. Medium-life cards are mounted on PVC, long-life cards on Polycarbonate or PET.

The card personalization is performed in batches for SIM and prepaid phone cards. The personalization process for banking cards and electronic ID cards has a batch size of one (see also Section 4.3). The optical and electrical personalization is followed by quality control and packaging for shipment. Products with a batch size of one can have also a letter shop process, where the cards come together with a letter and an envelope for mailing. In case of larger batch sizes, shipment is typically in trays.

---

[1] Clean rooms are rated as "Class 10,000" when there exist no more than 10,000 particles larger than 0.5 microns in any given cubic foot of air.

13.7 Conclusion

During the last 20 years smart card technology has emerged as the preferred identity solution, by offering mature technology, quality and an excellent performance/price ratio. The technology platform of smart cards allows for securely hosting and managing logical and physical identity credentials, well suited for both enterprise and government environments, including ID programs on a nationwide scale.

14 Identity and Access Management Technologies

Teodor Dumitrescu and Oliver Pfaff

After Chapter 5 introduced identity and access management solutions from a user-oriented perspective, this chapter examines the fundamental technologies used to build these solutions.

Identity and access management have become a critical component of enterprise IT systems:

- Identity management is concerned with the lifecycle of identity information for users as well as other system entities. This concerns unique entity identifiers (e.g. usernames) and supplementary attributes (e.g. group memberships or role assignments) as well as associated credentials for the purpose of authentication (e.g. passwords or public key certificates).

- Access management regulates access to resources based on authorization policies which consider properties of requested resources (e.g. security classifications) and requesting subjects (e.g. usernames, group memberships or role assignments). A usual authorization prerequisite is to demand authentication from requestors.

These services have a long history in enterprise security with a wealth of techniques developed and standardized. New identity and access management technologies are currently emerging on the basis of XML technologies and Web services. This chapter investigates traditional and emerging technologies.

14.1 Fundamental Concepts

14.1.1 Identity Management

Identity management supplies and maintains entity identifiers (digital identities), for example "*john.doe@siemens.com*", related attributes, for example "*Vice President Sales*" as well as authentication credentials for entities, for example passwords or public key certificates. This enables security services, such as authentication, Single Sign-On (SSO), authorization and other identity-enabled applications, such as corporate directories, personalization and presence services.

The challenge for identity management is to create, publish and maintain a consistent and accurate view of identities over the many different directories, user databases and application-specific repositories that make up the fragmented, heterogeneous enterprise IT environment. It involves the creation of a unique digital identity from the various authoritative sources of (partial) information, the maintenance of an integrated identity store and the provisioning with account and attribute information of all other systems. Identity management involves tasks and techniques common to system management, security management and EAI (Enterprise Application Integration).

Based on the technologies and architectures involved we distinguish between two broad classes of identity management applications:

- Two or three-tier, client/server applications with an LDAP/X.500 directory as persistence layer and a (mostly) Web-based presentation. They cover both end-user and administrator functionality such as: user self-services, user administration, delegated administration, password/credentials management, etc. Some of these activities may require the cooperation of more than one person (e.g. requesting privileges) and involve some form of workflow.

- Applications involving different heterogeneous components that use various, mostly complex, integration technologies. Metadirectories and user provisioning systems are typical examples for this.

Both types of applications can expose Web services interfaces, some of them standardized, and can be integrated in this way into a larger service-oriented landscape.

14.1.2 Authentication and Single Sign-On (SSO)

By verifying claimed identity (e.g. "*I am john.doe@siemens.com*"), authentication provides a fundamental security service. Authentication occurs between a claimant (e.g. an IT-system such as a Web browser used by *john.doe@siemens.com*) and a verifier (e.g. an IT-system such as a Web server in the domain of *siemens.com* or an external domain such as *osram.com*), also known as asserting and relying party respectively. In authentication systems, the following kinds of objects are distinguished:

- Authentication credentials such as shared secrets, shared secret keys or public keys that are used to corroborate claimed identities between claimants and verifiers. This is realized by authentication protocols such as HTTP basic authentication (shared secrets), Kerberos (shared secret keys), or SSL/TLS (public keys). These authentication credentials are assumed to be maintained by identity management, along with subject identifiers and other attributes. Note that public key certificates represent the authentication credentials that are based on public keys. Their maintenance is a task of a PKI system (cf. Chapter 12).

- Authentication statements such as "*Authentication authority says: this is john.doe@siemens.com*" which are created by authentication authorities. Authentication authorities represent a third type of entity in authentication systems – besides claimants and verifiers. They allow authentication systems – based on symmetric or asymmetric cryptographic techniques – to scale because they relieve claimants of the need to share authentication credentials with every verifier (and vice versa). Authentication authorities can be differentiated as:

    – Offline authentication authorities that are not involved in claimant/verifier inter-
actions in real-time. They issue long-lived authentication statements before such
interactions. For example, Registration Authority (RA) and Certification Authority (CA) in a PKI-based authentication system represent an authentication
authority of this type. PKI certificates represent authentication statements in
PKI-based authentication systems.

    – Online authorities that are involved in claimant/verifier interactions in real-time.
They issue short-lived authentication statements as such interactions happen.
For example, Kerberos is an authentication system with an online authentication
authority. Kerberos tickets represent authentication statements in Kerberos.

Authentication – as a means to establish evidence for subject identifiers – may occur
between claimants and verifiers residing in the same or in different security domains.
Note that authentication across heterogeneous security domains requires identity federation, a service that asserts the identity of an authenticated user across domain
boundaries.

Transferring authentication states between communicating entities in distributed cli-
ent/server or federated environments is known as SSO. SSO systems are based on
online authentication authorities issuing short-lived authentication statements.

Comparing Authentication Services

For reasons of scalability, most enterprise authentication systems rely on architectures
with offline and/or online authentication authorities. Thus, it is important to distinguish the fundamental security models for exchanging authentication statements:

- Bearer model: protect the authenticity of authentication statements but do not
require claimants to explicitly present confirmation data to establish proof-of-possession for authentication statements. I.e. relying parties can check whether
authentication statements were issued by the (claimed) authentication authority.
They cannot determine if they are presented by legitimate owners.

- Proof model: additionally require the presentation of confirmation data to establish
proof-of-possession for authentication statements. I.e. relying parties can check
whether authentication statements are presented by legitimate owners.

Important examples of authentication systems conforming to these security models
are:

- Web-SSO systems that exchange authentication statements (or references to them,
e.g. authentication statement artifacts) via HTTP cookie headers conform to the
bearer-model. This is due to the fact that HTTP cookies are set by Web servers and
passed back to them without modification. Identity theft attacks may be mounted
by attempting to intercept and replay authentication statements (or references to
them). This fundamental limitation of HTTP cookie-based Web-SSO systems
mandates additional measures such as SSL/TLS protection or the protected binding of meta-data such as current time, sequence numbers, originator IP addresses
with HTTP cookie contents to reduce the given exposure. Cf. [FSS01] for more
information.

- Kerberos-based SSO systems conform to the proof model. This is due to the fact that the Kerberos protocol requires claimants to supply valid authenticators when submitting Kerberos tickets (these are the authentication statement in Kerberos) to verifiers. These authenticators represent cryptographic confirmation data for the proof-of-possession of authentication statements. Cf. Section 14.2.4 for more details.

- PKI-based authentication systems also conform to the proof model. Note that – as an infrastructure technology – PKI itself does not define security protocols for the exchange of confirmation data for the proof-of-possession of PKI certificates. In PKI-based authentication systems this is achieved by security protocols such as SSL/TLS or S/MIME. These authentication protocols define the exchange of confirmation data in specific application scenarios such as Web or e-mail.

14.1.3 Authorization

Authorization systems prevent unauthorized access to resources. Authorization and cryptographic techniques together represent the lion's share of IT security mechanisms:

- Cryptographic techniques address scenarios where attackers have direct access to the raw bits that are representing information.

- Authorization addresses scenarios where access to raw bits has to pass through some layer of system functionality. This layer is called reference monitor below. Examples of reference monitors are operating systems, Web and application servers, as well as e-mail, collaboration or database applications in IT networks.

Authorization systems are based on the following building blocks:

- PEPs (Policy Enforcement Points) represent parts of reference monitors. They intercept access requests, send authorization decision requests to PDPs and enforce authorization decisions, i.e. allow or deny access.

- PDPs (Policy Decision Points) represent authorization authorities. They render authorization decisions for corresponding requests from PEPs. This is based on the governing authorization policies obtained from PMAs. Note that PDPs may be remote services or collocated with PEPs.

- PMAs (Policy Management Authorities) represent authorization policy authorities. They create, supply and maintain authorization policies in an authorization system.

Comparing Authorization Technologies

This section presents various classification criteria for benchmarking authorization technologies. It focuses on the authorization policy expressiveness:

- Identity-centric authorization: based on subject and resource identifiers, for example *Only john.doe@siemens.com may access https://www.siemens.com/board/secrets.pdf*. Note that authentication systems supply information on the authenticated subject identity.

- Category-aware authorization: adds support for structuring the sets of subjects and resources independently of one another, for example *Sales-team members may read files beneath https://www.siemens.com/sales.* Compared to identity-centric authorization, this may require the retrieval of subject attributes (e.g. group memberships or role assignments) from other sources than authentication systems as well as the retrieval of resource attributes (e.g. resource classifications or resource properties such as being served by a specific container) from other sources than the access request.

- Relationship-aware authorization: adds support for jointly structuring subjects and resources, for example *Sales team members may read documents beneath https://www.siemens.com/sales/contracts if customer resides in the same region as the requestor.* Compared to category-aware authorization, this requires the ability to express conditional relationships between subject and resource attributes and to evaluate them at runtime.

Corresponding authorization policies can be represented in various ways including programmatic and declarative approaches. ACLs (Access Control Lists), permissions and privileges are examples of declarative approaches. Authorization can also be performed on various levels of resource granularity, for example network, application or object access. These aspects represent assessment criteria that are orthogonal to the considered expressiveness. Federation support is a further criterion. Note that federated environments may require access management services to be capable of processing subject identifiers and related attributes from external security domains. The assignment of PMA responsibility is yet another criterion. Authorization systems that manage access to enterprise resources often assign this responsibility to dedicated administrators while systems that manage individual resources and enhance privacy often demand end user-managed authorization policies, for example to enable explicit consent.

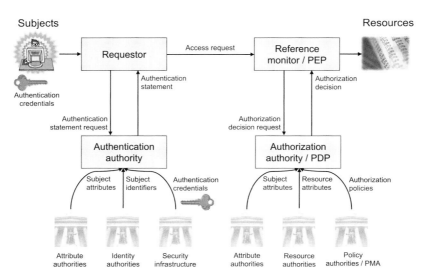

Figure 14.1 Identity and access management reference model

14.1.4 Identity and Access Management Reference Model

The reference model (Figure 14.1) serves as a framework for the investigation of identity and access management technologies. It focuses on the usage of identity information in authentication, Single Sign-On (SSO) and authorization. Note that the authentication and authorization authorities may use different subject attributes. The attributes relevant for authorization decisions (e.g. group membership, permissions, roles, etc.) are denoted collectively as entitlements.

14.2 Traditional Technologies

Various technologies have evolved over the last decades that are now used in building identity and access management solutions. This chapter examines the most representative of these traditional technologies.

14.2.1 LDAP

LDAP (Lightweight Directory Access Protocol) provides the fundamental technology to implement general-purpose, standards-based directory services. Directories are highly distributed and replicated, hierarchical object stores. They represent specialized databases optimized in providing object naming on a large scale in a network environment. In particular, directories are supposed to have:

- A large read-to-write ratio, i.e. to contain largely static data
- A flexible schema that can be easily extended to support a large variety of applications
- A good performance for complex search operations even in distributed environments.

Despite its name, LDAP is more than a protocol. LDAP defines:

- The LDAP protocol, a standard, extensible, client/server Internet protocol for accessing directory services. It is message-oriented; the client sends requests to the server that is responsible for performing the necessary operations in the directory and returning the results or errors. The protocol supports nine basic operations for interrogation (search, compare), update (add, delete, modify, modify DN) as well as authentication and control (bind, unbind, abandon). It provides extensibility through three methods: LDAP extended operations (entirely new operations, e.g. StartTLS), LDAP controls (which alter the behavior of existing operations) and SASL (Simple Authentication and Security Layer), a framework to accommodate multiple authentication methods. The wire protocol is not entirely text-based; it uses a simplified version of ASN.1 BER (Basic Encoding Rules), even if many data types inside the payload are string-encoded. LDAP PDUs (Protocol Data Units) are directly mapped to the TCP/IP stream.
- The LDAP directory information model, which together with the LDAP naming and functional models, is based on the X.500 (1993) ITU-T recommendations

(cf. Section 14.2.2). The LDAP directory is a collection of entries that model real-life objects, called object entries, and entries that point to object entries, called alias entries. Entries are arranged into a hierarchical structure, called DIT (Directory Information Tree). An entry consists of a set of attributes; each attribute consists of a type and one or more values. The directory content is policed by the schema, a set of rules describing the structure of entries in terms of attributes and the attribute properties including their syntaxes and matching rules. A special entry called root DSE (DSA-Specific Entry) allows clients to discover the schema and the features supported by the server.

- The LDAP naming model that describes how the hierarchical, inverted-tree structured directory is building unique names for its entries: each entry has a unique Distinguished Name (DN), which is the concatenation of the Relative Distinguished Names (RDNs) of all the entries from the root of the tree to and including the considered entry. Each entry builds its RDN as a set of one or more (type, value) pairs, the involved attributes being called naming attributes. All RDNs below a node are unique and by recurrence so are the DNs in the whole directory (see Figure 14.2; the entry with the DN *cn=Joe Doe, dc=siemens, dc=com is an alias to cn=John Doe, O=Siemens, C=DE*).

- The LDAP functional model that describes the operations supported by the protocol including the request parameters, behavior of the server and format of the response. From the mentioned operations, search is the most powerful one; it allows retrieving a set of entries which match an LDAP filter (a Boolean combination of type-value assertions) subjected to additional restrictions. As far as the service is concerned, an LDAP server has to behave according to the X.500 (1993) recommendations. This does not require the use of any X.500 protocols, for example LDAP can be mapped onto any other directory system as long as the X.500 data and service model are observed.

- The LDIF (LDAP Data Interchange Format, RFC 2849), a text-based format that describes the content of directory entries (LDIF content file) or the changes applied to various directory entries (LDIF change file). The format is record-oriented and includes the DN of the entry, the change operation (only for change files) and a set of attribute type value pairs. It is widely used to exchange data between various LDAP servers, for backup and recovery purposes or as an interface to other applications like metadirectories and synchronization services.

- The LDAP security model (Figure 14.2) that covers the client/server authentication methods and the usage of TLS together with LDAP. Since LDAP is stateful, clients can authenticate at bind time and enjoy the privileges associated with their identity for all the subsequent operations on this connection. In addition to the simple DN plus password authentication, LDAP defines multiple authentication mechanisms through SASL (RFC 2222), Digest-MD5 (RFC 2831) and External that can employ TLS authentication. TLS can be started on existing LDAP connections with an extended LDAP operation (StartTLS) and can provide certificate-based client and server authentication as well as transient message authentication and confidentiality. Note that LDAP does not define an authorization model.

Started in 1993 as a simple, low-footprint protocol to access X.500 directories, LDAP has evolved to protocol version 3 (LDAPv3) and has become the standard for directo-

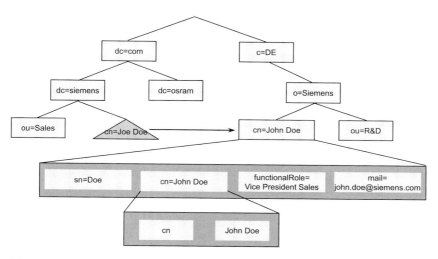

Figure 14.2 LDAP information and naming model

ries and identity repositories. LDAPv3 is a proposed Internet standard, approved in 1997 and augmented with the security model in 2000. The specification is covered by RFCs 2251-2256, 2829-2830 and 3377. RFC 3377 is the technical specification of the standard and refers to the other RFCs. At the time of writing, the IETF working group LDAP (v3) Revision (ldapbis) is updating the specifications and expects to promote LDAPv3 to Internet draft standard by the end of 2005 or beginning of 2006 (cf. www.ietf.org). In addition to the LDAPv3 activity, other IETF working groups and individual contributors have published extensions to LDAP in various areas (extended operations, controls, schemas, APIs, etc.) and standardized the usage of LDAP for other services and protocols (there are over 60 LDAP-related RFCs and Internet drafts). In addition to the already mentioned documents, some of the most important are listed below:

- The paged result control (RFC 2696) allows a client to retrieve a larger search result in smaller pages. The server-side sorting control (RFC 2891) requires the server to sort the search results according to a list of attribute types and matching rules provided by the client. Combined, these controls dramatically optimize the usage of computing resources in an environment where many clients perform large search operations.

- Unfortunately no universal registry exists for publishing LDAP schemas, but various standard schemas are available. In addition to LDAPv3/X.500 (RFC 2256) there are:
  - RFC 2247 defines an algorithm and schema elements that allow Internet DNS names to be represented as LDAP DNs.
  - RFC 2798 and its update RFC 3698 define the Internet Organizational Person object class (inetOrgPerson), the de facto standard for person-related information used by most LDAP deployments.

- RFC 2587 defines a minimal schema to support PKI based on PKIX. It defines object classes like pkiUser, pkiCA, cRLDistributionPoint and deltaCRL.

- RFC 3703 and its update RFC 4104 define an LDAP schema for the objects of Policy Core Information Model (PCIM), an access policy modeling standard (RFC 3460) developed jointly by IETF and DMTF.

• The Internet Draft draft-behera-ldap-password-policy-09 (work-in-progress) defines both schema elements and controls to implement password policies for LDAP directories. These are rules to make sure that users change their passwords periodically, that passwords meet certain strength requirements, that old passwords are not reused and users are locked out after a certain number of failed login attempts.

LDAP directories are supporting various tasks in the IAM context:

• In identity management, LDAP directories are used as repositories for digital identities and their attributes. This provides user-friendly naming, powerful searching capabilities and the building of groups. Through standard interfaces, protocols and information models they facilitate the location and sharing of identity information among users and network applications.

• In authentication and Single Sign-On (SSO) services, LDAP directories supply keying information to relying parties. In particular they are an enabling infrastructure for PKI deployments as repositories of both X.509 certificates and Certificate Revocation Lists (CRLs).

• In authorization services, LDAP directories provide persistence for authorization policy information and support its exchange between PMAs and PDPs.

LDAP has become a major topic with many technical, deployment and operational issues, see [HSG03] and [SS02] for a more detailed explanation. Many vendor and some open source initiatives provide LDAP-based directory products, tools, libraries, etc. making the adoption and deployment of LDAP directories and the development of LDAP-enabled applications both easy and attractive for enterprises. Newer XML-based technologies like DSML and SPML (cf. Section 14.3.6) are extending the reach of LDAP directories to Web services and XML applications.

14.2.2 X.500

X.500 was the first standardized directory system designed to be general-purpose, global in scope, distributed and replicated. It predates LDAP and constitutes the basis for much of the initial LDAP modeling. The standardization work is done jointly by ITU-T (Recommendations X.500-X.530) and ISO/IEC JTC 1 (ISO/IEC 9594-1 to 9594-10, common text with the X.500 recommendations). Today liaison and close cooperation is maintained with the IETF, particularly in the area of LDAP. The X.500 series was first published in 1988 and was extensively revised in 1993, 1997, and 2000/2001.

X.500 defines the directory as a collection of servers called DSAs (Directory System Agents) that cooperate to hold a logical database of information collectively known as the DIB (Directory Information Base). Users access the directory through clients called DUAs (Directory User Agents) and can read or modify the information, subject

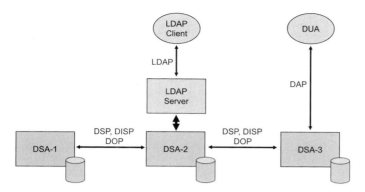

Figure 14.3 X.500 distributed and replicated directory

to having permission to do so. The distribution of the information is transparent to users. A DSA provides access to the DIB to DUAs and/or other DSAs and may use information stored in its local database or interact with other DSAs to carry out requests. The general architecture is illustrated in Figure 14.3.

In order to provide these functions, the standard defines a number of models (X.501) and protocols (X.519):

- The directory user information model, which addresses the information put into directory and managed by the user (or on his behalf). It is the same object and naming model as the one used by LDAP and described in Section 14.2.1. It consists of objects entries, aliases, attributes, the DIT, distinguished names, etc. (see also Figure 14.2). The structure of the user information is schema controlled. In order to encourage schema reuse by different applications, a number of useful object classes and attribute types are defined (X.520, X.521).

- The directory operational and administrative model, which extends the user information model with operational attributes and subentries. Operational attributes (e.g. access control, time stamp, administrative role, subtree specification, has subordinates, etc.) control directory operations while subentries associate the values of a set of attributes (e.g. collective attributes) with specific subtrees. This provides the basic modeling for the specification of access control, collective attributes and distributed schema/subschemas.

- The DSA information model, which deals with the information a DSA must hold in a distributed environment in order to perform name resolution, operation evaluation, shadowing (replication), etc. The DSA views its own portion of the DIB as a collection of DSEs, with various DSE types defined. Among these, knowledge references (superior, immediate superior, subordinate, non-specific subordinate and cross references) play a crucial role in finding the appropriate DSAs to perform distributed requests.

- A directory functional model, also called abstract service definition (X.511), and a distributed operations model (X.518). The functional model describes the operations supported by the client protocol DAP and, as mentioned in the previous section, are the basis for the LDAP functional model. There is close correspondence between the LDAP and DAP operations, their parameters, results, errors, etc. (there are two additional operations in DAP, read and list which in LDAP are covered by search). The distributed operations model extends the server behavior to the case when the DIB is distributed. The DSAs interact with each other, for example by chaining the requests and merging the results before returning them to the client.

- A directory replication model (X.525), which the standard calls shadowing: one instance of each replicated entry is identified as the master copy, the others as shadows (single-master replication model). Before shadowing can occur, an agreement between the involved DSAs is required. It covers the conditions under which shadowing may occur and defines among others which subtree or set of entries and which attributes will be replicated (partial and filtered replication).

- The access protocol between a DUA and a DSA called DAP (Directory Access Protocol) and three server/server protocols between two DSAs:
  - DSP (Directory System Protocol) extends the client/server protocol elements to other DSAs, and provides for distribution transparency for clients.
  - DISP (Directory Information Shadowing Protocol) defines the exchange of replication information between two DSAs.
  - DOP (Directory Operational Management Binding Protocol) defines the exchange of administrative information between two DSAs.

  The mentioned protocols are specified in X.519 with protocol conformance statements defined in X.583-X.586. The X.500 protocols rely heavily on ASN.1 and other OSI upper layer protocols.

- A framework for public key certificates and attribute certificates (X.509), which defines public key certificates and CRLs (Certificate Revocation List) needed for PKI (see Chapter 12) as well as attribute certificates and their revocation lists, which provide a secure way to transmit privileges.

With LDAP directories widely adopted and deployed, X.500's most common role is as backend technology for LDAP servers. Its strength resides in its standardized and proven capabilities which go beyond LDAP in the area of distribution and replication, access control and administration. The close relationship between LDAP and DAP on one hand and the common user information model on the other hand allow for good integration of LDAP in X.500 servers. Implementations range from LDAP to DAP gateways, over optimized LDAP-server-DSA tight coupling to LDAP ports integrated in the DSA. X.500 is a large and technically complex subject in itself, with the standard as authoritative reference; see also [Cha94] for a good overview of the 1993 version.

14.2.3 Metadirectory and Provisioning

Both metadirectory and user provisioning deal with the issue of inter-connecting heterogeneous identity management systems that have different data formats, different semantics for data and operations, different protocols, APIs written in different programming languages, use different databases or directories as repositories and run on different operating systems. Like in all integration scenarios, a hierarchy of layers is involved, each layer increasing the integration depth, adding new functionality and value:

- Platform integration has to deal with hardware and operating system diversity. Interconnectivity protocols like various RPCs, message queue buses, CORBA, SOAP, etc. are used to bridge this gap.
- Data integration is concerned with the syntactic and semantic differences in data and metadata (schemas). The ETL (Extract-Transform-Load) paradigm and technologies developed in connection with data warehouses (see [KC04]) are also well suited for identity data integration. This approach is oblivious to the application logic of the various systems.
- Application integration deals with bridging the application logic and functional models of the identity systems and may involve integrating events, transactions, etc. across them.
- Business process integration adds the ability to coordinate processes and workflows across the various systems.

In this picture, the metadirectory deals mostly with platform and data integration, while provisioning covers application and business process integration. Provisioning can be built on top of a metadirectory or can provide its own connectivity and data transformation services.

As discussed in Chapter 5, metadirectories perform two basic services:

- The directory "join", which creates unique, global digital IDs with their attributes from multiple authoritative sources and publishes them in a central, LDAP-based identity store (also sometimes called a metadirectory).
- Synchronization services between the identity store and individual repositories, or directly between pairs of repositories.

Metadirectories are in general batch oriented, with data written to files at different stages in the processing flow (the other option is streaming data flow). In line with ETL methodology, the extraction step deals with source data models (schemas), connection and access to data, attribute filtering, scheduling the extraction and capturing changed data (deltas). It has to accommodate at least LDAP directories, relational databases, flat and XML files, popular operating systems, groupware and packaged applications user stores as possible sources. The transform step involves both cleaning of the extracted data and conforming to the target schema. It is the step where the metadirectory logic and complexity reside (entry joining, attribute mapping and merging, ownership issues, etc.) and value is added to the data. It provides correct, consistent and complete data for the identity store. Operational aspects of the metadirectory include job scheduling and execution, exception handling and recovery, monitoring and auditing.

Provisioning deals with the process of managing (creating, modifying, deleting, suspending, and restoring) user accounts and related attributes, especially entitlements, within various target systems (e.g. Windows domains). Provisioning systems allow account and entitlement management to heterogeneous enterprise resources in a timely, deterministic and auditable fashion based on a central user and entitlement model that reflects the enterprise business-rules. They rely on the native authentication and authorization mechanisms (PEP and PDP) of the integrated target systems to enforce enterprise business rules automatically and consistently. Provisioning is narrower in scope than metadirectory, because it focuses on a centralized authorization management system for the enterprise and has a tighter integration with the target systems. Some aspects of provisioning are standardized by OASIS in SPML (see Section 14.3.6). Provisioning systems implement:

- A central user identity store as identity and attribute authority, created and maintained through a combination of metadirectory integration, self-management and delegated administration.

- An authorization model for structuring the users and their entitlements according to their business roles and role permissions (e.g. according to NIST RBAC or extensions to it, see Section 14.2.5: Role Based Access Control). This model must be general enough to encompass the variety of native authorization models present in the various target-systems.

- Both automatic and manual processes for assigning user to privileges through provisioning policies, request workflows and administrator actions, based on user attributes and privilege templates/parameters.

- The business logic to map this authorization model onto the user accounts and their entitlements (e.g. account attributes, groups, roles, etc.) in target systems. Note that provisioning systems are not aware of the target system resources; they deal only with the users and their structuring. The target system PMA allows the association with resources, which in turn enables authorization enforcement through the native PEP and PDP.

- The middleware to manage the life-cycle for these accounts and entitlements in the target systems.

From an architectural point of view, provisioning systems are client/server-based, event- and transaction-aware systems and have higher requirements for performance (e.g. zero-latency) than metadirectories.

14.2.4 Kerberos

Kerberos is a framework for authentication in client/server environments. It distinguishes between the following parties: clients, Kerberos KDCs (Key Distribution Centers) and target servers. In Kerberos, initial authentication is performed between clients and KDCs while subsequent authentication is performed between clients and target servers:

- Clients represent users or other applications performing authentication. They act as claimants for (initial and subsequent) client authentication and verifiers for server authentication (Kerberos KDC and target servers).

- KDCs represent authentication authorities in Kerberos. They act as verifiers for (initial) client authentication and claimants for server authentication. They issue authentication statements in the form of Kerberos tickets.

- Target servers include all network application servers (Web, e-mail, ftp servers, etc.) which consume these authentication statements. They act as verifiers for (subsequent) client authentication and claimants for server authentication.

Kerberos provides SSO and key management services as well as support for authorization:

- Kerberos specifies the initial authentication schemes between clients and Kerberos KDCs by itself. Kerberos supports initial authentication based on shared secret keys (so called passkeys which are derived from passwords) and public keys represented by PKI certificates (the Kerberos PKINIT option).

- Kerberos tickets conform to the proof model: valid authenticators need to be provided when presenting a Kerberos ticket to a target server or to the Kerberos TGS (Ticket Granting Service). Kerberos authenticators include the current time and other fields that are encrypted under a short-lived key, which is sent to the client encrypted and has to be decrypted by client with its passkey or private key. In other words, authenticators in the Kerberos protocol ensure that the client is part of the underlying keying association with the Kerberos AS (Authentication Service).

- Kerberos assigns short-lived symmetric session keys to clients and target servers on the basis of long-lived keying associations between clients and KDCs as well as between target servers and KDCs. Applications may use these short-lived session keys to protect their communications.

- Kerberos tickets can carry authorization information (whose contents are not defined by Kerberos). The security architecture of Windows domains uses this capability to transfer proprietary PACs (Privilege Attribute Certificates) from Windows domain controllers to target services. PACs are signed objects comprising operating system-specific data. They describe group memberships of the authenticated user. PACs are currently documented in Internet drafts only.

Kerberos originated from the MIT Athena project and was brought into IETF standardization resulting in the Kerberos v5 specification RFC 1510 (and its update RFC 4120) plus several supplementary specifications (cf. [KPS02] or [DeC04] for an overview on Kerberos). It is worth noting that the Kerberos authentication framework represents the foundation for authentication in Windows domains (starting with Windows 2000 servers). Thus, it enjoys widespread use in the enterprise infrastructure. Kerberos is also available and widely deployed in UNIX environments. Note that the technical development of Kerberos is still continuing. For example, Microsoft recently introduced Kerberos S4U (Service for User) extensions for enhanced impersonation services on Windows Server 2003. Currently, there is also an active IETF working group working on Kerberos extensions, for example public key cryptography for initial authentication in Kerberos and AES encryption for Kerberos (RFC 3962).

Kerberos can be used in federated environments but its federation support has limitations:

- Kerberos is not generic in reporting authentication events:
  - It tightly couples initial and subsequent authentication since Kerberos defines and performs initial authentication.
  - Kerberos tickets lack metadata on the initial authentication, for example they do not report the method of initial authentication.
- Kerberos requires the same subject identity in communications between Kerberos clients and KDCs and between Kerberos clients and target servers.
- Kerberos tickets are scoped to dedicated targets and cannot be presented to arbitrary target servers.

14.2.5 Traditional Authorization Techniques

DAC (Discretionary Access Control), MAC (Mandatory Access Control), and RBAC (Role Based Access Control) represent traditional concepts for authorization that are implemented in a variety of IT systems. ACLs and capability lists are examples of authorization mechanisms that are based on these concepts.

Discretionary Access Control

The concept of DAC is based on the model of individual resource ownership. DAC provides owner-controlled resource sharing by allowing resource owners to grant resource access to other subjects. In strict DAC, only the resource owner has a discretionary authority to grant resource access. In a liberal DAC model, owners can delegate authority for granting resource access to other users, for example in multi-level grants. To a large extent, the authorization support in mainstream enterprise IT systems is based on DAC:

- Controlling access to UNIX operating system resources is at the discretion of the resource owner. This is realized on the basis of file permissions that grant read, write and execute rights for resources on the basis of the subject notions of owner, owner group and others. Due to limitations of this basic permission model, ACLs have also been developed for UNIX systems by the POSIX 1003.1e/1003.2c working group. These ACLs extend the basic UNIX file permissions by allowing resource owners to authorize named users and groups. This is currently limited to user and group identifiers from the local domain. These ACL concepts are implemented in a variety of UNIX systems but the corresponding POSIX documents have not been formally approved by the IEEE. Cf. [Gru03] for further information.
- Controlling access to Windows operating system resources is at the discretion of the resource owner. This is based on security descriptors, which provide information about the resource owner and contain ACLs that specify access rights for other users or groups. Authorized subjects are described by SIDs (Security IDentifiers), which uniquely identify users and groups. Note that SIDs comprise an authority part identifying the domain as well as a relative identifier identifying the entity relative to an authority. Thus they are not limited to the local domain but to Windows domains. In order to access Windows protected resources, subjects from non-Windows Kerberos domains or from PKI domains need to be mapped to Windows

domains via proxy accounts in the Active Directory (cf. [DeC04] for more details). Note that besides identity mapping, inter-realm trust needs to be established between the non-Windows Kerberos domain or the PKI domains and the Windows domain.

• Controlling access to X.500 directory entries is at the discretion of directory administrators. This is based on operational attributes called ACI (Access Control Information). Directory access control represents an ACL-type authorization that describes authorized subjects based on X.500 distinguished names. This mechanism delivers category-aware authorization and supports authorizations on various levels of resource granularity. It was introduced by the second edition of X.500 (1993) while LDAP v3 does not specify access control. Thus, LDAP servers use various proprietary access control mechanisms. Cf. [Cha00] for further information.

• Controlling access to Java platform resources by native Java means is performed by the security manager and is based on granting permissions via Java policy files. Grants authorize entities to perform certain actions on resources. Permissions can be granted to a codebase (Java files downloaded from specified URLs) or subjects, which are described by name strings and Java classes that process them. Related subject authentication is performed through JAAS (Java Authentication and Authorization Service). Note that controlling access to Java policy files relies on the operating system, i.e. the ability to modify Java policy files provides the discretion to manage authorization for Java platform resources. Cf. [And02] for more details.

• Controlling access to Apache Web server resources (by native means) is based on configuration settings in httpd.conf (per server) and .htaccess (per directory). The basic Apache access control allows the description of requestors based on client hostname, IP address, and other HTTP request characteristics (here: mod_access directives Allow and Deny) plus authenticated users on the basis of the notions of resource owner and owner group as well as other users or groups that are named by identifiers (here: mod_auth directive Require). The Apache policy configurations do not explicitly specify the resources for which access is controlled; this is implicitly derived from the placement of the configuration files. In general, access restrictions apply to all HTTP methods. Note that controlling access to Apache configuration files relies on the operating system, i.e. the ability to edit Apache configuration files provides the discretion to manage authorization for Apache Web server resources.

Capability lists represent another type of DAC mechanisms. They comprise lists of resources together with access rights that may be accessed by a subject.

Originally, DAC was an identity-centric authorization technology. Since identity-centric authorization has scalability issues when managing enterprise resources, several enhancements to basic DAC have been made, for example, to support the handling of categories of subjects and resources.

Mandatory Access Control

The concept of MAC is based on the model of organizational resource ownership. It serves an organization-controlled sharing of information by restricting information flows. In traditional MAC, access to resources is restricted based on the sensitivity of the information contained in the resource (classified by a security label) and the authorization of the requesting subject (classified by a security clearance). MAC realizes authorization via comparison of security labels and clearances. MAC-based authorization is mostly used in government and military IT systems. Since the mainstream operating systems are based on the concept of DAC, MAC support demands variants of commercial operating systems, for example Trusted Solaris from Sun Microsystems. Open operating systems have also started to support MAC. Adding MAC support to LINUX is a major theme behind SELinux (cf. [LS01]). Moreover, FreeBSD 5.X offers MAC support on the basis of the POSIX 1003.1e/1003.2c drafts (cf. [Wat01]).

MAC represents a category-aware authorization technology, but it lacks expressiveness for more complex scenarios where an individual belongs, for example, to more than one category.

Role-Based Access Control

The concept of RBAC provides a model to structure the subject population for access management purposes. This concept is based on subject roles and role permissions:

- Roles are representations of job functions within an organization.
- Permissions are approvals to perform operations upon RBAC-protected objects.

In other words, RBAC employs a 2-level indirection assigning permissions to subjects via roles. The NIST is a driving force behind the development of RBAC (cf. csrc.nist.gov/rbac). The NIST model for RBAC is published as ANSI/INCITS standard 359-2004 (February 2004, cf. also [FKC03]). The following RBAC profiles need to be distinguished:

- Core RBAC: defines user / role assignment and role / permission assignment. Note that RBAC permissions implicitly grant access rights (in contrast to e.g. the Java system notion of permissions).
- Hierarchical RBAC: supports role inheritance based on a superiority of roles.
- Static separation of duty: places constraints on the assignment of roles to avoid conflicts of interest.
- Dynamic separation of duty: similar to static separation but based on time or other dynamic factors.

Windows Server 2003 introduced RBAC support with the Windows Authorization Manager. It comprises a management console plug-in as PMA and a runtime dll as PDP. The GUI allows administrators to define role-based authorizations for enabled applications, which have to implement a corresponding PEP. The authorization policies use a proprietary encoding that persists either in XML files or as Active Directory entries. They describe access conditions on the basis of abstractions, such as roles, tasks and operations. Note that this requires coordination with the business logic of the PEP.

The authorization information base of RBAC systems refers to subject roles and abstract permissions. As defined by NIST, RBAC represents a category-aware authorization technology. It is not well-suited to managing relationship-aware authorizations since this would require the modeling of resource-specific roles, for example *manager of company A*, *manager of company B*, etc. The single dimension of roles in RBAC does not scale when the assignment of authorizations depends on multiple factors, such as functional subject role (e.g. *manager*) and resource affiliation (e.g. *company A, company B resources*).

Some of these limitations can be overcome by extending the RBAC model and allowing for parameterizable/template roles: attributes can be assigned to the subject role associations (either as explicit values or through the subject's attribute types) which then influence the role permission resolution. Another resolution strategy is to rely on a more expressive authorization technology and embed RBAC support in it. An example of this approach is XACML (cf. XACML Section 14.3.4), which is capable of supporting identity-centric, category as well as relationship-aware authorization models in parallel and embeds RBAC as a profile. The RBAC profile of XACML is optional and covers the specific needs of certain applications.

Common Properties – Federation Support

DAC, MAC and RBAC can serve federated environments but their federation support has several limitations:

- DAC, MAC, and RBAC realize identity-centric or category-aware authorization models. Without extensions, they do not cover relationship-aware authorization which is typically required in federated environments to support mainstream use cases, such as *Resource must be assigned to company A, B, etc. to allow access for a company A, B, etc. manager.*

- The traditional realizations bind early, i.e. their decision making logic is rather simple and not capable of performing runtime evaluation on the basis of configurable predicates for subject, resource and action attributes, such as authentication quality and conditional contexts between them.

- Present realizations have scoping and expressiveness limitations in describing authorized subjects. For example, subjects need to be from the local domain (UNIX), from a Windows domain (Windows) or from a directory population (X.500). This usually requires mapping external user identities to local user accounts in order to operate in federated environments. Moreover, operating system authorization has limitations in expressing authorized users based on application-specific attributes.

- The traditional realizations also lack support for distributed authorization policy management where, for example, multiple, independent subjects – such as end users and administrators – author policies for authorization resources. This requires the support of meta-data for example for policy synthesizing and conflict resolution.

14.2.6 Further Initiatives

Various other initiatives have contributed traditional identity and access management technologies including:

- The ITU-T recommendation X.812 or ISO/IEC international standard 10181-3 describes an access control framework based on an application-dependent access enforcement function (AEF, corresponds to PEP), an application-independent access decision function (ADF, corresponds to PDP) and access control information (ACI).
- The IETF developed various identity and access management technologies including:
  - A reference model for authorization services on the Internet (RFCs 2903, 2904, 2905, 2906).
  - RADIUS (Remote Authentication Dial In User Service, RFC 2865) describes a protocol for exchanging authentication, authorization and configuration information between network access servers and an authentication server. RADIUS servers can act as proxies to other RADIUS servers or interact with other kinds of authentication servers.
  - Diameter defines another authentication, authorization and accounting framework for network access and IP mobility (RFC 3588, 4004, 4005).
  - The COPS protocol (Common Open Policy Service, RFC 2748) describes the exchange of authorization decision requests and responses between PEPs and PDPs.

14.3 Emerging Technologies

The traditional identity and access management technologies focus on intra-enterprise scenarios since they tend to implicitly assume that identity and resource providers reside in one enterprise. They do not cover the requirements for distributed identity and access management needed for inter-enterprise scenarios. This limitation is becoming critical with the advent of the federation paradigm. Federation aims at allowing enterprises to extend their existing identity and access management systems to accommodate interactions with partner organizations. This chapter examines emerging identity and access management technologies that address federated inter-enterprise services.

14.3.1 SAML

SAML (Security Assertion Markup Language) is a fundamental technology for transferring identity-related security information between domains to enable cross-domain SSO as well as identity federation. SAML defines:

- An XML-based syntax to express declarations of facts about subjects (called assertions). SAML assertions may carry multiple statements of the following types:

- Authentication statement: the subject was authenticated by a particular means at a particular time.
- Attribute statement: the subject is associated with certain attributes.
- Authorization decision statement: the subject may (or may not) access a named resource with a specified action.
- An XML-based syntax to acquire SAML assertions in a request/response protocol as well as bindings for this protocol via HTTP and SOAP-over-HTTP.
- Profiles for cross-domain SSO in Web environments.

SAML is developed by an OASIS technical committee (www.oasis-open.org/committees/ security). Its current specification release (version 2.0, March 2005) is published as an OASIS standard. This version improves on SAML 1.x and incorporates Liberty-Alliance contributions (by adopting functionality, not syntax). The main properties of SAML are:

- SAML does not define initial authentication by itself. SAML authentication statements do not constrain the methods of initial authentication. They carry information on this method as well as further meta-data about the context of initial authentication (e.g. the length of authentication keys).
- SAML does not specify attribute vocabularies. It supports arbitrary application-defined attributes, i.e. it is generic with respect to attributes that can be carried.
- It is not mandatory to scope SAML assertions to dedicated targets, i.e. a SAML assertion may be submitted to various relying parties.
- SAML relies on XML Signature and XML Encryption for object protection and supports bearer as well as proof models in associating assertions with their owners.

SAML is a key technology for identity federation. Its marshalling of identity-related security information enables SAML applications, such as Shibboleth and Liberty-Alliance, to deploy various identity federation models (cf. Section 14.4.3). Moreover, it defines SSO profiles for Web applications which can be used as basis for interoperable implementations. In these profiles, SAML assertions may carry attribute statements, i.e. identity providers can push attributes to resource providers. Note that these Web-SSO profiles do not define the attributes to be exchanged, the related identity mappings and the underlying agreements between the participating security domains. These issues are matters of SAML applications.

14.3.2 Shibboleth

Shibboleth (*Hebrew – refers to criteria that test if an individual belongs to a group*) is a technology framework for identity federation and distributed authorization in Web environments. Shibboleth is a SAML application that specifies interactions between identity and resource providers for attribute exchange and distributed authorization:

- Shibboleth extends the SAML Web-SSO profiles by supporting attribute pull. Shibboleth also specifies an additional WAYF (Where Are You From) service. This service supports resource providers in identifying the home domain of a requestor.

- The Shibboleth protocol exchanges transfer information about subject authentication and subject attributes. For this purpose, Shibboleth specifies a standard attribute vocabulary based on the LDAP object class eduPerson.

Shibboleth is developed as part of the Internet2 initiative (shibboleth.internet2.edu; also cf. [MCC04]). In contrast to other initiatives considered in this section, the Shibboleth project delivers both specification and open source software (cf. shibboleth.internet2.edu/release). Version 1 of the Shibboleth system was provided in June 2003 and builds upon SAML 1.1. The main properties of Shibboleth are:

- Shibboleth represents a functional superset of the SAML 1.1 Web-SSO profiles. It mainly adds cross-domain attribute exchange for the purpose of authorization where resource providers pull attributes from identity providers via the SAML request/response protocol.
- The privacy of participating users is addressed through pseudonyms and user consent:
  - Identity providers use pseudonyms in the form of subject handles to assert the identity of an authenticated user to a resource provider. A subject handle is opaque to resource providers and can only be resolved to the actual subject identity by the corresponding identity provider.
  - User consent concerns the supply of attribute information to requestors. It is expressed in the form of personal attribute release policies maintained in the identity provider domain. In addition to end users, Shibboleth administrators also have authority to govern certain aspects of attribute release.
- The choice of the deployed authentication and authorization techniques is at the discretion of the corresponding identity and resource providers. Shibboleth explicitly aims at extending – not replacing – existing identity and access management systems. In particular, Shibboleth relies on existing Web-SSO systems for maintaining mutual authentication state between a browser and the domain of the identity provider as well as the resource provider. Moreover, Shibboleth relies on existing Web authorization systems to manage access to resources in the resource provider domain.

14.3.3 Liberty-Alliance

The Liberty-Alliance provides a technology framework for identity federation in Web and Web services environments. The Liberty-Alliance specifications define:

- A framework for identity federation (ID-FF – IDentity Federation Framework) that enables federation through account linkage, SSO and session management features.
- A framework for identity-based Services (ID-WSF – IDentity Web Services Framework) that supports the location and invocation of Web services that provide access to identity-related information of a user (e.g. *my presence data*).
- A collection of interface specifications for identity services (ID-SIS – IDentity Service Interface Specifications), for example personal identity profile and presence.

The Liberty-Alliance specifications are developed by an industry initiative (www.projectliberty.org). Version 1.0 of the Liberty-Alliance phase 2 specifications represents the most recent release (May 2005). The main properties of these specifications are:

- The identity federation model supported in ID-FF is based on end-user consent and linkage of already present user accounts. The last ID-FF specification 1.2 is based on SAML 1.1. It was contributed to OASIS and blended into SAML 2.0. Note that the Liberty-Alliance maintains ID-FF in Version 1.2 but does not plan further enhancements for this specification. Thus, SAML will replace ID-FF in the long-term.

- The ID-WSF specification supports identity-based discovery of Web services, permission-based attribute sharing and an interaction service. The identity-based discovery service supports resource providers in discovering the identity provider of a user. The profile access mechanisms allow identity providers to perform access control for user attributes based on the user's permissions. Note that identity services may have to obtain permissions from a user to supply personal information to requesting services. The interaction service describes protocols and profiles that allow services to carry out such actions. ID-WSF also describes requirements and profiles for securing the discovery and use of identity services.

14.3.4 XACML

XACML (eXtensible Access Control Markup Language) is a powerful technology that is well suited to building authorization systems. XACML defines:

- An XML-based syntax to express authorization policies. This language is based on subject, resource, action and environment characteristics described via generic, application-defined attributes.

- An XML-based syntax to express authorization decision requests and responses, which is aligned with the authorization policy language.

XACML is being developed by an OASIS technical committee (www.oasis-open.org/committees/xacml). Its current specification release (Version 2.0, February 2005) is published as an OASIS standard. The main properties of XACML are:

- XACML authorization policies support conditions that represent rule predicates that are evaluated at runtime. Conditions provide a means of indirection:
  - Condition: $c(S,R,A,E) \rightarrow \{true, false\}$, where S, R, A, and E denote subject, resource, action and environment attributes
  - If true, then rule: $r(S,R,A,E) \rightarrow \{permit, deny\}$

  This is fundamental for implementing relationship-aware authorization. It allows conditional relations to be described between subjects, resources and other relevant attributes, which are evaluated during decision making. This supports, for example, authorization use cases that require:
  - Categorizations of subjects and resources (e.g. *group, role* and *folder, classification*) that are independent of one another
  - Relations between subjects and resources (e.g. *self, owns*)

- Relations between subjects (e.g. delegation models, such as *is-proxy-of* or *secretary-of*, *manager-of*).

• XACML supports obligations that are returned with authorization decisions. Obligations represent agreements between PMAs and PEPs that have to be fulfilled with the enforcement of authorization decisions (e.g. *notify resource owner, needs to be authenticated through SSL/TLS client certificates*).

• XACML supports attribute information that is pushed into PDPs via XACML authorization decision requests as well as pulled by PDPs from other sources, such as attribute authorities, for example information on role assignments, which is fetched from role enablement authorities.

• The XACML policy model allows authorization policies to be structured and supports distributed as well as federated policy management, for example multiple sources for policy information. It is possible to locate policies in distributed environments, to federate administration of policies about the same resource and to synthesize a policy information base from multiple sources. The support for policy synthesis allows privacy scenarios to be addressed where authorization policies are authored by end users to implement consent as well as administrators to address organizational governance. Attribute release policies in Shibboleth (cf. section Shibboleth) as well as recent IETF work on authorization for presence information illustrate this capability.

XACML is a general-purpose authorization technology based on application-defined attributes. It supports federated environments and allows addressing of identity-centric, category-aware and especially relationship-aware authorization scenarios. XACML possesses a flexible authorization model and is especially capable of accommodating the traditional access management concepts such as DAC, MAC, RBAC and ACLs, capability lists. Cf. [LPL03] for further information on XACML.

XACML had a predecessor, XACL, developed by IBM to address the problem of fine-grained authorization for parts of XML documents. This work was brought into OASIS and was superseded by XACML, which is capable of controlling access to parts of XML documents but is not limited to XML-based resources.

The remainder of this section considers the relationship between XACML and SAML, two central technologies for modern access management systems.

XACML and SAML

XACML and SAML are complementary technologies, which both have the capability to express authorization decisions and corresponding requests:

• The XACML context syntax defines a canonical form to express authorization decision requests against XACML-PDPs and their responses.

• SAML expresses authorization decision requests and responses in form of SAML queries and assertions with authorization decision statements.

The two technologies can be integrated in a layered architecture since the design of XACML explicitly supports the accommodation of non-XACML authorization deci-

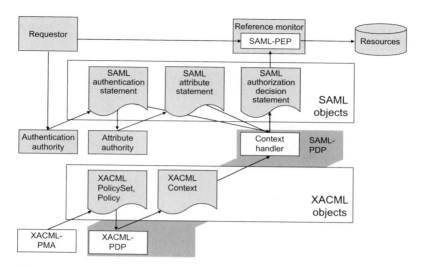

Figure 14.4 Integration of XACML and SAML

sion request and response formats. This integration is illustrated in Figure 14.4 (note that the use of SAML is optional for XACML and vice versa).

XACML also defines a profile for the use of SAML in exchanging XACML policies as well as XACML authorization decision requests and responses. This profile particularly supports PDPs in pulling XACML policies from PMAs. It defines how to map SAML attribute elements when creating XACML authorization decision requests (cf. Figure 14.4).

14.3.5 Web Services Security (WS-Security)

WS-Security defines a framework for Web services (short: WS) security that includes technologies for identity and access management. These technologies are investigated here. Note that WS-Authorization, a specification announced in the WS-Security roadmap, was not released until the time of writing.

WS-Federation

WS-Federation is a technology framework for federation in Web and Web service environments. It comprises:

- The WS-Federation specification that defines mechanisms for the federation of identity, authentication and authorization information across security domains.
- The passive and active requestor profiles that specify the use of WS-Federation mechanisms by Web browsers and SOAP client applications respectively.

WS-Federation and its corresponding profiles are developed by a private initiative of various vendors. It currently does not represent a standardization effort of a public body. The most recent specification release from July 2003 is copyrighted by their authors. Main WS-Federation properties are:

- WS-Federation describes a federation model for Web services together with the related meta-data.
- The passive requestor profile describes how standard Web browsers perform sign-on, attribute exchange and sign-out in federated environments. The protocol exchanges of this profile are based on HTTP. The active requestor profile describes corresponding exchanges for SOAP.

Web-SSO

The Web-SSO meta-data exchange protocol (WSSOMEX) and its corresponding interoperability profile enable SSO between security domains that use Liberty ID-FF and WS-Federation:

- WSSOMEX defines how a service can query an identity provider for meta-data that describes the identity-processing protocol suites supported by that provider.
- The corresponding interoperability profile defines subsets of the SAML Web-SSO profiles, Liberty-Alliance ID-FF and the WS-Federation passive requestor profile that a WSSOMEX-compliant system has to support.

These specifications are developed by a private initiative of Microsoft and Sun Microsystems. They currently do not represent a standardization effort of a public body. The most recent specification release from April 2005 is copyrighted by their authors.

WS-Policy and WS-SecurityPolicy

WS-Policy is an XML-based syntax for describing meta-data about Web services (e.g. service features, security requirements ...). In addition to WS-Policy, WS-SecurityPolicy specifies security-specific artifacts for use in WS-Policy, for example to express requirements on confidentiality. Together with its companion specifications WS-PolicyAssertions and WS-PolicyAttachment, WS-Policy allows service consumers to look-up provider preferences. This can provide among other things a quality-of-protection coordination between service providers and service consumers.

WS-Policy and WS-SecurityPolicy are developed by private initiatives. Their most recent releases from September 2004 and December 2002 are copyrighted by their authors. Note that WS-Policy does not specify authorization policies and thus is complementary to authorization technologies such as XACML:

- WS-Policy is a language for describing service meta-data that allow service providers and consumers to coordinate their preferences.
- XACML is a language for describing authorization information that allows service providers to decide whether to grant requests for resource access from consumers.

WSPL

WSPL (Web Services Policy Language) also describes Web services meta-data for the purpose of coordination between Web service providers and requestors. WSPL supports policy-based quality-of-protection negotiation and represents a profile of the

XACML policy syntax. But WSPL uses a different evaluation model to native XACML:

- WSPL determines the mutually acceptable sets of attributes – given two policies.
- Native XACML determines an authorization decision – given an authorization decision request and authorization policy.

WSPL is currently a working draft of the OASIS technical committee on XACML. It is a competitor of WS-Policy. Cf. [And04] for more information on WSPL.

14.3.6 SPML

SPML (Service Provisioning Markup Language) provides an XML-based technology and Web service for provisioning services, which it defines as: "the automation of all the steps required to manage (setup, amend & revoke) user or system access entitlements or data relative to electronically published services". SPML defines (cf. Figure 14.5):

- A provisioning domain model consisting of RAs (Requesting Authorities), which issue SPML requests to service points, PSPs (Provisioning Service Points), which listen for, process and return the results for SPML requests, and PSTs (Provisioning Service Targets) which are the endpoints for provisioning actions (cf. Figure 14.5). Examples of PSTs are directories, databases, NT domains, individual machines, applications or groups of applications.
- An operational model of clients performing protocol operations against servers through the exchange of SPML documents. RAs act as clients with PSPs as servers and PSPs in turn can act as clients with PSTs or other PSPs as servers. Note that a PST operates as a full service point responsible for a single service or resource, the target system itself.
- SPML provisioning schemas as a standardized and reusable way of describing, in an XML-based syntax, the attributes involved in the exchanges between clients and servers as well as the corresponding SPML protocol to request and receive a target schema.

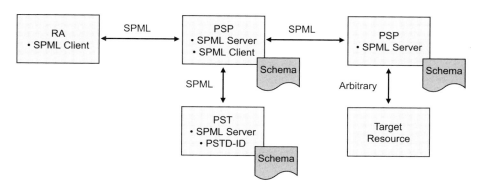

Figure 14.5 SPML provisioning model

- XML-based syntax to describe the provisioning operations against a provisioning schema at a service point. They comprise simple mandatory requests and responses to add, modify, delete and search objects and extended ones that allow for schema exchange and asynchronous batch requests (getSchema, batch, status, cancel).

- SOAP-over-HTTP protocol binding, including the corresponding WSDL (Web Service Definition Language) document, which describes the SPML service as a Web service as well as file binding for SPML requests and responses.

SPML is being developed by an OASIS technical committee (www.oasis-open.org/committees/provision). Its current specification release (Version 1.0, October 2003) is published as an OASIS standard. At the time of writing this, the OASIS provisioning committee is working on a revised and expanded SPML version 2, which is planned to become standard at the end of 2005.

The main properties of SPML are:

- SPML provisioning schemas use an object class definition and attribute sharing model that is based on the X.500 object model. Moreover, SPML follows an open-content approach allowing applications to extend XML elements defined by SPML.

- The service point is responsible for publishing the services it supports, both simple and extended, and performing the client-requested actions. A PSP may use non-SPML communication to interact with actual provisioning targets (e.g. JDBC to a database, LDAP to a directory, etc.).

- Target systems maintain a PSTD-ID (Provisioning Service Target Data Identifier), a unique identifier for the data on a PST (e.g. the UID on UNIX/Linux server or a distinguished name for a directory).

- SPML requests can be singleton or batch (multi-requests) and both can be executed synchronously or asynchronously based on the client and server capabilities. In the asynchronous case, the server has to support status-request and cancel-request operations. Batch requests can be executed sequentially or in parallel upon request.

SPML does not have any normative security defined even if security plays a crucial role in provisioning systems: SPML services will themselves be a subject for access management since administration of assets via SPML will demand an adequate authentication and authorization of requestors. The SOAP-over-HTTP binding describes some methods to achieve message authentication and confidentiality.

As an open protocol, which does not impose any restriction on the implementation of the provisioning system or any unnecessarily hard constraints for conformance, SPML has the potential for wide adoption. This in turn will foster the development of a large variety of new, provisioning-enabled applications which among others may:

- Push identity information from the application to a target, for example a metadirectory.

- Supply keying information to relying parties in authentication and SSO services.

- Provide authorization policy information from a PMA to a policy repository or a PDP and to manage it as part of an authorization service.

SPML reuses another XML-based identity management standard, DSML (Directory Services Markup Language) by including its name space and schema. The remainder of this section considers the relationship between SPML and DSML.

SPML and DSML

DSML specifies an XML language for querying and modifying directory contents and for representing structural content. DSML was developed by an OASIS technical committee (www.oasis-open.org/committees/dsml) and is published as OASIS standard (Version 2.0, April 2002).

DSMLv2 specifies directory operations and basically translates the ASN.1 grammar of LDAP into an XML schema. It focuses on extending the reach of LDAP directories to XML environments, for example to applications that might not want to use the full LDAP stack. DSMLv2 defines two normative bindings: a SOAP request/response binding and a file binding that serves as the DSMLv2 analog of LDIF.

DSML is a good candidate to implement a powerful PST for LDAP directories, since it exposes the full directory functionality including schema access and management and can be easily blended into the SPML framework.

14.3.7 Further Initiatives

Various other initiatives are involved in the development of emerging technologies for identity and access management. These include:

- Grid computing aims at enabling the coordinated sharing of distributed resources owned by various organizations. This especially mandates advanced authorization services. Authorization in Grid computing is based on identity federation and the concept of virtual organizations. Various projects develop authentication and authorization solutions for Grid computing, which employ the emerging technologies that were considered before. This includes research projects, such as Akenti, Cardea, CAS, GridShib, PERMIS, and PRIMA. Corresponding technology development usually proceeds in the context of the Globus toolkit for Grid computing (www.globus.org) and OGSA (Open Grid Services Architecture), a service-oriented baseline architecture for Grid computing developed by the Global Grid Forum (www.ggf.org). Cf. [Sie03] and [WSF03] for further information on GRID security.

- EPAL (Enterprise Privacy Authorization Language) is a private initiative by IBM that was contributed to the W3C as a member submission and is published as a W3C note. EPAL specifies an authorization policy language with a focus on privacy services. As an authorization technology, EPAL essentially provides a subset of XACML functionality (cf. [And05]).

- OATH (Open AuTHentication) describes a framework for authentication. This framework represents an umbrella for authentication services focusing on the accommodation of existing authentication mechanisms, protocols and infrastructure. It is developed by an industry consortium (www.openauthentication.org).

• Rights markup languages, such as XrML (eXtensible rights Markup Language, cf. www.xrml.org) and ODRL (Open Digital Rights Language, cf. www.odrl.net) facilitate the binding of rights meta-data with actual resource contents. These DRM technologies are complementary to authorization technologies, such as XACML, since they aim to control the usage of a dedicated resource on a local system rather than to control access to a variety of resources offered on a networked server.

14.4 Applications and Examples

This section discusses enterprise scenarios employing traditional and emerging technologies. They illustrate the IAM reference model presented in Section 14.1.3.

14.4.1 Provisioning Windows Domain Accounts

This first example examines the provisioning of user accounts in Windows domains and their use in accessing Web resources through IIS (Figure 14.6).

This scenario is based on an authoritative source of identity information that resides outside the Windows domain (e.g. a human resource data base). It uses provisioning

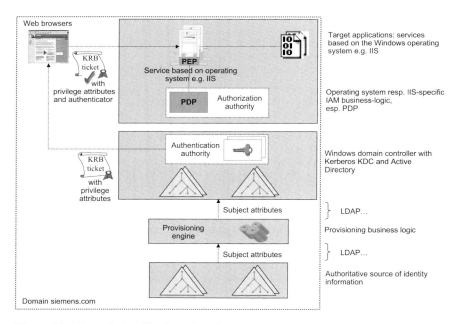

Figure 14.6 Provisioning Windows domain accounts

business logic and technology to establish user accounts in the Active Directory of a Windows domain based on information from the authoritative source. Authentication and authorization are performed through native Windows means:

- The provisioned accounts are used through a Kerberos-based Windows domain logon (cf. Section 14.2.4). The Kerberos KDC issues tickets with a PAC. Together with a Kerberos authenticator, that represents confirmation data for the ticket, it is presented to a target service. In case of Web resources served by IIS, this is performed through Kerberos-in-HTTP (Negotiate / SPNEGO, cf. RFC 2478).

- IIS natively allows the enforcing of IP address restrictions as well as so-called Web site permissions. The IIS Web site permissions allow administrators to define read-only or execute-only access for virtual directories. For this authorization service, PEP and PDP are provided by the IIS.

- Since Version 6.0, IIS supports URL-based authorization through the Windows authorization manager (see Section 14.2.5). Here, the PEP is provided by the url-auth.dll plug-in to IIS with the PDP provided by the Windows authorization manager runtime.

- For static resources served through IIS, IIS also supports file-oriented authorization through the native Windows operating system mechanisms (cf. Section 14.2.5). In this case, PEP and PDP reside in the Windows operating system. Note that this only applies to users with a valid Windows account.

For authorization purposes, this example is restricted to resources that are served by native Windows services or by services that employ the native authentication and authorization mechanisms of Windows. The following scenario addresses identity and access management in heterogeneous IT environments.

14.4.2 Web-SSO and Authorization

This Web-SSO and authorization scenario (Figure 14.7) considers a heterogeneous IT environment with Web and application servers from various vendors, static and dynamic Web resources as well as HTTP and SOAP-based resource accesses in a single security domain. The architecture considered illustrates the fundamental role of declarative access policies and policy engines as central elements of modern policy-based authorization systems.

The location of the PEPs depends on the resources served and the required granularity of authorization:

- For Web servers serving static resources, PEPs are realized as Web server plug-ins.

- In case of Web applications providing dynamic resources or application servers hosting business logic services, PEPs may be integrated as plug-ins in the underlying container (Web or application server) or with the business logic of the application.

PEPs interact with the IAM business logic that accommodates an online authentication authority and a PDP. We consider XACML for authorization in this scenario:

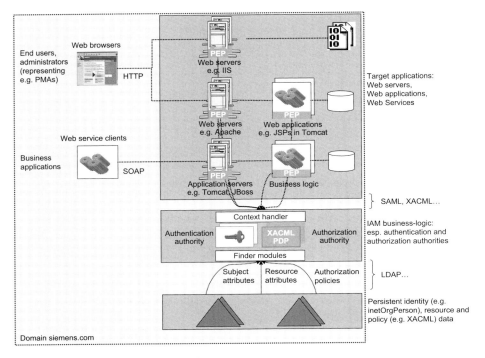

Figure 14.7 Web-SSO and authorization

- XACML supports the integration of various authorization decision formats through a context handler (cf. Figure 14.4 for an illustration with respect to SAML).
- XACML can manage the required authentication via obligations. In classical Web environments, this is enforced through PEPs by requesting a specific authentication protocol via HTTP error responses or redirects. In Web services environments, PEPs may employ negotiation frameworks, for example WS-Policy or WSPL.

The corresponding authentication protocol takes place between the client (Web browser or SOAP client) and server (Web or application server). In the case of successful initial authentication, the authentication authority is responsible for issuing authentication statements that are used for subsequent authentication. Note that the authentication part of the Windows provisioning scenario may be integrated with the considered scenario. This externalizes the authorization from Windows while retaining the authentication features of Windows domains.

The transfer of short-lived authentication statements (or references to them) by means such as HTTP cookie headers provides SSO to the Web servers in the domain. If authentication statements are exchanged within a single domain, the contents, format and security model of the authentication statements are at the discretion of this domain. They may employ SAML for instance. Authentication statements should carry meta-data on the initial authentication to facilitate authorization decisions based on the method of initial authentication. They may also carry subject attributes, such as group memberships, or role assignments that are used by authorization or personalization services. Web service clients can be handled in a similar way as Web clients, since the SOAP security extensions allow authentication statements to travel in SOAP headers.

XACML supports identity-centric, category and relationship-aware authorization models. The deployment of an adequate model is at the discretion of the application that implements authorization services. With respect to this integration, a distinction needs to be made between the strategy of integrating PEPs with the underlying container (Web or application server) or with the business logic of the application:

- The integration with the underlying container can be addressed through off-the-shelf PEP plug-ins for mainstream Web and application servers. It allows the actual business logic of the application to remain authorization-unaware. Note that this strategy may process URLs (including the application-specific query part) but has limitations with respect to processing application-specific semantics. (e.g. query parameters in the URL, which refer to supplementary information that is not included in the URL but is relevant for authorization decisions).

- The integration with application business logic requires the application to be authorization-aware. Note that off-the-shelf support for this strategy is limited to PEP development toolkits.

This example is limited to a single security domain. The next scenario deals with identity federation between security domains.

14.4.3 Identity Federation

The identity federation scenario (Figure 14.8) considers distributed authorization based on identity federation with the identity provider and the resource provider residing in different security domains. It focuses on cross-domain SSO and identity mappings. Note that the identity federation scenario may be combined with the Web-SSO and authorization scenario to address SSO and authorization in each of the federated domains.

This scenario can be implemented by federation protocols, such as the SAML Web-SSO profiles, Shibboleth, Liberty Alliance ID-FF or WS-Federation passive requestor profile. It uses federation protocol endpoints residing in the identity and resource provider domains:

- The outbound authentication endpoint in the identity provider domain is responsible for issuing authentication statements (e.g. SAML assertions) for consumption by foreign domains. Depending on the federation protocol used, it may support authentication statement lookup by artifact or attribute pull from resource provider domains. The federation business logic and corresponding finder modules provide identity mapping and attribute exchange through pull or push. In order to support SSO as well as authorization locally in the identity provider domain, the outbound authentication endpoint may include a PEP (not shown; cf. Figure 14.7 for an illustration) integrated with the local IAM business logic.

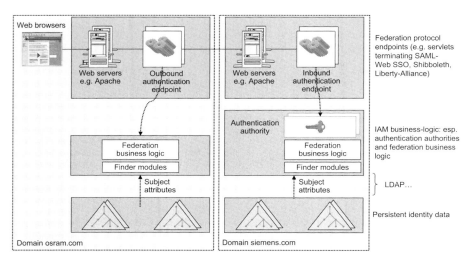

Figure 14.8 Identity federation

- The inbound authentication endpoint in the resource provider domain is responsible for processing authentication statements obtained from foreign domains. In order to support SSO locally in the resource provider domain, the inbound authentication endpoint may also comprise a PEP (not shown; cf. Figure 14.7 for an illustration) to obtain an authentication statement for the resource provider domain. The inbound authentication endpoint usually redirects the browser to the actually requested resource. Note that authorization is regarded as an optional feature for an inbound authentication endpoint since resource access authorization typically needs to be enforced on the Web or application servers serving the requested resource. This requires the authorization system to be capable of supporting relationship-aware services in order to address federation use cases (e.g. *Resource must be assigned to company A, B, etc. to allow access for a company A, B, etc. manager*).

The following strategies of identity mapping need to be distinguished in identity federation:

- Injective: different subject identities in the identity provider domain correspond to different subject identities in the resource provider domain. This can be achieved by mapping external identity information via local user accounts in the resource provider domain or by directly processing the external identity information:
  - Account-based injective identity mapping relies on user accounts that exist a priori. As a mapping mechanism, it may employ alternative subject identifiers maintained as subject attributes in the destination repository. This identity mapping strategy is supported by SAML Web-SSO. The Liberty-Alliance ID-FF specification is based on this strategy.
  - Account-less injective identity mapping does not require users from external domains to have entries in a user repository of the resource provider. It requires

the authentication and authorization services of the resource provider to directly accommodate the information supplied by the external identity provider. The identity mapping strategy is also supported by SAML Web-SSO. The Shibboleth specification is based on this strategy.

- Non-injective: multiple subject identities in the identity provider domain (e.g. *john.doe@siemens.com ...*) correspond to a virtual subject in the resource provider domain (e.g. *siemens.com employee from sales*). Via abstraction, non-injective mappings may be deployed on the basis of federation protocols that support injective mappings. Corresponding virtual subjects in the destination may or may not reside in the form of user accounts in the destination repository. Note that a non-injective mapping based on user accounts in the destination domain will use non-individual accounts.

Identity mappings are also encountered in traditional authentication technologies, such as Kerberos or PKI-based authentication. They typically require identity mappings when they are used to assert authenticated user identity between security domains. The corresponding mappings are usually injective and require user accounts to exist a priori in the resource provider domain (e.g. mapping users from PKI domains to Windows domains via alternative security identifiers in the Active Directory, cf. Section 14.2.5).

14.5 Conclusion

Identity and access management services are critical components across enterprise IT systems. They provide a common enabling infrastructure for the enterprise applications. A wealth of identity and access management technologies have emerged and various bodies have developed standards for them.

Section 14.2 examined the most important traditional technologies in identity and access management. These technologies mainly address intra-enterprise scenarios, i.e. distributed systems within an enterprise.

Significant innovation is currently taking place in the area of XML and Web services technologies. This concerns identity and access management in particular. Section 14.3 analyzed the most relevant emerging technologies in identity and access management. The emerging technologies mainly address inter-enterprise scenarios, i.e. loosely-coupled, distributed systems in federated environments. To a large extent, the emerging identity and access management technologies complement the traditional ones. They should be regarded as an extension of the traditional technologies rather than a replacement.

15 Information Security Management Systems

Steve O'Reilly

This section describes strategies and methods for establishing and maintaining information security management systems, together with specific guidance on third party assurance.

Protecting business-critical or sensitive information is vital for any organization, whether sole trader, SME or large corporation. Effective information security embraces much more than technical know-how; so this chapter is not a 'technical' document. It provides practical, business-oriented guidance and reference material aimed at the business professional with a need to protect the confidentiality, integrity and availability of information, as well as those charged with planning, developing and implementing information security management systems (ISMS).

The guidance draws on practical experience of implementing ISO/IEC 17799, The Code of Practice for Information Security Management [ISO17799], in both the public and private sectors. It is fully consistent with the Standard, which is rapidly being adopted by businesses around the globe as they recognize the need to demonstrate effective protection of their own and customers' information.

15.1 The Need for and Relevance of Information Security

15.1.1 Introduction

Information exists in many formats; in paper-based records, on mobile phones, on film, as well as in IT systems, on electronic storage devices, disks and tapes. Information security has evolved therefore as a discipline comprising a broad range of concepts, designed to protect an organization's information assets. In addition to technical controls related to IT, it also encompasses many supporting subjects such as personnel security, physical and environmental security, third party contracts and business continuity management.

The purpose of Information Security is to preserve the confidentiality, integrity and availability of an organization's information assets. Compromise of one or more of these attributes could threaten the reputation or perhaps the continued existence of even the largest corporate entities and may be a breach of statutory or regulatory obligations.

A risk assessment and proper classification of an information asset will determine its sensitivity and result in the implementation of appropriate safeguards to ensure its confidentiality, integrity and availability. Security of information will then be achieved by implementing a suitable set of controls. These could be technical, procedural, defined by policy or personnel related. An effective security strategy will comprise a combination of these.

15.1.2 Business Drivers for Information Security

There are many parallel and overlapping business drivers for achieving compliance with best practice and demonstrating information security or 'assurance'. Confidentiality, integrity and availability of information are today of the utmost importance, both from a service delivery and regulatory perspective.

Operational Risk

Operational risk (financial or otherwise) can occur due to failings of information systems, business processes or internal controls. This might be faulty software, incorrect data entry, natural disasters or failure to react to and meet regulatory changes. Whilst operational risk clearly encompasses the provision and use of IT, it implicitly covers perhaps every other manifestation of risk, including risks to the security of information itself. Assessing risks to information assets is therefore vitally important in demonstrating compliance with best practice.

Companies need to have a clear understanding of the meaning of risk and this needs to be defined and communicated effectively. A 'system of control' should be evidence of a commitment to ensuring that staff across the organization understand and can manage risk in their areas, to exploit the benefits of new technology. This is reliant on having an organizational structure that will facilitate the management of all operational risks.

Corporate Governance, Legal and Regulatory Requirements

Information security is often treated solely as a technology issue, when it should be viewed as a corporate issue and a governance challenge. Businesses today face increased scrutiny when it comes to corporate governance, accountability and ethics. In the fast-changing regulatory environment, information security is now seen as a fundamental part of managing operational risk, in support of effective corporate governance.

Firms now have to react quickly to ensure that their information processes comply with the myriad regulatory requirements, paying particular attention to auditing processes. An efficient and cost-effective way to meet these obligations will be through the establishment of efficient information security management systems (ISMS, see below), as failure to be pro-active may leave businesses prone to severe financial penalties.

In addition, legislative and regulatory requirements demand that directors and senior managers now need to be aware that they are responsible and accountable for risks to the security of information in every part of the business and that managing information risks does not fall squarely to the IT managers. It is important to note that compliance with a standard does not of itself confer immunity from legal or regulatory obligations; however, there are distinct advantages.

Security as a Business Differentiator

A trusted and secured operational environment can become an important competitive metric in demonstrating to clients and trading partners, through the process of regular audit, that the security régime meets an industry-recognized standard of best practice.

Many organizations still equate information security with IT security. Significantly, some companies still do not have a fully documented and formal information security policy, and where it does exist, it often is owned by the IT department, addressing largely IT issues alone.

Recent experience shows that both the investment community and regulatory authorities do not see information security as merely an IT problem and regard the lack of governance as a significant commercial risk. Information security violations can now be one of the most important factors that impact an evaluation of a company and information security governance is now a significant criterion when deciding whether to buy or sell company shares.

Reduce Incident Recovery Costs

No matter how thoroughly an organization tries to safeguard its people and operations, there will always be disruptive events outside its control; from power blackouts, severe weather, fires, floods and terrorism to systems malfunctions and incorrect data entry. In order to remain competitive, businesses need to react in an effective manner, applying consistent and appropriate measures, in order to streamline responsiveness and cut costs. An effective ISMS will provide the structure and capability to manage incidents of any magnitude and to manage and reduce incident recovery costs.

Improved Efficiency of Business Operations

When properly designed and implemented, information assurance efforts can not only increase security, but also can even improve the efficiency of operational processes and the achievement of business objectives. Improving process efficiency, reducing losses, improved customer confidence, increased employee participation are all benefits of successfully implemented information assurance programs.

Customer Assurance

Over the past years, with the increasing implementation of web-based, public-facing applications, there has been any number of embarrassing breaches across different market sectors. Many companies have launched a range of Internet based services, confident that websites and the supporting Internet technology are secure, however, public perception of this type of transaction is often that use of the Internet is inherently insecure. In order to demonstrate their confidence to customers, many organizations have achieved independent certification to ISMS standards, such as BS 7799 [BS7799b].

Compliance with or indeed certification to such standards has given customers the assurance that they can use Internet based services without fear of potentially sensitive information being intercepted, changed or accessed in any way by other, unauthorized Internet users. Therefore, ISMS certification is becoming an important strategic target for companies offering such high technology services.

Third Party Trading Requirements

Great care must be taken when selecting a service provider. Their own information security practices should be above reproach and operated in a secure and trusted manner. In addition, these practices should be regularly audited against a recognized 'best practice' standard such as ISO/IEC 17799 (see Section 15.5).

15.1.3 Business Issues

In general, security incidents have two costs: Direct cost related to the effort required to restore a system and indirect costs related to the interim loss of service. Security therefore should be viewed as a business 'enabler' rather than a costly overhead.

More and more companies are beginning to look at the business case for information security, considering the return on investment they might earn and the advantages it might bring. As discussed earlier, security can be a business differentiator. For example, if you were interested in online banking and one of the two banks you were considering had a security breach, which would you be more likely to choose?

Increased regulation will also influence the 'security spend'. For example, the new Basel II Capital Accord [Bas04] encourages banks, through improved risk management (including information security controls), to reduce minimum capital requirements – the corollary being increased funds available for cash flow and investment.

Demonstrating conformance to best practice should bring its own benefits. An example being the approach of insurance risk managers who now look for lower and discounted rates based on the robustness of business continuity planning within their organizations; thus recognizing that security spending needs to be balanced against the benefits in protecting data and the supporting technology.

15.2 Focussing on Security Critical Business Processes

Managing risk has always been both an explicit and implicit fundamental management process, especially in the financial services sector. Today, however there is ever more pressure to avoid things going wrong whilst continuing to improve corporate performance in the new environment.

Growing reliance on technology, outsourcing, online services and complex financial products have all conspired to introduce an environment in the increasingly regulated financial sector which is encountering mounting demands to satisfy the authorities that operational risks are being managed effectively.

In most business environments operational risk manifests itself in the usual background of technical and IT systems' problems, regulatory variations, market changes and demands. The dependence on information systems and networks means that organizations are more vulnerable to security threats; the interconnecting of public and private networks and the need to share information has increased levels of risk whilst weakening central control.

It is important therefore to clarify where good security is most needed and to qualify (and quantify where possible) the level of assurance required.

15.2.1 Setting a Management System Scope

It is important to understanding the real business objectives for security, to ensure that improvement activities are focused in areas that will maximize the benefit to the enterprise in the most cost efficient manner. It is the identification of these business objectives which dictate the scope of the *Information Security Management System* (ISMS). Incorrect or ill-defined scope is a common area of difficulty in achieving compliance and establishing and maintaining effective security.

There are many different objectives that drive a business to improve security:

- Satisfy/impress customers
- Improve security, through effective risk management (operational risk, corporate governance)
- Satisfy trading partners, particularly for eCommerce
- Fear of legal action
- Business efficiency gains
- Industry peer pressure
- Government initiative

In UK government circles, e.g., the objective has been to provide both internal and external assurance in information processing and this is reflected in the following statement of scope:

- The ISMS supporting the Provision of IT and networking services to all business functions within the Department.

In the commercial sector however the focus has been on satisfying trading partners and regulators and gaining a marketing advantage. This is reflected in the following statement of scope:

- The ISMS supporting the Provision of Internet Access, to enable customers to conduct banking remotely.

The scope of an ISMS can be defined in terms of the organization as a whole, or parts of the organization, covering all relevant assets, systems, applications, networks and other information processing technology employed to process, store or communicate information. There are five key elements that need to be documented and that comprise 'scope' in this context:

People, working in a *Location*, using *Information*, supported by *Technology*, to carry out one or more *Business Processes*.

In addition, there are a number of important internal third parties upon which the effective security management of the business process is dependent. These (discussed further in section five below) include, but are not limited to:

- Personnel, for staff recruitment, vetting, disciplinary and other related aspects;
- Facilities, for building/site security.

15.2.2 Scoping and Security Assurance Strategies

Compliance with ISO/IEC 27001 [ISO27001] or BS 7799 Part 2 [BS7799b] involves establishing an ISMS to support a specified part of an organization focusing on critical business processes (the 'Scope'), and then making any necessary security improvements within this scope to comply with the standard.

The most cost effective way in which to implement ISO/IEC 27001 for an organization in a controlled manner is to develop an initial ISMS, supporting a well defined set of key business processes and to progress towards compliance in this area first. It is more practicable to start with those areas which are considered to be the most crucial. Following this, the scope can be extended to cover other business functions. Small organizations can realistically aim to have a single ISMS supporting the entire organization, but a staged approach is still recommended in order to realize this objective.

Under normal circumstances, it is not recommended that the scope of an ISMS is limited to specific sites, locations or departments, or even sections, in their entirety but instead should reflect the provision of a corporate function to defined business processes or functions. For instance, it may transpire that parts of an organization perform hundreds of business processes and that gaining compliance for those considered least important may be time-consuming and costly and perhaps derive little in the way of business benefit. Caution should be exercised before attempting to gain corporate-wide or departmental-wide compliance in one pass.

Experience has shown that limiting the scope in the way described is a valuable exercise, since following compliance or certification being gained for a specific process, lessons learned can be used to apply a similar approach to other elements of the organization.

Similarly, whilst having gained compliance for the provision of a corporate function such as IT to a nominated section or sections, it is often found that a great deal of benefit is derived by all other sections also supported by IT. This is because a significant amount of the work has already been completed during the initial stage (for example, in terms of Information Security Policy, Security Organization, Personnel Security,

Physical Security, Network and Systems Access Controls, etc. as presumably these are consistently applied across all business areas).

Some companies have sought ISMS certification for critical business processes whilst the remainder of the organization benchmark their security related activities against the certified compliant ISMS. This has helped to reduce certification costs whilst ensuring enterprise-wide consistency in the application of security controls.

The following questions provide a good test of whether the chosen scope will provide the required business benefits:

- Does the scope reflect business objectives?
- Is an initial scope a sensible proposition?
- Is the scope boundary clearly defined?
- Will the existing management structure support this ISMS?
- Are all interfaces understood?
- Are third parties known (internal/external)?

15.3 Establishing an Effective Information Security Structure and Culture

15.3.1 Management System Development

It is vital to have senior management participation in the development and maintenance of the ISMS, underpinning the 'Plan' and 'Do' in the PDCA model illustrated in Figure 15.1. There should be a senior management security representative (preferable at board level) acting as a 'champion'. It is important that the senior management demonstrates commitment and leadership, setting the direction and then providing support, budget and resources to ensure that all concerned understand that information security is a critical business issue which affects the long term success and survival of the company.

Whether an SME or large corporation, it is recommended that senior management teams:

- Recognize that drawing up an information security policy is now effectively a legal requirement, as well as being sound practice in protecting the organization's information assets and its position in the event of a security incident.
- Commission a suitable group (which could be drawn from the group also responsible for the information strategy, perhaps augmented in technical expertise) to undertake this task.
- Promote and support the security policy, once agreed, at the highest level.

The key to establishing an information security culture in an organization is in the creation of an ISMS. ISO/IEC 27001 illustrates this process using the 'Plan-Do-Check-

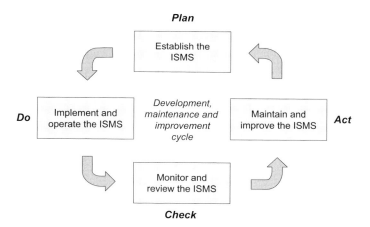

Figure 15.1 The PDCA model

Act' model (see Figure 15.1). To demonstrate ongoing compliance with ISO/IEC 27001 it is necessary for an ISMS to be operating effectively and to be properly managed.

Ideally, an ISMS should be established as soon as possible. Aspects of the management system that are absent or deficient would be identified during a *Gap Analysis* exercise (see below). In addition, the output from a risk assessment (also described below) provides further guidance on the implementation of the ISMS. For additional information see also Chapter 2.

15.3.2 Information Security Assessment and Improvement

Conducting a *Gap Analysis* is an effective way of assessing the current state of the 'health' of information security within an organization. It provides an assessment, at a high level, of the status of security (and ideally should be against the controls in ISO/IEC 27001, Annex A).

A Gap Analysis is an information gathering activity covering many aspects of the business including IT operations, facilities, business continuity and personnel. It is essential that the correct individuals are identified for this exercise, i.e. those that can speak with authority about the areas in question. Likely interviewees would include security staff, facilities and HR managers, business managers and IT operations staff.

It is also of great importance that the right questions are asked, in order to get an accurate picture of the organization's status. A good rule of thumb is to use the RIDE acronym – asking four simple questions in relation to each control:

R – Is responsibility for the control clear?

I – Is the control implemented fully and appropriately?

D – Is there appropriate documentation that would satisfy an auditor?

E – Is there evidence of effective implementation that would satisfy an auditor?

Once the analysis has been completed, an organization has a much clearer idea of both weak and strong areas of security. From this a report can be developed that details not only the findings but also the interpretation and analysis of the findings, resulting in a set of broad recommendations for security improvement.

Once agreed with all parties, a plan of discrete actions can be documented (a *Security Improvement Programme* – SIP), which will describe what needs to be achieved to reach a level of compliance with best practice. This plan should assign priorities and responsibilities and estimate the effort involved in implementation.

15.3.3 The Information Asset Register

In order to identify which information requires to be protected, an organization should prepare an *Information Asset Register* (IAR). This register does not need to itemize every individual document or data types, but instead should identify the broad categories of information that support the organization's business processes.

The IAR should detail the format of the information (Word, Excel, hard copy, electronically stored), the owner and its location (on the system, in removable media, secured in a fireproof safe, etc.) and any interim protective marking (i.e. 'Management in Confidence', 'Staff in Confidence', 'Restricted', etc.).

The IAR provides significant input into the risk assessment as the value of the information assets will assist in determining the controls to be implemented and the final requirements for ensuring confidentiality, integrity and availability.

15.3.4 Selecting Risk Justified Controls

Assessing risks to information assets is crucially important in demonstrating compliance to regulators. Best practice in managing information risks dictates that organizations should assess risks to their data and supporting infrastructure and identify the objectives and underpinning controls which are most appropriate to their needs. The objective of this exercise is to ensure a balanced approach to security and to establish where existing security controls may need to be improved, or to justify decisions to exclude certain controls. For example, a secure information processing product being used in an open office environment may provide a similar level of security as an unprotected personal computer locked in an office with restricted personnel access.

The risk assessment must demonstrate to third parties, such as auditors, how the company's assets have been valued and how the perceived threats and any identified vulnerabilities to those threats, have been considered in a methodical manner.

Both the Gap Analysis and Risk Assessment exercises may be undertaken using either a tools-based or paper-based approach. This decision depends on the:

- Nature of the business process being assessed
- Number of separate business functions
- Complexity of those functions
- Dependence on other complex processes.

Consistency in applying information protection controls across the organization will also provide internal as well as external assurance in exchanging and storing data and assistance in ensuring compliance with statutory and regulatory obligations.

Assessing and managing risk is also a mandatory aspect of compliance with ISO/IEC 27001. Based on a business impact assessment, the likelihood of threats and the level of vulnerability to threats, an organization must measure how significant a risk is in terms of its likelihood and its consequences. Countermeasures mapped to the controls within ISO/IEC 27001 can then be determined to manage these risks. ISO/IEC 27001 emphasizes the need to manage risks (i.e. both assess and treat them) on an ongoing basis as circumstances change. The risk assessment provides a level of detail not found in the Gap Analysis.

15.3.5 Implementing Controls

There are a number of different ways that risks can be managed or 'treated' in accordance with their severity:

- Transferring some or all aspects of the risk – insurance or outsourcing (note that reputation risk cannot be transferred).
- Avoiding the risk – by doing things differently and thus removing the risk where it is feasible to do so.
- Accepting the risk – perhaps because nothing can be done at a reasonable cost to mitigate it. In this instance the decision will have to be explained to auditors. The risk must be monitored to ensure that the level of risk remains tolerable.
- Treating the risk:
  - Implementing risk reduction – actions which lessen the likelihood of the risk or the consequences and applied *before* the risk materializes.
  - Contingent actions – reducing the impact of the risk *after* the risk materializes.

The risk assessment will confirm the controls that need to be implemented, and these will be included in the *Security Improvement Plan* (SIP). Once the SIP has been finalized, a project plan can be determined including an approximate date for achieving compliance.

15.3.6 Security Documentation

There are three distinct categories of documentation associated with a fully compliant ISMS, containing various categories of information, each with different purposes, characteristics, audiences, classifications and sensitivities:

- Process documentation
  This consists of policies, procedures and standards that describe and support business processes. These documents detail what is done, how it is done, when it is done, by whom and to what standard or specification. This documentation will exist at a corporate, group and local level.

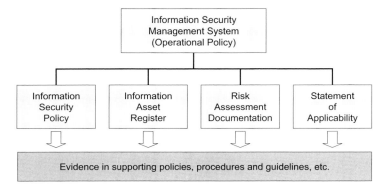

Figure 15.2 Information security management system

- Evidential documentation
  This is documentation that provides evidence that the business processes are operating according to specification and best practice. It would include management documentation, contracts and system logs. Such documentation should be controlled using standard records management procedures such as for version and change control, retention and disposal.
- ISMS documentation (mandatory for ISO/IEC 27001) comprising:
  - A Statement of Applicability, describing how best practice has been adopted
  - Risk management documentation, describing the analysis and treatment of risks
  - An Information Security Policy (see below)
  - The Information Asset Register
  - An ISMS Operational Policy (see below).

The control of all three types of documentation is specified as required within the standard ISO/IEC 27001. Compliance with the ISO 9000 series of standards is one way of raising assurance that documentation is being managed effectively (cf. Figure 15.2).

15.3.7 Security Roles and Responsibilities

Responsibility for security management in most organizations falls across a number of different areas of the business – physical security, personnel security, environmental issues relating to server rooms, compliance with regulation and legislation, etc. The role of *Information Security Manager* is of the utmost importance and includes responsibility for security co-ordination, attendance at the *Security Forum* (see below) and managing the ISMS documentation.

In addition, there should be nominated individuals responsible for physical security, personnel security issues (such as recruitment), data protection compliance and IT security as well as staff who can provide specialist advice, for example on legal issues.

From a practitioner perspective, all compliance activities should probably be concentrated under one department, with links into every business area through local representation. Ideally, information security should be part of annual performance plans with specific requirements for all levels of staff and management.

15.3.8 Information Security Management Forum

The overall responsibility for the ISMS will rest with the *Information Security Management Forum* (ISMF). This should be established as early as possible with representatives from across the enterprise, including:

- Staff with direct information security responsibilities;
- A senior manager
- A representative from the business
- A representative from HR
- A representative from facilities
- A representative from IT operations.

During the development of the ISMS the Forum would be responsible for managing the Security Improvement Programme, creating a security management baseline, establishing key mechanisms such as incident reporting, awareness training etc. Importantly, the Forum should monitor accepted risks and maintain the 'Risk Acceptance Register or 'Risk Log' (see below).

15.4 Maintaining Effective Security

15.4.1 ISMS Maintenance

Corporate Governance compliance should not necessarily be viewed as a project in its own right or an end in itself but rather it is an iterative process, reacting to ever changing risks in the business environment. Similarly compliance with an ISMS standard is an ongoing process.

Once an ISMS has been successfully established (the 'plan' and 'do' in the PDCA model) it then has to be successfully maintained. This is achieved through monitoring and reviewing the ISMS (the 'check' in the model) and improving the ISMS (the 'act' in the model). An organization is required to demonstrate that it is dealing proactively with potential security weaknesses as well as responding reactively to incidents and audit findings.

15.4.2 Raising Security Awareness

This is a fundamental aspect in the effective management of information security and can be a difficult objective to achieve, particularly where large numbers of employees are involved.

A useful starting point for awareness is the corporate Information Security Policy. This should be a brief, high level policy which defines security, staff responsibilities and the importance of security to the organization as a whole. It should also identify security staff. It can refer to more detailed security-related policies such as for the use of e-mail and the Internet, remote working and so on.

If appropriate, organizations can require all staff to sign the policy to raise assurance that they are familiar with its contents and agree to adhere to them.

An effective way to ensure an appropriate level of staff understanding of the importance of security and how it is addressed within the organization is to ensure information security is included during induction of new staff. As a minimum, staff should be made aware of the Information Security Policy, where to find further information on security, such as via an intranet, and key security contacts.

It is also important that existing staff are aware of security, particularly if changes to policies are made. Ongoing awareness can be maintained in a number of ways including formal training sessions, articles in newsletters, poster campaigns, computer based training modules and via a corporate intranet.

15.4.3 Security Incident Reporting and Management

Organizations need to demonstrate that they are constantly improving security controls by reacting to events. Incident reporting therefore becomes an important mechanism. Many organizations will already have an IT helpdesk and someone to whom physical security incidents can be reported. ISO/IEC 27001 requires that the Security Forum has visibility of all kinds of incidents, defined as anything which can directly or indirectly affect the availability, confidentiality or integrity of information. This would include instances of unauthorized access, IT failures, software bugs, thefts of equipment and environmental damage to the IT infrastructure from fire or water.

It is especially important to monitor the trend of incidents and react accordingly. If there is an increase in the number of damaging viruses found on the network, then a stronger technical solution may be required or as a baseline measure, a procedural change to how the system is monitored in the interim.

15.4.4 Security Assurance Mechanisms

What has become apparent through the kind of disasters, calamities and misfortunes that we all know about is that the traditional audit model is possibly inadequate. Inconsistent measurement processes, inadequate sampling and poor evaluation have all contributed. So, to be effective in supporting the information security effort, the audit framework needs to take account of all aspects of physical and environmental security, personnel security, the adherence to policy and standards and the technical environment supporting key business processes.

This can be identified as two distinct parts:

- Accounting Systems – those systems that maintain reporting on the financial health and management of the company and support the corporate governance effort and regulatory effort

- Business Usage – those systems that support the business, in order to demonstrate assurance in information processing.

The challenge in auditing is to be confident that the information contained within the different business systems is consistent across the organization and most importantly accurate. It is important therefore that objective assurance that security is being managed effectively can be demonstrated.

Internal audits should check on the effectiveness of existing controls, against the security baseline described in an organization's *Statement of Applicability*. A framework and schedule for carrying out such audits needs to be developed. This should be carried out by someone independent of security staff and not directly involved in implementing security controls.

Technical testing (mandatory for ISO/IEC 27001 compliance) should focus on the effectiveness of the security of the IT infrastructure. This can be done as penetration testing (i.e. from external to the network) or intrusion detection (internally on the network itself) and preferably both. The use of an independent (third party) tester using specialist tools is a better way of raising assurance.

As well as formal audits, spot checks by security staff, without users being prewarned, can be a useful way of testing compliance. An example would be checks to ensure that an organization's clear desk policy is being followed.

It is important for compliance to focus on the overall effectiveness of a control, not just its existence. A good example of this is in the area of Business Continuity. For true compliance, it is not enough to have business continuity plans, they also need to have been tested to demonstrate their appropriateness and effectiveness.

15.4.5 Operating the ISMS

Once the ISMS is fully operational, the focus of the Security Forum changes from the development phase (managing the SIP and establishing security mechanisms) to now looking at security incidents and the results from auditing activities. It should have full visibility of both of these in order to be able to review the adequacy of policy and procedures and the currency of the risk assessment and other key ISMS documentation, in the light of incidents arising.

The organization needs to demonstrate that it is reacting to any changes, both planned and unforeseen. The performance of third parties, such as outsourcing companies with responsibility for some security measures, should also be reviewed by the Forum.

The evidence demonstrating progress and improvements will be contained within the minutes of the Forum, tracking any necessary actions, known areas of weakness, outstanding and accepted risks. These should be important points of focus for the Forum.

The effectiveness of the ISMS itself, including how effective the Forum is at handling changes, should be reviewed as part of the auditing process, as should the risk assessment and Statement of Applicability, on at least an annual basis, or after a major organizational change.

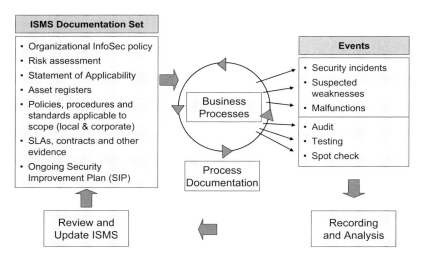

Figure 15.3 ISO/IEC 27001 compliant ISMS model

Figure 15.3 describes an ISMS model compliant to ISO/IEC 27001.

15.5 Assurance in Third Parties and Outsourcing Issues

15.5.1 Typical Third Party and Outsourcing Scenarios

In Section 15.2, the issue of assurance was examined. This section expands on the concept and describes in practical terms how assurance can be gained from third parties.

Third parties can be internal or external, for example:

- Security (e.g. guards)
- Cleaning
- Waste disposal (e.g. shredding)
- Bespoke software development
- Equipment maintenance
- Telecommunications
- Customers (e.g. users)
- Facilities management (e.g. Internet service providers).

Managing third party relationships to achieve effective security is one of the most important areas of compliance. Certainly, implementation of ISO/IEC 27001 is usually more about determining correct 'division of responsibility' than about debating the relevance of each of the controls. This means that an organization must either take direct responsibility for a security control or raise assurance that the control is covered adequately by the relevant third party. This can be achieved through the development of a contract review checklist or matrix, where the parties work through each control assigning responsibility or agreeing how each control will be shared.

Internal Third Parties

Figure 15.4 describes a relationship between the IT department and internal third parties, where the scope of the ISMS is 'provision of IT services' and where that provision is reliant on internal third parties to provide security-related services, such as secure buildings and adequately screened and vetted staff.

Staff involved in delivering these 'internal services' are outside the defined scope of the ISMS however, the IT function depends on them for their various services, for its own overall information security. The proposed ISMS must therefore obtain assurance that these services are being delivered appropriately.

This assurance is obtained by putting in place documented agreements with the various internal third parties. These forms of *Operational Level Agreements* (OLAs) define the expected security relevant service, as indicated in ISO/IEC 27001.

A key element of the agreements will be the right by the IT function to carry out, or commission, independent audits of these internal third parties against the definition of the expected services. The audits will form a key element of the IT function's ongoing internal compliance program as part of operating its ISO/IEC 27001 compliant ISMS.

Specifically, for each ISO/IEC 27001 control that is addressed by departments outside the scope of the ISMS, the following needs to be in place to support the ISMS:

- Clear, documented responsibility for the aspect of information security which is that subject of that control
- Confirmation from the relevant departmental manager that the relevant control is in place and effective
- Documentary evidence (records/logs in either electronic or hardcopy format), which can be inspected at agreed intervals on a sampling basis.

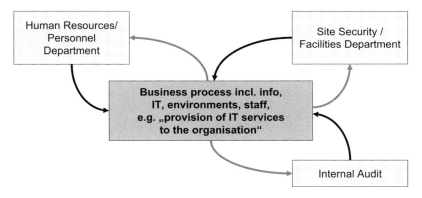

Figure 15.4 ISMS Scope Boundary

Beyond obtaining assurance for the IT function's ISMS that the relevant services are being provided correctly, there is no claim being made about the compliance of any internal third parties therefore, although desirable, it is not actually necessary for the activities of internal third parties to be supported by documented policies, standards and procedures. Neither is it necessary for the functions provided by these internal third parties to be themselves compliant beyond those that have been specifically identified in the documented agreement with the IT function.

So, in this case an internal OLA would be appropriate to manage the relationship; the OLA being the necessary security control at the scope boundary (in the case of an external service provider this would take the form of a legally binding contract, including the appropriate security requirements relating to confidentiality, integrity and availability issues).

In summary, in order for the processes within the scope to be compliant with best practice the ISMS supporting them needs to have 'assurance' that:

- The various third parties accept responsibility for the aspect of information security that they are providing, e.g. vetting of staff, physical security of the building.
- There is a common understanding of the manner in which these services are provided, e.g. some form of written description.
- Where appropriate, there is evidence that the services are actually being provided, and that this evidence is being periodically examined.

External Third Parties

Under the rules of the BS 7799 Scheme laid down by the United Kingdom Accreditation Service (UKAS), 'other legal entities' (i.e. external third parties) cannot be included within the scope of an ISMS, therefore any contract with an external third party needs to clearly identify security requirements in addition to system/functional requirements and these must be demonstrably risk justified.

An example might be where the IT function receives security relevant services from external third parties as part of delivering its business functions. Examples within the scope of the ISMS are the services received from:

- External connectivity to trusted partners
- Bespoke software development
- Web site hosting
- Graphic design for websites.

For such external third parties, the approach taken should be to ensure that there is a clear contract in place that enumerates all of the key aspects of information security that are part of the defined service expected to be delivered through the contract, including the right to audit. The adequacy of the specified security requirements must be demonstrable through risk assessment.

In a similar manner to internal third parties, audits will be carried out periodically to confirm that the various clauses are being adhered to. This is the way in which assurance will be raised, again as a key element of the compliant ISMS.

As a key control, it will be necessary to put in place a register of third parties remembering that for both internal and external third parties, the documented agreement/contract forms the boundary of the ISMS.

15.5.2 Achieving and Measuring Security Assurance

This section provides advice on measuring assurance levels, both internally and externally. By following these principles, you can ensure that the risks to your organization are minimized. Assurance needs to be achieved or demonstrated in four distinct areas. The areas and supporting actions can be summarized as follows:

Internal Organizational Assurance

* Define ISMS(s) according to security requirements and business needs
* Develop a suitable information security policy
* Undertake a risk assessment for each ISMS within the organization
* Select an appropriate set of controls to manage the identified risks
* Where appropriate and necessary undertake a formal ISO/IEC 27001 certification.

Communications Assurance

* Assess the levels of vulnerability related to the assets
* Calculate the impacts of security breaches
* Assess the levels of risk to the system
* Select controls from ISO/IEC 27001 to reduce the risks.

Service Provider Assurance

* Check your service provider's security policy and ensure that it matches the rigor of your own
* Check the legal, regulatory and contractual measures relating to the service and the service provider
* Assess the 'trustworthiness' of the technologies and business processes involved
* Ensure that the contract with the service provider includes an appropriate set of security requirements
* Assess assurance level (based on compliance with ISO/IEC 27001) either through a formal ISO/IEC 27001 certification or through an audit carried out by your organization.

Trading Partner Assurance

* Ensure that your partner has a published security policy that matches the rigor of your own
* Assess the organizational security of the trading partners (based on compliance with ISO/IEC 27001) either through a formal ISO/IEC 27001 certification or through an audit carried out by your organization

- Ensure that contracts are in place describing all controls that should be in place to provide appropriate security

15.6 Conclusion

Information security should be a corporate business driver. Compliance in information security is now an integral part of managing operational risk and securing your information is of the utmost importance. It is clear that many benefits accrue from an appropriate and successful risk driven information security improvement programme.

Both the 'business' and supporting IT departments need a greater understanding of customer and regulatory requirements and how the business needs to react.

In order to meet these requirements, organizations will need to apply an extensive programme of activity:

- Reviewing controls
- Improving resilience
- Speeding up recovery
- Determining unacceptable levels of loss
- Consolidating data.

Once all that is accomplished, companies will need to assess whether they have achieved their security objectives. Consideration of the guidance given in ISO/IEC 17799 shows that there is no 'best' approach to achieve the security objectives of your organization. A balance is needed between technical and organizational controls. Experience has shown that there are a number of factors which are critical to the successful implementation of information security within any organization:

- Security policy, objectives and activities that reflect business objectives
- An approach to implementing security that is consistent with the organizational culture
- Visible support and commitment from management
- A good understanding of the security requirements, risk assessment and risk management
- Effective marketing of security to all managers and employees
- Distribution of comprehensive guidance on information security policy and standards to all employees and contractors and carrying out training and education
- A comprehensive and balanced system of measurement which is used to evaluate performance in information security management and feedback suggestions for improvement.

Glossary and Abbreviations

Access control	Protection of system resources against unauthorized access; a process by which use of system resources is regulated according to a security policy and is permitted by only authorized entities (users, programs, processes, or other systems) according to that policy (RFC 2828).
Accountability	The property that ensures that the actions of an entity can be traced uniquely to the entity.
ACI	Access Control Information
ACL	Access Control List
ADF	Access Decision Function
Advanced Encryption Standard (AES)	A symmetric block encryption mechanism providing variable key length specified as Federal Information Processing Standard (FIPS) 197 [FIPS197].
AEF	Access Enforcement Function
APDU	Application Protocol Data Unit
AS	Authentication Service (Kerberos)
ASIC (Application-Specific Integrated Circuit)	An integrated circuit (IC) customized for a particular use, rather than intended for general-purpose use. As gate sizes have shrunk and design tools improved over the years, the maximum complexity possible in an ASIC has grown to over 100 million gates.
ASN.1	Abstract Syntax Notation No. 1
Asset	Anything that has value to an organization.
Authentication	The process of verifying an identity claimed by or for a system entity. An authentication process consists of two steps: Presenting an identifier to the security system (identification), and presenting or generating authentication information that corroborates the binding between the entity and the identifier (verification) (RFC 2828).
Authenticity	The property that ensures that the identity of a subject or resource is the one claimed. Authenticity applies to entities such as users, processes, systems and information.
Authorization (administrative connotation)	An authorization is a right or a permission that is granted to a system entity to access a system resource. To authorize means to grant such a right or permission (RFC 2828).

Authorization (operative connotation)	The process of determining whether a subject is allowed to have the specified types of access to a particular resource (SAML).
Authorization decision	The result of an act of authorization. The result may be negative, that is, it may indicate that the subject is not allowed any access to the resource (SAML).
Authorization policy	Policy for rendering authorization decisions.
BER	Basic Encoding Rules
BS 7799-2	British Standard BS 7799 Part 2 "Information security management systems – specification with guidance for use" is a management standard, and explains how to build, maintain and improve an Information Security Management System (ISMS). It is predicated on risk assessment and the Plan-Do-Check-Act model.
CA	Certification Authority
Certificate Holder	The end user (system) that is the subject of a certificate. Certificate holder can be a human person, a legal entity (e.g. company) or an end-system (e.g. Web-server).
Certificate Policy (CP)	A document provided by the operator of a specific PKI that describes a kind of a certificate usage regulation. The PKI typically defines certificate classes and the CP prescribes which certificates shall be used for what purpose.
Certificate Practice Statement (CPS)	A document provided by the operator of a specific PKI that describes the procedures controlling how certificates are issued and administered within the framework of the PKI.
Certificate Revocation List (CRL)	A list of certificates which have been revoked, are no longer valid, and should not be relied upon by any system user. A CRL is always issued by the CA which has issued the corresponding certificates.
Certificate	A document or data structure containing a public key that is digitally signed by a well-known authority (the Certification Authority), certifying that the public key belongs to the owner specified in the document or data structure.
Certification Authority (CA)	An organization trusted by both ends of a communication link, whose public key is widely published. A certification authority uses its private key to digitally sign certificates attesting that certain public keys belong to certain organizations and/or devices.
CIM	Common Information Model
CMS	Card Management System
Common Criteria (CC)	An international standard [ISO15408] for product and system security. The Common Criteria allow users to specify their security requirements, developers to specify the security attributes of their products, and evaluators to assess if products or solutions actually meet their claims.

Confidentiality	The property that information is not made available or disclosed to unauthorized individuals, entities, or processes.
COPS	Common Open Policy Service
Credential	A proof of qualification, role, or clearance that is attached to a person.
Cryptographic Service Provider (CSP)	A software module that carries out cryptographic operations. The CSP interface is the standard Windows interface for smart cards with a cryptographic co-processor.
DAC	Discretionary Access Control
DAP	Directory Access Protocol
Data Encryption Standard (DES)	A symmetric block encryption mechanism designed in the 1970s [FIPS46]. Due to its short key length DES was replaced by the AES, but is still used in multiple encryption mode, e.g., 3DES or Triple DES (FIPS 46-3).
Data Integrity	The property that data has not been altered or destroyed in an unauthorized manner.
DIB	Directory Information Base
Digital Signature	A cryptographic transformation of a data unit that allows a recipient of the data unit to prove the origin and integrity of the data unit. Moreover it protects the sender and the recipient of the data unit against forgery by third parties, and the sender against forgery by the recipient.
Directory Service	A service to search and retrieve information from a catalogue of well defined objects, which may contain information about certificates, telephone numbers, access conditions, addresses, etc.
DISP	Directory Information Shadowing Protocol
DIT	Directory Information Tree
DMTF	Distributed Management Task Force
DN	Distinguished Name
DOP	Directory Operational Management Binding Protocol
DRM	Digital Rights Management
DSA	Directory System Agent
DSE	DSA-Specific Entry
DSML	Directory Services Markup Language
DSP	Directory System Protocol
DUA	Directory User Agent
EAI	Enterprise Application Integration
EER	Equal Error Rate

End Entity	User of PKI certificates and/or end user system that is the subject of a certificate (certificate holder).
EPAL	Enterprise Privacy Authorization Language
ETL	Extract-Transform-Load
Evaluation Assurance Level (EAL)	Predefined sets of Common Criteria assurance requirements. Common Criteria EALs are numbered 1 to 7 with higher EAL levels gaining more assurance.
FAR	False Acceptance Rate
FPGA (Field-Programmable Gate Array)	A programmable semiconductor device used to process digital information. It utilizes gate array technology that can be reprogrammed after it is manufactured, rather than having its programming fixed during manufacturing.
FRR	False Rejection Rate
FTC	Failure to Capture Rate
FTE	Failure to Enroll Rate
Gramm Leach Bliley Act (GLBA)	GBLA is a US law requiring financial institutions to protect the security, integrity and confidentiality of consumer information. GLBA requires an advanced level of security understanding and awareness.
Health Insurance Portability and Accountability Act (HIPAA)	HIPAA is a comprehensive US legislation that governs privacy, security and electronic transactions concerning healthcare data. HIPAA stipulates that patients have significant rights to understand and control how their health data is used, and it obliges healthcare providers to provide an explanation of how they comply with privacy regulations.
IAM	Identity and Access Management
Identity	The unique identifier for a person, organization, resource, or service along with optional supplementary information (e.g., privileges, attributes, ...).
ID-FF	IDentity Federation Framework (Liberty Alliance)
ID-SIS	IDentity Service Interface Specifications (Liberty Alliance)
ID-WSF	IDentity Web Services Framework (Liberty Alliance)
IEC	International Electrotechnical Commission
IETF	Internet Engineering Task Force
Information Security Management System (ISMS)	An ISMS is a management system to establish policies and objectives for information security within the context of the organization's overall business risk and the means by which these objectives can be achieved.
International Civil Aviation Organization (ICAO)	An agency of the United Nations, developing the principles and techniques of international air navigation and fostering the planning and development of international air transport (www.icao.org).

IoC	Identifier on Card
ISO	International Organization for Standardization
ISO/IEC 17799	International Standard ISO/IEC 17799 "Code of practice for information security management" provides 132 information security guidelines structured under 11 major headings to enable readers to identify the security controls which are appropriate to their particular business or specific area of responsibility. As well as giving detailed security controls for computers and networks, ISO/IEC 17799 also provides guidance on security policy, staff security awareness, business continuity planning, and legal requirements.
ISO/IEC 27001	International Standard ISO/IEC 27001 "Information security management systems – Requirements specification" is an updated and revised version of BS 7799-2:2002. This international ISMS standard is currently being finalized and expected to be available by the end of 2005.
ITU-T	International Telecommunication Union – Telecommunication Standardization Sector
JAAS	Java Authentication and Authorization Service
KDC	Key Distribution Center
LDAP	Lightweight Directory Access Protocol
LDIF	LDAP Data Interchange Format
MAC	Mandatory Access Control
Minutiae	A fingerprint is made up of a pattern of ridges and furrows as well as characteristics that occur at Minutiae points (ridge bifurcation or a ridge ending).
MoC	Matcher on Card
NIST	National Institute of Standards and Technology
Non-Repudiation	The ability to provide evidence that an action or event has taken place, so that this event or action cannot be repudiated later.
OASIS	Organization for the Advancement of Structured Information Standards
OATH	Open AuTHentication
OCSP	Online Certificate Status Protocol
ODRL	Open Digital Rights Language
OGSA	Open Grid Services Architecture
PAC	Privilege Attribute Certificate
PC/SC	A specification for integrating smart cards and smart card readers in computing environments developed by the PC/SC Workgroup (www.pcscworkgroup.com).
PCIM	Policy Core Information Model

PDP	Policy Decision Point
PDU	Protocol Data Unit
PEP	Policy Enforcement Point
Personal Security Environment (PSE)	A security environment, where the private key and other PKI related information (e.g. certificate of the trusted CA) can be stored securely, such that e.g. only the certificate holder is able to use the corresponding private key.
PIN	Personal Identification Number
PKCS	Public-Key Cryptography Standards (PKCS) are specifications developed by RSA Laboratories in cooperation with worldwide experts for the purpose of accelerating the deployment of public-key cryptography. PKCS documents are available from http://www.rsasecurity.com/rsalabs/
PKI	Public Key Infrastructure
PKINIT	Public Key cryptography for INITial authentication (Kerberos)
PKIX	PKI for X.509 Certificates
PMA	Policy Management Authority
Policy Decision Point (PDP)	A system entity that makes authorization decisions for itself or for other system entities that request such decisions. A PDP is an authorization decision authority (SAML).
Policy Enforcement Point (PEP)	A system entity that requests and subsequently enforces authorization decisions (SAML).
Policy Management Authority (PMA)	A system entity that creates and manages authorization policies (also called PAP – Policy Administration Point in XACML).
Policy	A logically defined, executable and testable set of rules of behavior (Liberty Alliance).
POSIX	Portable Operating System Interface
Pretty Good Privacy (PGP)	PGP provides cryptographic privacy and authentication and was originally designed and developed by Phil Zimmermann in 1991. Algorithms and data formats of PGP have been standardized by the IETF in a specification known as OpenPGP.
Privacy	The right of an entity (normally a person), acting in its own behalf, to determine the degree to which it will interact with its environment, including the degree to which the entity is willing to share information about itself with others (RFC 2828).
PSP	Provisioning Service Point (SPML)
PST	Provisioning Service Target (SPML)
PSTD-ID	Provisioning Service Target Data Identifier (SPML)
RA	Requesting Authority (SPML)

Radio Frequency Identification (RFID)	A method of storing and remotely retrieving data using devices called RFID tags. An RFID tag is a small object that can be attached to or incorporated into a product, animal, or person. RFID tags contain antennas to receive and respond to radio-frequency queries from an RFID transceiver. Passive tags require no internal power source.
RADIUS	Remote Authentication Dial In User Service
RBAC	Role-Based Access Control
RDN	Relative Distinguished Name
Registration Authority (RA)	An optional PKI component to which a Certification Authority delegates certain management functions such as identification of certificate holders and checking of certificate holder data.
Repository	A system or collection of distributed systems that stores certificates and CRLs and serves as a means of distributing these certificates and CRLs to end entities.
Resource	Data contained in an information system as well as a service provided by a system, an item of system equipment or a facility that houses system operations and equipment (SAML).
Risk Analysis	The systematic process of identifying security risks, determining their magnitude, and identifying areas needing safeguards.
Risk Management	The process of assessing and quantifying risks, and establishing an acceptable level of risk for an organization.
S4U	Service for User (Kerberos extension, Microsoft)
SAML	Security Assertion Markup Language
Sarbanes-Oxley Act (SOA, also known as SOX)	US law established in 2002 to strengthen corporate governance, and to restore public trust and investor confidence in accounting practices. SOA was sponsored by US Senator Paul Sarbanes and US Representative Michael Oxley.
SASL	Simple Authentication and Security Layer
SID	Security IDentifier (Microsoft)
Single Sign-On (SSO)	A system that enables a user to access multiple computer platforms or application systems after being authenticated just one time (RFC 2828).
SME	Small and Medium Sized Enterprises
SoC	System on Card
SPML	Service Provisioning Markup Language
SPNEGO	Simple and Protected NEGOtiation
SSL	Secure Sockets Layer
Subject	A system entity that causes information to flow among objects or changes the system state (RFC 2828).

Symmetric crypto-graphic technique	Cryptographic technique that uses the same secret key for both the encryption and the decryption transformations.
Target of Evaluation (TOE)	An IT product or system and its associated guidance documentation that is the subject of a Common Criteria evaluation.
TGS	Ticket Granting Service
TGT	Ticket Granting Ticket
TLS	Transport Layer Security
ToC	Template on Card
Trust Center	Particular physical and organizational measures required for ensuring that the critical central hardware and software components of a PKI operate securely.
Trusted Third Party	A security authority, or its agent, trusted by other entities with respect to security related activities.
Virtual Private Network (VPN)	A private network utilizing shared networks, e.g., a network established via cryptographic tunneling protocols operating over another network infrastructure.
VoIP	Voice over IP
WAYF	Where Are You From (Shibboleth)
World Wide Web Consortium (W3C)	An international consortium (www.w3c.org) to develop Web standards and guidelines published as W3C Recommendations.
WS	Web Services
WSDL	Web Service Definition Language
WSPL	Web Services Policy Language
WSSOMEX	Web-SSO Metadata EXchange protocol
XACL	XML Access Control Language
XACML	eXtensible Access Control Markup Language
XML	eXtensible Markup Language
XML Encryption	A W3C Recommendation specifying how to encrypt the content of an XML element.
XML Signature	A W3C Recommendation specifying how to digitally sign the content of an XML element.
XrML	eXtensible rights Markup Language

References

[Ada99]   C. Adams and S. Lloyd: Understanding Public-Key Infrastructure, Macmillan Technical Publishing, 1999.

[And02]   A. Anderson: Java Access Control Mechanisms. Technical Report TR-2002-108, Sun Microsystems. March 2002.

[And04]   A. Anderson: An Introduction to the Web Services Policy Language. Proceedings 5th IEEE International Workshop on Policies for Distributed Systems and Networks (Policy 2004). New York, June 2004.

[And05]   A. Anderson: Key Differences between XACML and EPAL. Workshop NCAC – New Challenges for Access Control 2005. Ottawa, April 2005.

[Aus01]   T. Austin: PKI – A Wiley Tech Brief, Wiley Computer Publishing, Wiley & Sons, 2001.

[Bas04]   Basel Committee on Banking Supervision: International Convergence of Capital Measurement and Capital Standards – A Revised Framework, June 2004.

[BBB92]   C. Bennett, F. Bessette, G. Brassard, L. Savail, and J. Smolin: Experimental quantum cryptography, Journal of Cryptology (1) 5 (1992), 3-28.

[BR00]   P. S. L. M. Barreto and V. Rijmen: "The Whirlpool Hashing Function", First open NESSIE Workshop, Leuven, Belgium, 13-14 November 2000.

[Bra93]   G. Brassard: Cryptography column – Quantum cryptography: A bibliography, Sigact News (3) 24 (1993), 16-20.

[BS7799a]   BS 7799-1: Information security management systems – Code of practice, 1999.

[BS7799b]   BS 7799-2: Information security management systems – specification with guidance for use, 2002.

[BSI03]   BSI: IT Baseline Protection Manual, 2003 (available via http://www.bsi.bund.de/gshb).

[Cha00]   D. W. Chadwick: Secure Directories. In: W.S. Schneider, B. Jerman-Blazic, T. Klobucar (editors): Advanced Security Technologies for Insecure Networks, pages 123-131. IOS Press 2000.

[Cha94]   D. W. Chadwick: Understanding X.500 – The Directory. Chapman & Hall, 1994, (out of print, online version available at http://sec.cs.kent.ac.uk/x500book/).

[CSI02]   Computer Security Institute: CSI/FBI Computer Crime and Security Survey, 2002.

[Dat04]   The ROI case for smart cards in the enterprise. The benefits of a converged logical and physical access solution, Datamonitor, 2004

[DBP96]   H. Dobbertin, A. Bosselaers, and B. Preneel: "RIPEMD-160, a strengthened
            version of RIPEMD", Proceedings Fast Software Encryption - FSE'96, Springer
            LNCS 1039 (1996), 71-82.

[DeC04]   J. DeClerq: Windows Server 2003 Security Infrastructures. Elsevier 2004.

[Deu85]   D. Deutsch: "Quantum Theory, the Church-Turing Principle, and the Universal
            Quantum Computer", Proceedings of the Royal Society of London, Series A,
            Vol. 400 (1985), 97-117.

[DH76]   W. Diffie and M. E. Hellman, "New directions in cryptography", IEEE Trans.
            Inform. Theory, IT-22:6 (1976), 644-654.

[Dob98]   H. Dobbertin: "Cryptanalysis of MD4", Journal of Cryptology 11:4 (1998),
            253-271.

[DR00]   J. Daemen and V. Rijmen: The Block Cipher Rijndael. In: J.-J. Quisquater and
            B. Schneier, eds: Smart Card Research and Applications, Springer LNCS 1820
            (2000), 288-296.

[ECR05]   ECRYPT Yearly Report on Algorithms and Keysizes (2004), 2005 (available via
            http://www.ecrypt.org).

[EEMA04]   European Forum for Electronic Business: PKI Usage within Corporate Organi-
            zations, Version 2, April 2004.

[ElG85]   T. El Gamal, "A public key cryptosystem and a signature scheme based on
            discrete logarithms", Springer LNCS 196 (1985), 10-18.

[FIPS113]   FIPS Publication 113: Computer Data Authentication, 1985.

[FIPS140]   FIPS Publication 140-2: Security Requirements for Cryptographic Modules,
            2001.

[FIPS180]   FIPS Publication 180-2: Secure Hash Standard (SHS), 2002.

[FIPS186]   FIPS Publication 186-2: Digital Signature Standard (DSS), 2000.

[FIPS197]   FIPS Publication 197: Advanced Encryption Standard (AES), 2001.

[FIPS198]   FIPS Publication 198: The Keyed-Hash Message Authentication Code
            (HMAC), 2002.

[FIPS46]   FIPS Publication 46-3: Data Encryption Standard (DES); specifies the use of
            Triple DES, 1999, withdrawn May 19, 2005.

[FKC03]   D. F. Ferraiolo, D. R. Kuhn, R. Chandramouli: Role-Based Access Control.
            Artech House, Computer Security Series, 2003.

[FSS01]   K. Fu, E. Sit, K. Smith, N. Feamster: Dos and Don'ts of Client Authentication
            on the Web. Proc. 10th USENIX Security Symposium August 2001.

[Gro96]   L. K. Grover: "A Fast Quantum Mechanical Algorithm for Database Search",
            Proceedings of the 28th Annual ACM Symposium on the Theory of Computing
            (1996), 212-219.

[Gru03]   A. Grünbacher: POSIX Access Control Lists on Linux. Proceedings of the 2003
            USENIX Annual Technical Conference. San Antonio, June 2003.

[Hou01]   R. Housley and T. Polk: Planning for PKI – Best Practices Guide for Deploying
            Public Key Infrastructure, Wiley & Sons, 2001.

[HSG03]   T. A. Howes, M. C. Smith, G. S. Good: Understanding and Deploying LDAP
             Directory Services, Second Edition, Addison-Wesley, 2003.

[ISO10116]   ISO/IEC 10116: Modes of operation for an n-bit block cipher, 1997.

[ISO10118b] ISO/IEC 10118-2: Hash-functions – Part 2: Hash-functions using an n-bit block
             cipher, 2nd edition 2000.

[ISO10118c] ISO/IEC 10118-3: Hash-functions – Part 3: Dedicated Hash-functions,
             3rd edition 2004.

[ISO10536]   ISO/IEC 10536 Identification cards – Contact-less integrated circuit(s) cards –
             Close-coupled cards (Parts 1 to 3).

[ISO13335]   ISO/IEC TR 13335: Guidelines for the management of IT Security (5 parts),
             1996-2001.

[ISO14443]   ISO/IEC 14443: Identification cards – Contact-less integrated circuit(s) cards –
             Proximity cards (Parts 1 to 4).

[ISO14888b] ISO/IEC 14888-2: Digital signatures with appendix – Part 2: Integer factoriza-
             tion based mechanisms, 1999.

[ISO14888c] ISO/IEC 14888-3: Digital signatures with appendix – Part 2: Discrete loga-
             rithm based mechanisms, 1999.

[ISO15408]   ISO/IEC 15408: Evaluation criteria for IT Security (3 parts), 1999.

[ISO15693]   ISO/IEC 15693: Identification cards – Contact-less integrated circuit(s) cards –
             Vicinity cards (Parts 1 to 3).

[ISO15946b] ISO/IEC 15946-2: Cryptographic techniques based on elliptic curves – Part 2:
             Digital signatures, 2002.

[ISO15946c] ISO/IEC 15946-3: Cryptographic techniques based on elliptic curves – Part 3:
             Key establishment, 2002.

[ISO15946d] ISO/IEC 15946-4: Cryptographic techniques based on elliptic curves – Part 4:
             Digital signatures giving message recovery, 2004.

[ISO17799]   ISO/IEC 17799: Code of practice for information security management, 2005.

[ISO18033b] ISO/IEC 18033-2: Encryption algorithms – Part 2: Asymmetric ciphers, 2005.

[ISO18033c] ISO/IEC 18033-3: Encryption algorithms – Part 3: Block ciphers, 2005.

[ISO18185]   ISO 18185: Freight containers - Electronic seals (7 parts).

[ISO27001]   ISO/IEC 27001: Information security management systems – Requirements
             specification, 2005.

[ISO7816]   ISO/IEC 7816: Identification cards – Integrated circuit(s) cards with contacts
             (Parts 1 to 6).

[ISO9796b]   ISO/IEC 9796-2: Digital signature schemes giving message recovery - Part 2:
             Integer factorization based mechanisms, 2002.

[ISO9796c]   ISO/IEC 9796-3: Digital signature schemes giving message recovery - Part 3:
             Discrete logarithm based mechanisms, 1999.

[ISO9797a]   ISO/IEC 9797-1: Message Authentication Codes (MACs) – Part 1: Mecha-
             nisms using a block cipher, 1999.

[ISO9797b]	ISO/IEC 9797-2: Message authentication codes (MACs) - Part 2: Mechanisms using a dedicated hash-function, 2002.
[KC04]	R. Kimball, J. Caserta: The Data Warehouse ETL Toolkit, Wiley Publishing, Inc., 2004.
[Kob87]	N. Koblitz: "Elliptic curve cryptosystems", Mathematics of Computation, 48 (1987), 203-209.
[KPS02]	C. Kaufman, R. Perlman, M. Speciner: Network Security: Private Communication in a Public World. Prentice-Hall, 2002.
[LPL03]	M. Lorch, S. Proctor, R. Lepro, D. Kafura, S. Shah: First Experiences Using XACML for Access Control in Distributed Systems. Proceedings of the ACM Workshop on XML Security. Fairfax, October 2003.
[LS01]	P. Loscocco, S. Smalley: Integrating Flexible Support for Security Policies into the Linux Operating System. Proceedings of the 2001 USENIX Annual Technical Conference. Boston, June 2001.
[LV01]	A. Lenstra and E. Verheul: "Selecting Cryptographic Key Sizes", Journal of Cryptology 14 (2001), 255-293.
[MCC04]	R. L. Morgan, S. Cantor, S. Carmody, W. Hoehn, K. Klingenstein: Federated Security: The Shibboleth Approach. EDUCAUSE Quarterly, Volume 27, Number 4, 2004.
[Mil86]	V. Miller: "Uses of Elliptic Curves in Cryptography", Proceedings Crypto'85, Springer LNCS 218 (1986), 417-426.
[Nas01]	A. Nash, W. Duane, C. Joseph, and D. Brink: PKI – Implementing and Managing E-Security, RSA Press, Osborne/MCGraw-Hill, 2001.
[NIS01]	NIST: Key Management Guideline, Draft, October 2001.
[NR93]	K. Nyberg and R. A. Rueppel: A new Signature Scheme based on the DSA Giving Message Recovery, 1st ACM Conference on Computer and Communications Security, Fairfax, VA, November 1993.
[OECD02]	OECD Guidelines for the Security of Information Systems and Networks – Towards a Culture of Security, 2002.
[PKCS10]	RSA Laboratories: PKCS #10: Certification Request Syntax Standard, v1.7, May 2000.
[PKCS11]	RSA Laboratories: PKCS #11: Cryptographic Token Interface Standard, v2.20, June 2004.
[PKCS15]	RSA Laboratories: PKCS #15: Cryptographic Token Information Syntax Standard, v1.1, June 2000.
[RFC1319]	B. Kaliski: The MD2 Message-Digest Algorithm, IETF RFC 1319 (I), April 1992.
[RFC1321]	R. L. Rivest: The MD5 Message Digest Algorithm, IETF RFC 1321 (I), April 1992.
[RFC2040]	R. Baldwin and R. Rivest: The RC5, RC5-CBC, RC5-CBC-Pad, and RC5-CTS Algorithms, IETF RFC 2040 (I), October 1996.

[RFC2144]   C. Adams: The CAST-128 Encryption Algorithm. IETF RFC 2144 (I),
              May 1997.

[RFC2222]   J. Myers: Simple Authentication and Security Layer (SASL), IETF RFC 2222
              (PS), October 1997.

[RFC2247]   S. Kille, M. Wahl, A. Grimstad, R. Huber, S. Sataluri: Using Domains in
              LDAP/X.500 Distinguished Names, IETF RFC 2247 (PS), January 1998.

[RFC2251]   M. Wahl, T. Howes, S. Kille: Lightweight Directory Access Protocol (v3),
              IETF RFC 2251 (PS), December 1997.

[RFC2252]   M. Wahl, A. Coulbeck, T. Howes, S. Kille: Lightweight Directory Access Proto-
              col (v3): Attribute Syntax Definitions, IETF RFC 2252 (PS) December 1997.

[RFC2253]   M. Wahl, S. Kille, T. Howes: Lightweight Directory Access Protocol (v3):
              UTF-8 String Representation of Distinguished Names, IETF RFC 2253 (PS),
              December 1997.

[RFC2254]   T. Howes: The String Representation of LDAP Search Filters, IETF RFC 2254
              (PS), December 1997.

[RFC2255]   T. Howes, M. Smith: The LDAP URL Format, IETF RFC 2255 (PS), December
              1997.

[RFC2256]   M. Wahl: A Summary of the X.500(96) User Schema for use with LDAPv3,
              IETF RFC 2256 (PS), December 1997.

[RFC2268]   R. Rivest: A Description of the RC2 Encryption Algorithm, IETF RFC 2268 (I),
              March 1998.

[RFC2440]   J. Callas, L. Donnerhacke, H. Finney, R. Thayer: OpenPGP Message Format,
              IETF RFC 2440 (PS), November 1998.

[RFC2587]   S. Boeyen, T. Howes, P. Richard: Internet X.509 Public Key Infrastructure
              LDAPv2 Schema, IETF RFC 2587 (PS), June 1999.

[RFC2612]   C. Adams, J. Gilchrist: The CAST-256 Encryption Algorithm, IETF RFC 2612
              (I), June 1999.

[RFC2692]   C. Ellison: SPKI Requirements, IETF RFC 2692 (E), September 1999.

[RFC2798]   M. Smith: Definition of the inetOrgPerson LDAP Object Class, IETF RFC 2798
              (I), April 2000. (Updated by RFC3698)

[RFC2829]   M. Wahl, H. Alvestrand, J. Hodges, R. Morgan: Authentication Methods for
              LDAP, IETF RFC 2829 (PS), May 2000.

[RFC2830]   J. Hodges, R. Morgan, M. Wahl: Lightweight Directory Access Protocol (v3):
              Extension for Transport Layer Security, IETF RFC 2830 (PS), May 2000.

[RFC2831]   P. Leach, C. Newman: Using Digest Authentication as a SASL Mechanism,
              IETF RFC 2831 (PS), May 2000.

[RFC2849]   G. Good: The LDAP Data Interchange Format (LDIF) – Technical Specifica-
              tion, IETF RFC 2849 (PS), June 2000.

[RFC2994]   H. Ohta and M. Matsui: A Description of the MISTY1 Encryption Algorithm.
              IETF RFC 2994 (I), November 2000.

[RFC3280]   R. Housley, W. Polk, W. Ford, and D. Solo: Internet X.509 Public Key
            Infrastructure – Certificate and Certificate Revocation List (CRL) Profile,
            IETF RFC 3280 (PS), April 2002.

[RFC3281]   S. Farrell and R. Housley: An Internet Attribute Certificate Profile for Authori-
            zation, IETF RFC 3281 (PS), April 2002.

[RFC3377]   J. Hodges, R. Morgan: Lightweight Directory Access Protocol (v3): Technical
            Specification, IETF RFC 3377 (PS), September 2002.

[RFC3647]   S. Chokhani, W. Ford, R. Sabett, C. Merrill, and S. Wu: Internet X.509 Public
            Key Infrastructure Certificate Policy and Certification Practices Framework,
            IETF RFC 3647 (I), November 2003.

[RFC3703]   J. Strassner, B. Moore, R. Moats, and E. Ellesson: Policy Core Lightweight
            Directory Access Protocol (LDAP) Schema, IETF RFC 3703 (PS), February
            2004.

[RFC3766]   H. Orman and P. Hoffman: Determining Strengths For Public Keys Used For
            Exchanging Symmetric Keys, IETF RFC 3766 (BCP), April 2004.

[RFC3851]   B. Ramsdell: Secure/Multipurpose Internet Mail Extensions (S/MIME)
            Version 3.1 Message Specification, IETF RFC 3851 (PS), July 2004.

[RFC4132]   S. Moriai, A. Kato and M. Kanda: Addition of Camellia Cipher Suites to
            Transport Layer Security (TLS), IETF RFC 4132 (PS), July 2005.

[Riv90]   R. L. Rivest: "The MD4 Message Digest Algorithm", Proceedings of Crypto'90,
            Springer LNCS 537 (1990), 303-311.

[RSA78]   R. L. Rivest, A. Shamir, and L. Adleman: "A Method for Obtaining Digital
            Signatures and Public-Key Cryptosystems", Communications of the ACM 21
            (1978), 120-126.

[Sho94]   P. W. Shor: "Algorithms for quantum computation: Discrete logarithms and fac-
            toring", Proceedings of the 35th Annual IEEE Symposium on the Foundations
            of Computer Science (1994), 124-134.

[Sie03]   F. Siebenlist: Grid Security: Requirements, Plans and Ongoing Efforts. 2003
            ACM Workshop on XML Security. George W. Johnson Center at George Mason
            University. Fairfax, October 2003.

[SS02]   B. Sheresh, D. Sheresh: Understanding Directory Services, SAMS, 2002

[USS04]   U.S. Secret Service and CERT Coordination Center: Insider Threat Study -
            Illicit Cyber Activity in the Banking and Finance Sector, 2004.

[Wat01]   R. Watson: TrustedBSD: Adding Trusted Operating System Features to
            FreeBSD. Proceedings of the 2001 USENIX Annual Technical Conference.
            Boston, June 2001.

[Wei04]   B. Weis: The Use of RSA Signatures within ESP and AH, IETF draft, Novem-
            ber 2004.

[WSF03]   V. Welch, F. Siebenlist, I. Foster, J. Bresnahan, K. Czajkowski, J. Gawor,
            C. Kesselman, S. Meder, L. Pearlman, S. Tuecke.: Security for Grid Services.
            Proceedings of the 12th IEEE International Symposium on High Performance
            Distributed Computing 2003 (HPDC'03). Seattle, June 2003.

[WY05]   X. Wang and H. Yu: "How to Break MD5 and Other Hash Functions", Proceed-
            ings of Eurocrypt'2005, Springer LNCS (2005), to appear.

[WYY05]   X. Wang, Y. L. Yin, and H. Yu: "Collision Search Attacks on SHA-1", research
            summary, 2005.

[X500]   International Telecommunication Union – Telecommunication Standardization
            Sector, "The Directory: Overview of concepts, models and services," X.500
            (2001) (also ISO/IEC 9594-1:2001).

[X501]   International Telecommunication Union – Telecommunication Standardization
            Sector, "The Directory: Models," X.501 (2001) (also ISO/IEC 9594-2: 2001).

[X509]   International Telecommunication Union – Telecommunication Standardization
            Sector, "The Directory: Public-key and attribute certificate frameworks" X.509
            (2000) (also ISO/IEC 9594-8: 2001).

[X511]   International Telecommunication Union – Telecommunication Standardization
            Sector, "The Directory: Abstract Service Definition", X.511 (2001) (also
            ISO/IEC 9594-3: 2001).

[X518]   International Telecommunication Union – Telecommunication Standardization
            Sector, "The Directory: Procedures for distributed operation", X.518 (2001)
            (also ISO/IEC 9594-4: 2001).

[X519]   International Telecommunication Union – Telecommunication Standardization
            Sector, "The Directory: Protocol specifications", X.519 (2001)
            (also ISO/IEC 9594-5: 2001).

[X520]   International Telecommunication Union – Telecommunication Standardization
            Sector, "The Directory: Selected Attribute Types", X.520 (2001)
            (also ISO/IEC 9594-6: 2001).

[X521]   International Telecommunication Union – Telecommunication Standardization
            Sector, "The Directory: Selected Object Classes", X.521 (2001)
            (also ISO/IEC 9594-7: 2001).

[X525]   International Telecommunication Union – Telecommunication Standardization
            Sector, "The Directory: Replication", X.525 (2001)
            (also ISO/IEC 9594-9: 2001).

[X530]   International Telecommunication Union – Telecommunication Standardization
            Sector, "The Directory: Use of systems management for administration of the
            Directory", X.530 (2001) (also ISO/IEC 9594-10: 2001).

[XKMS]   P. Hallam-Baker and S. Mysore: XML Key Management Specification
            (XKMS 2.0), Version 2.0, W3C Recommendation, June 2005.

[XMLEnc]   D. Eastlake, J. Reagle, T. Imamura, B. Dillaway, and E. Simon: XML Encryp-
            tion Syntax and Processing, W3C Recommendation, December 2002.

[XMLSig]   D. Eastlake, J. Reagle, D. Solo, M. Bartel, J. Boyer, B. Fox, and E. Simon:
            XML-Signature Syntax and Processing, W3C Recommendation,
            February 2002.

Index

Berner, Georg
Management in 20XX

What will be important in the future – a holistic view

2004, 224 pages, 141 coloured illustrations,
17.3 cm x 25 cm, hardcover
ISBN 3-89578-241-6, € 37.90 / sFr 61.00

The book describes some remarkable future scenarios and ambitious visions.
It will help you come up with new ideas for the future of your company, and points
out the changes you will have to make in order to meet the challenges of the future.
There is plenty of emphasis on the new role people will play.

This book is both informative and inspiring.

"Management in 20XX" goes far beyond other business books. It drastically makes
clear how technical evolution will change our life, and how this evolutionary process will create totally new challenges for future business and management.

Davenport, Thomas H.; Probst, Gilbert J.B. (Editors)
Knowledge Management Case Book

Best Practises
With a Foreword by Dr. Heinrich von Pierer,
President and CEO of Siemens AG

2nd revised and enlarged edition, 2002, 336 pages,
79 illustrations, 4 tables, 17.3 cm x 25 cm, hardcover
ISBN 3-89578-181-9, € 39.90 / sFr 64.00

This book provides a perspective on knowledge management at Siemens – an
internationally recognised benchmark – by presenting the reader with the best of
the corporation's practical applications and experiences. For the second edition,
most of the cases have been updated; new cases have been added.

Presenting applications from very different areas, this practice-orientated book is
really outstanding in the broad field of KM literature.

Wiehler, Gerhard
Mobility, Security and Web Services

Technologies and Service-oriented Architectures
for a New Era of IT Solutions

2004, 219 pages, 68 illustrations,
17.3 cm x 25 cm, hardcover
ISBN 3-89578-229-7, € 49.90 / sFr 80.00

This book provides an insight into the exciting world of new technologies and
points the way ahead towards a new era of IT solutions. It describes complex
interrelations in a clearly comprehensible way. Concrete examples show how
companies can meet the challenges of the future and seize their opportunities.

This book is a must for all those who understand future-oriented IT solutions, who
can take the initiative and who want to enhance their market value, particularly
CIOs, CTOs, IT architects, consultants, project managers, network specialists,
application developers, IT decision-makers and heads of department in industry
or administration. Students of technical or business-related disciplines will also
find it highly interesting.

Gläßer, Lothar
Open Source Software
Projekte, Geschäftsmodelle, Rechtsfragen und Anwendungsszenarien –
was IT-Entscheider und Anwender wissen müssen

2004, 136 Seiten, 14 cm x 22,5 cm, kartoniert
ISBN 3-89578-240-8, € 29,90 / sFr 48,00

Dieses Buch gibt Anwendern und Entscheidern in Industrie und Verwaltung
einen Einblick in die Möglichkeiten des Einsatzes von OSS im Unternehmen.
Sie erhalten einen kompakten Überblick über die wichtigsten Open-Source-Pro-
jekte aus den Bereichen Betriebssystem (z. B. Linux), Office (z. B. OpenOffice),
Middleware (z. B. Projekte der Apache Software Foundation) und Entwicklungs-
werkzeuge (z. B. Eclipse, ArgoUML). Die verschiedenen Lizenzmodelle werden
vorgestellt und die rechtlichen Konsequenzen des Einsatzes von Open Source
Software erläutert.

Wagner, Johann; Schwarzenbacher, Kurt
Föderative Unternehmensprozesse
Technologien, Standards und Perspektiven für vernetzte Systeme

2004, 188 Seiten, 65 Abbildungen,
17,3 cm x 25 cm, gebunden
ISBN 3-89578-231-9, € 54,90 / sFr 88,00

Das Buch gibt IT-Managern, Beratern, Projektmanagern, Systemarchitekten und
Studenten einen umfassenden Überblick über die technischen Voraussetzungen
zur Automatisierung (globaler) betriebswirtschaftlicher Prozesse. In enger
Zusammenarbeit mit Produktherstellern entstanden, bietet es einen kompetenten
Einstieg in die Kernkonzepte der neuen Technologien und Standards zur Model-
lierung und Implementierung sowie dem Überwachen und der Adaption von
Prozessabläufen.

Wiehler, Gerhard
Mobility, Security und Web Services
Neue Technologien und Service-orientierte Architekturen
für zukunftsweisende IT-Lösungen

2004, 244 Seiten, 68 Abbildungen,
17,3 cm x 25 cm, gebunden
ISBN 3-89578-228-9, € 49,90 / 80,00 sFr

Das Buch gibt Einblick in die spannende Welt neuer Technologien und weist den
Weg in eine neue Ära von IT-Lösungen. Es stellt komplexe Zusammenhänge
verständlich dar und zeigt mit konkreten Hinweisen und illustrierten Beispielen,
wie Unternehmen die Herausforderungen der Zukunft bewältigen und Chancen
nutzen können.

Dieses Buch ist eine Pflichtlektüre für alle, die zukunftsweisende IT-Lösungen
verstehen, kompetent agieren und ihren Marktwert erhöhen wollen, insbesondere
CIOs, CTOs, IT-Architekten, Consultants, Projektmanager, Netzwerkspezialis-
ten, Anwendungsentwickler, IT-Entscheider, Fachabteilungsleiter aus Industrie
und Verwaltung sowie Studenten aus technischen und betriebswirtschaftlichen
Studiengängen.